D0935496

CONFESSIONS OF A GOLFAHOLIC

A Guide to Playing America's Top 100 Public Golf Courses

Paul Laubach

All statements, data and other information contained in this book are based upon the research, experience and opinions of the author. Reasonable efforts have been made to publish reliable data and information, but the author and the publisher cannot assume responsibility for the validity of all materials. The opinions expressed in this work are solely the opinions of the author and do not necessarily represent the opinions or thoughts of the publisher.

Editorial Content: AnnaMarie McHargue
Cover Designer: Bobby Kuber
Interior Layout: Leslie Hertling
Cover Photo and Additional Photography: Frank Lorey

Published by Elevate Publishing, Boise, ID

Printed in the United States of America

ISBN: 9781937498719

Dedication

To my parents, Peter and Charlotte Laubach,
who have long hoped I would make good on my "expensive" English degree. Regrettably it is not this book.

TABLE OF CONTENTS

PROLOGUE

Question: Which is more pathetic? Listening to golf on the radio, or watching a rerun of a golf tournament on television, months after the fact, and knowing the winner? Answer: Who cares? Either way, if you have partaken in either of these activities, you are a golf addict.

Here are some other indications you may have a golf "problem":

- If you know the difference between a Mashie and a Niblick.
- If you can read a stimpmeter. Bonus points if you own a stimpmeter.
- If you know how many grams your shaft weighs.
- If you know the difference between a movable and non-movable obstruction.
- If you still have a VCR player, so you can watch Al Geiberger's Cybernetics video.
- If you know the difference between gorse and heather.
- If you know how slope is calculated.
- If you know who Fluff and Bones are.
- If the ringtone on your phone is the theme for the Masters.
- If you actually inquired into purchasing Bubba Watson's hovercraft.

If you did not understand half the questions, then stop reading now. To the non-addict, the only thing more boring than playing or watching golf is reading about golf.

I am fully cognizant of my problem but have no intention of seeking help. Rather, each day represents a new opportunity to embrace the addiction. This work is the literary equivalent of the obnoxious golfing partner who analyzes each of his shots for you while playing, and then recaps the round in excruciating detail while you imbibe at the nineteenth hole.

Chapter 1

The Germ of an Idea

The headline screamed, "IRS Says 47 percent of U.S. Households Will Pay No Federal Income Tax for 2009." What?!

I had lost a small fortune in 2007 making a movie, with huge losses again in 2009 opening a restaurant. O.K., so I invested in two absolute sure-fire, losing propositions, but I was still handing over significant funds to the bloated government machine. Clearly I needed something else if I were to join the ranks of those smart enough to get someone else to pay their way. I needed to become the "high maintenance," hot-looking girlfriend of Uncle Sam.

I was mulling over the dilemma while hacking my way through another early morning round at the La Costa Resort and Spa, which is both near my home and where a large chunk of my earnings finds a home each year. Retirement would be a viable option, but not to a classic obsessive-compulsive personality like myself. I couldn't help but wonder, "How can I obtain massive tax write-offs while enjoying myself?"

After carding a disappointing 84 on the north course, I began the 10-minute trek back to my office, listening to the Golf Channel on XM Radio, when it occurred to me: what type of idiot listens to golf on the radio? Clearly, I had a problem. So what? I have plenty of other issues. The radio hosts were rehashing the recently completed Masters. You may remember the battle of good versus...not so good. Phil winning another Major in Tiger's return to the tour, after a brief exile following some Thanksgiving-night shenanigans. As a long-time Mickelson fan, I had been gloating to the Tiger apologists since Sunday.

The 2010 Masters was a fantastic event won by someone I don't know over someone I don't care to know, but it was not going to help me with my tax issues. What I needed was another junket to Pebble Beach. A $500 round on the best golf course in the world would not help my tax issues or my pocketbook, but it would bring me five hours of peace. (Note: the recommended pace of play is four hours and fifteen minutes.) If only I could write off the trip. And then it hit me…

Send to: PS@myaccountingfirm.com
Subject: Personal Taxes (do not want to pay)

PS,

Don't laugh…I have decided it is imperative that I play the 100 best golf courses available to the public (in the U.S.)…probably a five-year ordeal (middle of Nebraska and North Dakota are on the itinerary). It is my intent to document the travels and write a book. Can I deduct my costs (i.e. travel, food, green fees, etc.)?

Thanks,
Paul L.

Subj: RE: Personal Taxes (do not want to pay)
Date: May 14, 2010
From: PS@myaccountingfirm.com
To: Plaubach@golfingidiot.com (not my real email address)

Paul,

A tough question. Probably not. Personal motives versus profit motives. There are numerous cases where expenses related to writing are determined to be subject to the hobby loss rules (deductions only to the extent of revenue). Travel, hunting, sports, etc. have all been challenged. Since you are not a published author, and it will be 5 years before the book is completed, it would be very difficult to show a profit motive. However, that does not mean that you shouldn't keep records—just in case.

PS

Subj: RE: Personal Taxes (do not want to pay)
Date: May 14, 2010
From: Plaubach@golfingidiot.com
To: PS@myaccountingfirm.com

PS,

Thanks for your quick response. I will take that as a "yes." Hopefully, I will only be billed for 1/10th of an hour...I need to eat tonight. My understanding is that a hobby is an activity you enjoy. I can categorically state that I seldom enjoy golf (that would require shooting a score in the low 70s), but rather I am addicted. Seems like I also should be able to deduct my costs as treatment for my addiction, since I am hoping to kick the habit by running out of money.

Paul L.

Subj: RE: Personal Taxes (do not want to pay)
Date: May 14, 2010
From: PS@myaccountingfirm.com
To: Plaubach@golfingidiot.com

Paul,

Get a new accountant, you cheap bastard.

PS

O.K., I made up that last response. Since my accountant did not categorically say no, I am optimistic that we will find a way to make this work. Saving taxes and golfing the top 100 courses...the thought makes me giddy.

Ultimately, my mission to visit and chronicle rounds at the 100 top golf courses available to the public resulted from the convergence of two distinct events: annoyance with our screwed up tax system, and the "golfer's high" created by the 2010 Masters. Not very romantic, I admit. No muses, no desire to write the great American novel, no journey of self-discovery. Nope, the motivation was derived solely from the desire to create large tax losses while feeding my golf addiction.

I must also admit a second, less noble, motivation (O.K., the first reason is not very noble either). It is my fervent hope that an altruistic member at one of the nation's elite private clubs (Augusta National, Pine Valley, Cypress Point, etc.) will find my words to be sufficiently entertaining that they might wish to spend four to five hours hacking around their club with yours truly. I am, of course, willing to pay the guest fees, and buy dinner at the eatery of their choice. A great time is guaranteed for all, as well as a signed copy of this book.

Having set the stage, please join me on this golfing journey...Fore!!!

Chapter 2

A Logistical Nightmare

The past two weeks have been spent formulating ideas for the book in my mind, while gently breaking the news to my wife that not only will she be seeing less of me over the next few years (for her, this is actually a plus), but I also plan to waste more of our savings on another foolish endeavor. "Of course, this is nothing like the low budget movie I wrote and financed, which generated large losses, or the burger restaurant we opened where the only eating was into our joint savings," I assure her. Right, and I am the next Hemingway (Ernest, not Mariel). *Old Man and the Links* sounds like a perfect title. I sense some resistance to this new lunacy, until I consent to let her join me at Pebble Beach, Greenbrier, the Broadmoor, Hawaii, Hilton Head and a host of other great resorts and locations at which she can double my budget. Maybe she can write about the spas and we can deduct her costs as well. I assure her we will only be spending the kids' inheritances and not our retirement funds. This is, of course, a lie, brought on by my addiction. Nevertheless, she buys into the plan, allowing me to move on to the next obstacle.

The second challenge is to identify the 100 best courses available to the public. Thanks to Google (I have recently conquered the idiosyncrasies of Al Gore's inventive mind), I was whisked to *Golf Magazine*'s top "100 Courses You Can Play" article. Unfortunately, the rankings were done in 2008, meaning they are somewhat dated. Of course, if my journey takes five years, there will be any number of changes. Maybe that is good, as I would have a legitimate claim to deduct future golf travel costs for updated editions. Nevertheless, it will be like trying to hit a moving target, not dissimilar to playing a round after an evening with some of my serious drinking buddies.

Upon first reviewing the *Golf Magazine* list, I notice a striking error: Pebble Beach was not rated number one. Due to some obvious but unexplained flaw, the "best course in the world" was rated second. Since I believe Pebble Beach to be perfection, the only explanation would be a tie. Coming in at number one was Pacific Dunes in Oregon. The Bandon Dunes courses have a great reputation, and I am anxious to try them out, but better than Pebble Beach?

My review of the list indicates that I have previously played 15 of the named courses, most of which are located in California, Nevada and Arizona. Should I play them again? At an average cost of $300 per round, plus travel and accommodations, it will put quite a dent in the pocketbook. Nevertheless, it does seem unavoidable. Further, who would not want to spend another five days in 115-degree weather in Scottsdale? Did I mention I am cheap? The off-season rates may be too hard to pass up, especially in the desert communities, where savings of 60 percent to 70 percent are the norm during the summer.

Speaking of great locations, it looks like I will be making treks to such vacation meccas as Bismarck, North Dakota; Rhodes, Iowa; Biwabik, Minnesota; and Gothenburg, Nebraska. Are you kidding me? At least I have heard of Bismarck. Logistics are going to be an issue.

There is a disproportionate number of courses in the South and mid-Atlantic. That means more garden spots like Choctaw and Biloxi, Mississippi, and Opelika, Alabama. Offsetting this are trips to Kiawah Island, Pinehurst and several locations in the Blue Ridge Mountains that should actually be great.

There are as many courses in Maine (two) as there are in Texas, and neither offers convenient travel options. Further, with Maine, I have to find a way to get there during golf season, and I am usually busy during the month of July.

I always have been good at planning, so I can probably figure out the most efficient way to get this done. Not sure how my boss will feel about the time off from work, but being self-employed, I have a fifty-fifty chance of not getting fired.

That, of course, brings up the next issue: how to pay for this indulgence? Even planning for the tax losses, the process is likely to set me back—big time. Based on past travels, I would expect to pay $1,200 per course for greens fees, caddies, travel, accommodations and the requisite golf hat. Food is not included in this estimate. If my projections are right, I need to set aside $120,000 to $150,000 for this experience. At least it is less than financing the movie or opening the restaurant. The logical way to cover the costs is to convince my daughter to drop out of her overpriced, private East Coast college after her sophomore year. If not, liquidating my wife's retirement account might be the answer, but I will have to tread lightly with this one.

The preferred low-cost option is to play off-season—December in Minnesota and August in Las Vegas will save a few bucks on greens fees and accommodations.

There are going to be many challenges, but, hey, it sounds like fun, and my accountant says it may be tax-deductible—bring on Biwabik.

Chapter 3:

Why Am I Doing This?

The typical question I get from friends and family regarding this boondoggle is,"Why are you doing this?" The question arises so often that I have begun to ask myself the same thing.

First, and most obvious, is that I truly am addicted to the sport. I love all that is great about the game, including the "gentlemanly" traditions, which seem to be generally more obvious on private and upscale public facilities. I hate to find myself stuck on a municipal track with an unimaginative design and questionable course conditions. And let's not even talk about the riff raff in their cutoff jeans, who seem to care so little about the sport. Call me old and stodgy, but...well...I *am* old and stodgy and see no point at this time to change.

Secondly, I am still trying to justify my college education. Since I skipped so many of my classes, I feel like my father never got his money's worth. By the way, he agrees. Maybe if I can get published, the English Literature degree will be forgiven.

Another motivating factor is my desire to see the United States. O.K., I have as much interest in visiting North Dakota as I have in traveling to New Delhi, but this is a terrific country, and there is much to see. Can there be a better way to get a dose of Americana than golfing across the fruited plains? Of course there is, but I plan to golf anyway.

Lastly, and as mentioned before, an important side benefit of publishing this book is that I hope to gain access to people who are in a position to help me achieve my real goal. By necessity, this work can only address courses available to the public. If given a choice, I would prefer to golf the 100 best courses in the country. Specifically, this would include Cypress Point, Pine

Valley, and the penultimate golf addict's number-one bucket list course—Augusta National. If you are a member at one of these exclusive courses, feel free to contact me, and I will make the trek to New Jersey, Georgia or Northern California. Did I mention I will pick up the dinner tab?

So, why am I doing this? Are you kidding? This is the coolest thing ever.

Chapter 4

Weapons of Grass Destruction

The one thing every golf addict loves is an excuse to buy new equipment. TaylorMade, Callaway, Titleist, Nike, Cobra, Ping, Cleveland, etc. would all be out of business if those of us addicted to the sport were not convinced that a new piece of hardware could lower our scores by a couple of strokes per round. Alas, years of constant change have wrought longer drives, better spin control and straighter shots, but unfortunately, the scorecards remain the same.

Regardless, my decision to embark on a golf odyssey provided the perfect opportunity to check out my local golf store. My current bag contains the classic TaylorMade Bubble Burner driver. The grip on the club needs to be replaced, and I think I have detected the beginning of a crack in the face. Probably need a new driver.

My three metal and I have had a love-hate relationship for years. Ever since I cashed in some American Express points to acquire the club sight unseen, we have had issues. This TaylorMade club is prone to duck hooks. Given the age and inconsistency of the club (it cannot possibly be the operator), it will probably have to be replaced as well.

I just purchased a TaylorMade Bubble Burner hybrid with a 19-degree loft. It worked great in the store, hitting into the giant plastic wall, but has been inconsistent on the course. The club has a neutral face, which I like, but has a tendency to go right at the wrong time. As the club is only a month old, it may be salvageable.

My other hybrid is a Ping 22-degree lofted club. This one has a closed face and is very confusing compared to the other hybrid. I seldom use this club except to play from the gnarly rough that defines the area just outside the fairways at La Costa. For consistency, it probably has to go, too.

The irons, P through 4, are Callaway X-18s. I like these clubs, but am not sure they like me. Three years of hacking around have taken their toll. Further, the 9 iron is a replacement club, with a regular graphite shaft versus the stiff graphite ones belonging to the rest of the set. I am about to give up on the original 9 iron falling out of the pine tree located along the left side of the eleventh fairway of the La Costa North course. I do not recall the exact circumstances that resulted in the club ending up in the tree, but suspect it had something to do with back-to-back double bogeys. These clubs are likely to be replaced.

I have two Cleveland wedges. The 56-degree replaced another that found its way over the fence on the left side of No. 4. I believe this club was won in a raffle at some charity golf event. As a free club, I can attest that I am getting my money's worth. Too bad, as I use the club for everything under 75 yards to the putting green. I also have been known to use it for putting on those days when I cannot sink anything. The other wedge is 52 degrees and has been a disappointment, but seldom sees the light of day. I think some new wedges are in order as well.

Lastly: my putter. For the past year, I have been playing a Monza Spider. It is a 33-inch model that has actually helped my game. The enormous head eliminates the possibility of a whiff, and seems to put the ball generally on-line. I am currently on my second edition, the first having developed a mysterious bend in the shaft.

My shoes are new and I have plenty of golf gloves courtesy of the two-for-one deal from MG Golf. But my Rodney Dangerfield golf bag has a broken zipper, so that, too, has to go in favor of something new.

Armed with my wish list and some room on the Visa card, I head to Golf Galaxy.

Unfortunately, my love of new golf equipment is tempered by my frugality. A new set of irons with graphite shafts will set me back about $800. Another $350 for a driver, $225 for a three wood, $300 for two hybrids, and $250 worth of wedges seems excessive. I have no doubt that new clubs will be in the offing before my quest is complete, but not today.

On the positive side, the Callaway Tour i golf ball is on sale, as the current line is being discontinued. I buy out the remaining stock of five dozen for under $30 a box. This is a savings of $15 per dozen from the usual price, and should give me at least 20 rounds worth of lake balls.

My final purchase is the most important piece of equipment that any golfer can have in his bag. The proper use of this tool has saved many a disaster round. For a mere $30, I have acquired the Cadillac of ball retrievers; a Golf Galaxy, 12-foot model that comes with its own head cover. The contraption that retrieves the ball is unique. Hopefully, it will work better than my previous 10 other ball retrievers, all of which have broken. Now this is exciting. I already am looking forward to my next round, and the opportunity to fish a few Pro V1s out of the many lakes and creeks that comprise La Costa.

I package up my purchases and head back to the office. Disappointed I have not acquired any new clubs, but still excited about the ball retriever… maybe an afternoon round is warranted. I first need to check my emails. First thing I see is that Austad's is offering a special deal on personalized Titleist Pro V1s. Buy three dozen get one dozen free, with no-cost personalization. Let's see, at $45 per dozen and $6.99 shipping, the average cost is only $35.50 per dozen. That is a great deal for Titleists, although I do not really care about the personalization. Heck, I'm just going to lose them anyway (assuming I cannot drag them out with my new ball retriever). Not able to pass up a deal, I order another four dozen golf balls, inscribed with my golfing moniker "bogeyman." I feel a little bad for the 10-year-old kid that drags these balls out of the pond for the purpose of reselling them. Golf is a psychological game, and who wants to see a bogey looking them in the eye before they tee off?

Chapter 5

More Logistical Nightmares

Enough procrastination; it is time to start booking some trips. A cursory glance at the list indicates several destinations where one can complete three or four courses in short order.

One option includes the Kohler courses near Sheboygan, Wisconsin. Whistling Straits-Straits, Blackwolf Run and Whistling Straits-Irish are part of the same resort facility. Even more compelling is that the PGA Championship is scheduled for Whistling Straits in August. In addition, Erin Hills Golf Course, which is situated between Sheboygan and Milwaukee, has just been selected to host the 2017 U.S. Open.

The second option, and my own personal favorite, is the Pebble Beach junket. Pebble Beach, Spyglass Hill and The Links at Spanish Bay are available via a great, albeit expensive, package. It may also be possible to play Pasatiempo and CordeValle on the same trip.

Option 3 is Bandon Dunes along the Oregon coast. Pacific Dunes, Bandon Dunes and Bandon Trails provide the highest concentration of highly ranked courses in the United States. I also have learned that a fourth course (Old Macdonald) is scheduled to open in June. No doubt the *Golf Magazine* bias will land this one in the top 100 as well. This is a must trip, according to my golfing buddies who already have made the trek.

After much internal anguish and consultation with the ultimate decision-maker (my wife), the obvious decision is to book all three and to do it quickly.

The Kohler courses represent the most significant challenge. Who in the world wants to go to Milwaukee? I suppose this will be a recurring theme given some of the outlying locales. On the plus side, I have to go to Minnesota this summer for a family reunion with my in-laws. Minnesota is close to Wisconsin, and, with the brownie points earned for hanging with the "fam," I can negotiate a week to golf on my own. It also turns out that one of my best friends and former Little League teammate had the misfortune (my words, not his) to end up in the Milwaukee area. Scott Rand is a doctor and, therefore, by definition must also be a golfer... With sufficient warning he should be able to make the time for a few days on the links. My willingness to fly on July 4 results in a bargain airfare on Southwest of only $72.00, plus (and this is why I love Southwest) my golf clubs fly free. The cost to fly from Milwaukee to Minneapolis is somewhat more expensive, and I will have to pay for the clubs. It is then back on Southwest for the return to San Diego. Even better, Scott is able to go online and book two nights and three rounds of golf at Whistling Straits for less than $1,000 per person. Maybe I will figure it out when I get there, but for right now this looks like one of the better bargains around. There is only one negative. Erin Hills is now closed and will not be reopening until later in July, making a return trip to Milwaukee necessary.

Cool. Three courses the first week in July; only 97 to go. Make that 96. The family reunion is being held in Brainerd, Minnesota. Since I drive the in-laws crazy, they usually send me off to play golf when we're together. Deacon's Lodge is located in the Brainerd area, so I will head there that week as well. It turns out there is another top 100 course in Minnesota. The Quarry at Giants Ridge is located in Biwabik. (I misspelled this city four times before getting it right.) I have no idea where it is located, but figure it must be close to Brainerd, right? According to Google Maps, the distance is merely 158 miles. Given my driving style that would be two hours; however, Google says 3 hours and 7 minutes, so it is not all highways. A quick glance at the map shows the course to be north of Duluth, toward International Falls and near Thunder Bay, Ontario, Canada. Ouch! We will only be there for three days, and I am getting too old for six-hour round-trips. This venue will also need to be delayed.

Speaking of booking quickly: I finally am able to get a quorum from my three brothers on a date we can go to Bandon Dunes. Everyone is in agreement with leaving on Saturday, September 25. I pop up the website, and call for reservations. Ninety minutes later I have tentatively booked a guest cottage for Wednesday, September 28, and a round at Pacific Dunes that afternoon. We have two rounds scheduled for Thursday, starting on Bandon Trails and finishing on Old Macdonald. There are no carts, so we old men are going to be mucho tired. Friday morning we are reserved for Bandon Dunes. We're up to $8,500 for the group, and still need to cover airfare, car rental, food and caddies.

Chapter 6

And, the Winner Is…

If you are still reading, you are probably asking yourself, *What qualifies this guy to tell me what golf courses I should be playing?* In a word: Nothing. I am a 50-something, bespectacled, slightly overweight, above-average but not great, golfer. My handicap floats between 6 and 8, which means I score more often above 80 than below. I am a comparatively short hitter, with a pretty good short game. I have never studied the game of golf, nor have I taken a course in golf course architecture. I did not take up the game until college, when I needed an excuse to ditch class. As described earlier, I am a bit hyper, so I enjoy a course that is constantly "in my face." Ultimately, I am overly opinionated and firmly believe everyone is entitled to my point of view. So, qualifications? Who needs them?

On the other hand, I have extensive experience as a film critic (Netflix). I realize this has nothing to do with evaluating a golf course, but I am used to assigning 1 to 5 stars in a subjective manner. In fact, in reviewing my Netflix account, I was impressed, while simultaneously depressed, that I have amassed 1700 ratings. Imagine watching 1700 movies at 1.75 hours per film. Based upon the knowledge garnered during my MBA education, this suggests an accumulation of 2,950 hours, or more than 120 days without sleep. I would like to see you do that. On the other hand, it is depressing that I have wasted so much of my life.

As a rater, I am tougher than most. Perhaps it is my response to the rampant grade inflation afflicting our schools, which, after participation trophies, is the root cause of most of this country's problems. I ascribe to rating on a bell curve, with very few As and very few Fs. Of the 1700-plus movies I have rated on Netflix, only 10 have received 5 stars. This includes, in no particular order, *What About Bob?*, *My Cousin Vinny*, *Dirty Harry*, *Under Siege*, *Animal House*, *Scrooged*, *True Lies*, *Charlie Wilson's War*, *Fargo* and *Fast Times at Ridgemont High*, with honorable mentions for *The Wrong Guy* and *Big Trouble*. Not too many critically-acclaimed movies in this group. Thus, anything you read in this book should be taken with a grain of salt. Is it too late to return your copy? Give me credit for knowing what I like and not being afraid to defy convention. No need here for me just to follow the crowd.

So, how does my rating system work? Basically, my ratings reflect the "coolness" of a golf course. In other words, does it have a "wow" factor? My rating is on a 1 to 10 scale, with 10 (A+) being Pebble Beach, which is the "coolest" place on the planet. Any course deserving of a spot on the top 100 should get a minimum score of *7* (C).

Defining cool is always difficult, but I know it when I see it. Factors include physical setting, course condition, history, local amenities, facilities, staff and hat selection. O.K., maybe hat selection is not critical, but I think more courses should focus on providing an interesting and eclectic collection of headwear. The toughest job will be to look past weather in evaluating a facility, especially given my propensity to save money, and the likelihood I will play many of the courses during the swing or off-season. I tend to like desert golf and forest-lined fairways, and am not as keen on Florida golf or links designs. As many of the top-ranked courses are links style (including the Bandon Dunes and the Kohler courses), I could break with the experts early.

It is important to understand that the ratings will generally be based upon no more than one or two rounds. I am sure all of the venues are great. However, it would be impossible to ignore external influences that may, or may not be, relevant. For example, how does one address playing Innisbrook's Copperhead course in tournament-ready condition, two weeks before the PGA event and in great weather, versus Cog Hill played in driving rain, 25 mile-per-hour winds and frigid air?

In addition, I have included the category "Absolutely Must Play?" The answer is probably a resounding *yes* to all, but in the interest of helping the reader prioritize his schedule, some had to receive a *no*. Generally, this is based upon a combination of factors including cost, convenience and proximity to other venues, as much as the actual golf course itself. I firmly believe everyone should play Taconic, but the outlying location, as well as a reservation system that does not allow tee times to be booked more than one week in advance, makes this one less critical. Ultimately, this exercise is highly subjective.

Chapter 7

The Dry (and Hot) Run

Before venturing all the way to Sheboygan, I decide to have a dry run on a local course. My original intention was to visit Trump National in Los Angeles County; however, my logical golfing partner is busy for the next several weeks. Option 2 is to visit the Coachella Valley (Palm Springs area) for off-season rounds on several courses I have previously played. I know that green fees drop precipitously during the summer when temperatures hit triple digits. The site for the La Quinta Resort Mountain Course suggests that discounted rates are available beginning on June 1. The weather cannot be that hot then, can it? I bring up Yahoo! weather. High today (May 2) in Palm Desert is 95 degrees. Hmmm, well, I have played in toastier conditions. Friends Joe and Greta Strong agree to join us June 1, so I book heavily discounted rounds at La Quinta and the PGA West Stadium Course. I get a 7:45 a.m. starting time at La Quinta, but nothing is available until 9:30 at the Stadium Course. Unfortunately, this means we will experience the hottest part of the day. Oh, well, the price is right, and I always enjoy golfing in this area.

Chapter 8

Anticipation

There are only two weeks remaining until we hit the links at the La Quinta Resort Mountain Course. Yahoo! weather says the high in Palm Desert will be 93 degrees.

Though no clotheshorse, I have started thinking about my attire. Golf is one of the few sports, hobbies, vocations, etc. where sartorial splendor takes a backseat to gaudy, unconventional and the outright ridiculous. From Ryan Moore's ties, to Ian Poulter's extremes, no sport celebrates "fabulous" attire like golf. Of course, professional players cannot wear shorts. Go figure.

Unfortunately, given my age and body shape, I do everything I can to not draw attention to myself. As such, I am forsaking knickers. Given the weather in the desert, I will probably break down and wear shorts. This is less of a problem for me than my golfing partners, whom I will likely blind with the sun reflecting off my pasty white legs. But this also raises the question as to whether I should continue to wear my mid-calf (old dude) socks, or switch to those ridiculous women's anklets. After years of ribbing from members of the club, I tried the little socks last year for the first time. They were totally uncomfortable, and they caused my voice to hit new highs. My primary goal is to conform, but those damn socks make me very emotional. I will defer that decision.

Over the years I have played in numerous golfing events where the players are given free shirts (my favorite price), and I also have received from friends and family any number of golf shirts for birthdays and Christmas, so I am good to go. I have plenty of golf shoes, and my khaki and navy shorts are well-stocked. Bottom line is that there will be no shopping for new duds.

When it comes to golf, however, I do believe it is incumbent upon all of us to wear at least something unusual. Being severely follicly challenged, I must wear a golf hat. No visor for me. Over the years, I have purchased hats at every new course I play. At last count, there were nearly 200 golf hats occupying space in my closet. The upcoming adventure will add at least another 100 to the collection. Many of the existing hats have been worn on numerous occasions and have been virtually destroyed by sweat marks, so getting a few new lids is probably a good thing.

When I acquire new headgear, it is usually of a design or color that my daughter would be embarrassed to wear, and you should see the stuff she can pull off. Clashing with the rest of my wardrobe is preferred and fluorescent is ideal. Whenever possible, I seek out caps that can double as beacons in case I am lost in the woods or that at least can protect me from stray deer hunters by identifying my presence from several miles away. Alas, not all golf facilities share my need to be different. In fact, there seems to be an inverse relationship between the "class" of a facility and the attractiveness of the hats. For example, it usually takes a lot of looking to find something acceptable/ridiculous at the Pebble Beach courses.

Let the Games Begin!

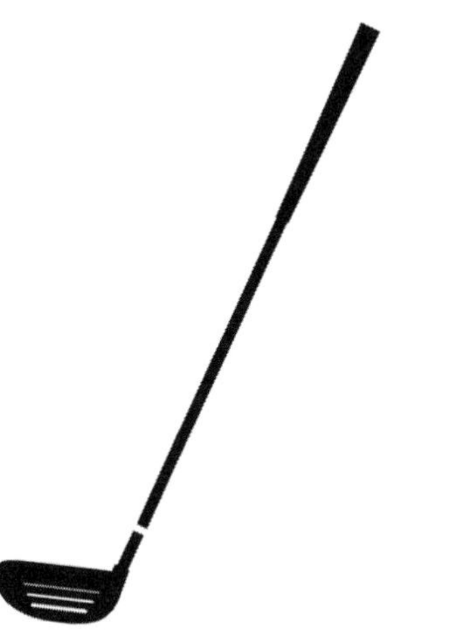

Chapter 9

The Sun Also Rises, and Boy Is It Hot

As a Southern California resident, I have often gravitated to the desert communities to satiate my need for winter golf. As an idiot, cheapskate and golf addict, I also find myself drawn to the desert during the off-season, when temperatures regularly exceed three digits but greens fees drop by 70 percent. Golfing early and with sufficient hydration (I learned the hard way that beer does not represent proper hydration) can make a round enjoyable, especially if you are nuts. Unlike northern climates, off-season golf in the desert is not only possible, but the condition of the courses is generally very good. Further, the ball rolls a lot further on a sunbaked fairway than through a snow bank.

When I grew up, the desert was collectively referred to as Palm Springs. As the region has developed, however, this golfing mecca is now primarily situated in the communities of Palm Desert, Indian Wells, Rancho Mirage and La Quinta. Within these four communities alone, there were 89 golf courses listed in a recent *Palm Springs Life* magazine article. Of these, 32 are open to the public. The remaining private courses are generally affiliated with residential developments. Coachella Valley occupies a large geographic area, and the commute from Palm Springs proper to PGA West can easily take 45 minutes, so I recommend staying in one of the new communities.

If you are looking to golf the two top 100 courses, they are not far from Palm Desert. PGA West Stadium Course is located about 15 miles away, but plan for 30 minutes of travel time. One annoying feature of the desert area is the incessant traffic signals that appear to be timed to maximum infuriation. This problem is compounded by the fact that it seems like half the people drive like they are 80 years old, which, of course, makes sense, since half of those people on the road are octogenarians. If you like Cadillac and Lincoln sedans, then your vacation will have an added benefit. But I digress. The second top 100 course is La Quinta Resort Mountain Course. This facility is situated less than 10 miles from the heart of Palm Desert.

The great thing about desert golf is the warm (sometimes hot) dry air, which allows shorter hitters to develop an inflated sense of power. It usually takes me three rounds to recalibrate when returning to my low-lying, heavy air, wet fairway, and sea-level home course. Desert play is often target golf, although many of the resorts have layouts that favor the directionally challenged. With the exception of the La Quinta courses, there is not much topographical change, but, like Florida, the courses are characterized by plenty of water.

When choosing a location to base in the desert, there are essentially two options. Palm Desert offers more alternatives to golfing. If the non-golfing spouse wants to get in a little shopping, you can send them over to the overpriced but exclusive El Paseo shopping district while you are on the links. If you have more control, direct them to the Cabazon Outlet Mall, about 30 miles to the west. This is one of the better outlet malls and the prices are more reasonable. Palm Desert also offers better access to the best restaurants in the Valley, and has superior proximity to several Indian casinos.

If on a golf excursion with the guys, especially if 36 holes a day are planned, La Quinta offers a second alternative. The courses along the Santa Rosa Mountains have more character, and potentially less wind. The downside is that the locale is more isolated. Nevertheless, as the area has expanded, more services are being provided.

Golf in the Coachella Valley is an absolute must for the passionate golfer. An extended vacation at one of the many seasonal rentals allows for an amazing array of golf, terrific weather during the winter, and day excursions to Los Angeles (about a two-hour drive) to hit Trump National, and/or to San Diego for Torrey Pines South (also about two hours). If you are trying to play the entire top 100, Rustic Canyon in Moorpark is situated just west of Los Angeles County, although it is a bit of a drive, and may require an overnight stay. One note of caution: the desert is prone to high winds and, despite the warm afternoon highs, there are frost delays. You never know what an off-season desert morning might bring.

ROUND 1 La Quinta Resort (Mountain)

Course Rank: 70

Date Played: June 2, 2010

Starting Time: 7:45 a.m.

Weather: It was 75 degrees when we teed off and 91 degrees when we putted out on 18.

My Score: 85

Number of Lost Golf Balls: 4, all on the front side. I hope this is not a trend.

Highlights: One birdie and eight pars

Lowlights: Two doubles and a quadruple

Excuse for Not Breaking 80: I suck. After a quick "kick in" par on No. 1, I hooked a ball into the lake on No. 2. Bad concentration on the front side, including four in the water, led to a 48 going out. Finishing with a 37, things improved dramatically on the much tougher inward nine. Welcome to my golf game.

Greens Fee: $79, discounted off-season rate.

Playing Partner(s): Joe Strong—longtime drinking buddy, Pebble Beach partner and consummate authority on all things sports and music.

Practice Facilities: Above-average driving range, hitting toward the Santa Rosa Mountains. Practice chipping and putting greens make it worthwhile to get there early.

My Rating: 7. I have played the Mountain Course on multiple occasions in the past, and was surprised to see it on the list. The front nine of the Mountain Course is pedestrian, and the good stuff does not start until

No. 14. The finishing holes are exceptional, running along the Santa Rosa Mountains.

Absolutely Must Play: No, but you absolutely must play in the desert, and this course offers good value and some really good holes, and the Santa Rosa Mountain setting is attractive.

Favorite Hole: Tough call between the par 3 No. 16 and par 4 No. 14. I love the elevated tee, and tight landing area on the par 3, but 14 appeals to the sadist in me. This is a difficult driving hole that begs you to hit left, where two large, steeply sloping sand traps gather up virtually all imperfect shots. The smart play is to hit right, but it makes this long hole even longer.

Location Characteristics: The primary attraction is the setting at the base of the Santa Rosa Mountains. On occasion, bighorn sheep may be seen grazing amongst the outcroppings. The course offers more topography than most in the desert, with a number of strategically placed lakes and a few decent views on the back nine.

Comments: Playing off-season meant some of the greens were dried out. With only a couple of exceptions, however, I felt they putted true, and were reasonably quick. The carts have an extensive GPS system that is helpful and an ice chest that is necessary. Water is available at many locations throughout the course. Homes line both sides of the fairway on Nos. 10 to 13, which can be disconcerting if you are not hitting accurate drives. The white tees seemed too short, with wedge shots into virtually all par 4s with a decent drive. On a good day, you could bring the course to its knees, but like most desert golf, you need to hit targets. Overall, the Mountain Course is a pleasant golf experience, but lacking any "wow" factor until you reach the final five holes.

ROUND 2 PGA West (Stadium)

Course Rank: 37

Date Played: June 3, 2010

Starting Time: 9:30 a.m.

Weather: 85 degrees to start, 97 degrees at finish. No significant wind, clear skies. I think I dropped three pounds despite drinking two gallons of water.

My Score: 82.

Number of Lost Balls: 2, both with an 8 iron, one on the signature Island Green at No. 17.

Highlights: 3 birdies and 7 pars

Lowlights: 5 double bogeys

Excuse for Not Breaking 80: The par 3s, which included three double bogeys and one bogey. I also blame Pete Dye for the sadistic design that disproportionately punishes mediocre shots.

Greens Fee: $109, discounted off-season rate (see weather). The premium greens fee in season is currently $199.

Playing Partner(s): Joe and I joined Joe and Ryoko, a cute Japanese couple who were celebrating their 25th anniversary.

Practice Facilities: PGA West is a massive facility with ample practice areas and a golf school.

My Rating: 8, as long as you like Pete Dye courses (I am a fan). Many of my friends do not care for this course given the quirky bounces that can cause a score to balloon, and the pros were apoplectic when they had to play from the black tees years earlier.

Absolutely Must Play: Yes. Pete Dye has created a crazy, sometimes gimmicky course that will drive you nuts, but occasionally provides a great reward. Even if you hate everything else, there is no denying the fun of playing No. 17, a par 3, island hole, that is reminiscent of No. 17 at Sawgrass.

Favorite Hole: No. 17. The par 3 is only 135 yards from the white tees, but is surrounded on all sides by water. Known as Alcatraz for the ample rock walls built into the sides of the green, any misplaced tee shot will be lost forever and send you to the drop area. I barely pushed my first one into the lake and reloaded. The second one landed safely in the middle, but it was my third double bogey on a par 3. Joe hit a career shot, 10 feet under the hole.

Location Characteristics: PGA West is situated "deep" in the city of La Quinta and is comprised of a residential golf community and six golf courses, of which three are open to the public. There are numerous undulations, moguls, swales, etc. that give the course character, but, at times, the water is overwhelming.

Comments: The most memorable part of my round was the three consecutive birdies on holes 7, 8 and 9, that led to a front side of 38. This, combined with my back nine 37 at the Mountain Course the day before, led to 18 consecutive great holes of golf. I was underwhelmed by the staff and general set up, especially relative to other top-rated courses. A probable bag drop area had no signage when we arrived, no staff, and no place to put the bags, so we had to walk around the clubhouse. The golf carts had great GPS, but there was no ice chest or water, which is generally common in the desert. For a first-class facility, they fell short. The golf itself can be terrific, especially for masochists like me. There are plenty of great holes, and you will be challenged. But bring your patience –the course plays slow (we took over five hours), and you will occasionally get bad breaks on good shots. This it is not necessarily a course for everybody.

Trip Summary:

I have always loved desert golf, although it is preferable when temperatures are below 85 degrees. The Mountain Course at La Quinta makes up for a slow start with a fabulous finish. The sadistic Pete Dye Stadium Course is not everyone's cup of tea, but will definitely test your game. If neither course is appealing, there are plenty of other options for all levels of golfers, making the Coachella Valley a great place to take the golfing wife. Even the golfing widow can find things to occupy her time. There is a plethora of excellent restaurants and, I am told, great shopping. The golf courses are usually in excellent shape. Green fees during the "season" (January to April) can be a bit stiff at the big-name courses, but discounted fees can be found on a number of Internet sites if you are willing to wait until the last minute. Off-season rates are very low, but they come with another type of price. Regardless of whether you are booking a golf junket with your usual foursome for a couple of days, or whether you are going to "winter" in the desert, the Coachella Valley has plenty to offer. Even if you are not interested in the top 100 courses in this area, no true golf addict should miss out on this regional experience.

Chapter 10

You're Aerifying When?

Frustration reigns as I attempt to schedule additional golf rounds. First, because of the U.S. Open at Pebble Beach, the resort is not offering any specials this year. My goal is to never pay retail, so my six-year consecutive run to the Monterey Peninsula will end in 2010. However, this opens up the end of August for another trip. I began looking at the Carolinas, but there are so many courses that my brain was unable to process a coherent schedule. I may need to take a week of vacation time just to wrap my arms around multiple trips to that region.

A review of the interactive map from *Golf Magazine* revealed a nice grouping of courses in Colorado. Having spent some time last summer in Park City, Utah, I have fond memories of golfing at altitude. In addition, the accommodations in skiing meccas can be terrific off-season, and at a fraction of the cost during the winter months. Connecting through the Red Sky Golf Club website, I found a terrific deal on a two-bedroom condominium in Beaver Creek. I figure I can make the trek to New Castle (Lakota Golf Course) and to Colorado Springs (Redlands Mesa) from that home base. I can supplement the trip by arriving a day early, and heading south of Denver to the Broadmoor resort.

First reservation is for golf and accommodations at Beaver Creek and Red Sky Ranch. Three nights and two rounds of golf set me back $1,250—not bad given the two- bedroom, two-and-half bath condominium. Next it is off to the Southwest Airlines site and the free baggage. Great deals are available on non-stop flights to Denver. This trip also qualifies as an anniversary gift for my wife, so another bullet dodged. The Broadmoor website is having issues, so I call the resort directly. I am able to book a standard room with golf for about $560. It is not a great deal, but it could be worse. They patch me through to the pro shop to make my golf reservation for Saturday.

"Which course do you want to play?" they ask. Broadmoor East is my reply.

"Uh oh," the pleasant voice responds. "We are aerifying the greens that week, and the East Course is closed...but our other courses are really nice."

"Give me back to reservations," is my only response.

My sunny disposition is being tested. At least Wisconsin is only two weeks away. I start thinking about that trip when it occurs to me that the upper Midwest junket is marred by the closure of Erin Hills. Two out-of-town trips booked and it looks like I will have to make return trips to both of these locales. I see dollar signs flash before my eyes, and start to rethink the timing. Is it too late to chase my back-up dream (i.e. visiting all of the Major League Baseball stadiums)?

Before getting too worked up, however, I need to get focused on the Senior Club Championship starting Friday at La Costa. Having recently passed the age 50 milestone, I now have a fighting chance for a top-three finish with all the old geezers. I will probably have the third lowest handicap of this year's entrants. Unfortunately, my game is a little off. My drives, which had been perfect, are now heading right. I am still trying to get my new irons dialed in, and the short game is inconsistent. I shot 73 last Monday, but could not break 80 the rest of the week. No time for these useless musings; I need a few hours on my backyard putting green.

Chapter 11

Bratwurst, Beer and Another Snafu

It is 7:00 a.m. on July 4, and I am in the Southwest Airlines terminal in San Diego. Next stop is Milwaukee after a plane change in Las Vegas. Good old Southwest; there is no charge to check through the clubs and everything I need for nine days and 12 rounds of golf.

Part one of the trip includes three days at the Kohler Courses outside Sheboygan, Wisconsin, followed by several days of golf in Milwaukee, and then to Minnesota for the in-laws' family reunion. It should have been done in reverse order.

My expectation for Kohler golf is very high. Whistling Straits is ranked number three on the *Golf Magazine* list. This means it is one spot below Pebble Beach, and theoretically better than Spyglass Hill. Blackwolf Run, another part of the package, is number 12. For good measure, the Whistling Straits Irish Course is rated 68.

Despite hosting the PGA this year, the Kohler people offered a fantastic package including three rounds of golf, two-night accommodations, two days of caddies, and free replays for under $1,000 per person. This is unlike Pebble Beach, which hosted the U.S. Open and eliminated all in-season package deals for 2010.

I am joining childhood friend Scott Rand, who somehow found his way to Milwaukee. Given that both he and his wife are from California, the journey to the middle of America seems strange. I recently learned Dr. Rand has become a golf addict. I was expecting one round each at the Kohler courses, and an additional round at the former site of the Greater Milwaukee Open (Brown Deer), but once he learned about the free replays, all hell broke loose. We are scheduled to drive there on Monday and play our first round at 12:00 noon. Given that the days are longer up near the North Pole, he seems to think we can complete a replay that day as well. As we are going to be walking the courses, I am less sure. With a 9:00 a.m. tee time on Tuesday at Straits, a replay is guaranteed. On Wednesday, we have another 9:00 a.m. tee time. Scott has also booked 3:00 p.m. at Brown Deer, but we may do another replay instead. He has a Thursday time at some local course, early in the morning, and another time booked at Brown Deer that afternoon.

Lastly, we have an early morning time on Friday at another venue. I am sure we would have played later that day as well, but my flight leaves for Minneapolis at 2:30. Nine rounds in five days. This is intense even for me. I have packed 50 ibuprofen and 50 aspirin, in addition to the usual assortment of bandages, heating pads, ice packs and salves. It does not get much easier in Minnesota, where I already have committed to four rounds in three days. Depending upon the madhouse with the in-laws, I have an option for a fifth.

The excitement is tempered by some bad news. I started perusing the weather reports ten days in advance. (I strongly recommend against this as the weather changes every seven minutes in the Midwest.) Unfortunately, the immediate weather report is calling for iffy conditions. Apparently, some tropical storm has been moving up from the South. Scattered and isolated thunderstorms are predicted for virtually the entire Wisconsin portion of the trip. The last time I was in this part of the world, it was a tornado. How can anybody live there?

I like the people of the Midwest. As a group they have always been friendly, if not a bit goofy. They remind me of my Canadian relatives: self reliant, honest, hard-working and generous. However, the pace of life is slower. There is no such thing as a Type "A" personality. In fact, they define laidback. For me, a great place to visit, but I would go crazy even if the weather was golf tolerable year-round. All you really need to know about Wisconsin residents is that they wear cheese on their heads.

The dining choices are likely to be interesting as well. I am far from a health nut, but the girth of a typical Midwesterner suggests a heavy reliance on meat and potatoes. Throw in goodly amounts of cheese, beer and bratwurst and my arteries will need weeks to recover. The last time I was in the area, all they spoke about was walleye. I am not very risky in my food choices, and generally am not partial to lake fish, so I passed last time. Perhaps I can be persuaded to take the plunge this go-round.

More bad news. Upon arriving at our accommodations in Sheboygan (the Inn at Woodlake, which is cheaper than The American Club), we received our itinerary. It turns out that Blackwolf Run is being renovated for an upcoming LPGA tournament. As such, the only availability is a mix of holes from the River and Meadow Valley courses. Alas, another return trip is now necessary. I suppose it could be worse, as I need to return to play Erin Hills; however, this is starting to get ridiculous.

ROUND 3 Whistling Straits (Straits)

Course Rank: 3

Date Played: July 6, 2010

Starting Time: 9:00 a.m.

Weather: 80 degrees, humid, with chance of thunderstorms. There was moderate wind, which kept shifting direction…into my face.

My Score: 91

Number of Lost Balls: 0 (*Yippee!*)

Highlights: 1 birdie (first hole, always bad luck) and 6 pars

Lowlights: 3 double bogeys, 1 triple bogey and 1 quintuple bogey

Excuse for Not Breaking 80: The 1,000-plus waste areas and bunkers, in which I spent an inordinate amount of time.

Greens Fee: $340 quoted rate. We played the course as part of a stay-and-play deal that offered great value.

Playing Partners: Scott Rand and Jason, our caddie.

Practice Facilities: Very good, but we were hitting into the wind, which threw off my tempo.

My Rating: 9+, based upon the terrific views of Lake Michigan, imaginative holes, great par 3s and being a major championship venue.

Absolutely Must Play: Yes, this is a definite must, especially with the other affiliated courses.

Favorite Hole: 18, and not just because I parred it. This is a very long hole back into the clubhouse, with a huge waste area in front. (Bubba Watson found this area during the playoff at the 2010 PGA. This is also the hole where Dustin Johnson learned about sand traps.) I also liked Nos. 8, 11, 12, 13 and 17.

Location Characteristics: Whistling Straits is situated along Lake Michigan. For golf purists, it is not technically links, as the undulations come from man-made efforts, rather than the natural wind and sand buildup that characterizes a "true" links design. Personally, I could not care less how the course is created. Those holes along the lake are exceptional, with the par 3s being particularly exciting. The course is littered with bunkers, most of which are played as waste areas except for the pros (see Dustin Johnson). Wayward shots find their way into very high, but often playable heather.

Comments: Whistling Straits is ranked number three for a reason. The setting is awesome, and the golf extremely challenging. No lost balls, no penalty strokes, and I could still not break 90. Our caddie indicated that 75 percent of the people he caddies for do not break 100, and only 5 percent break 90. The par 3 holes are especially memorable with elevated tee boxes and forced carries, not to mention severe slopes toward Lake Michigan if you miss on the wrong side. This is a penultimate Dye design that severely penalizes mediocrity, let alone poor play. And yet the course is very playable if you hit perfect shots. The greens putt true. You must walk the course, so a caddie is highly recommended. I loved the way the caddies (who, by the way, are top notch) line up with the player's bags in anticipation of their arrival at the facility. The clubhouse is tasteful, without being over the top. Hope for a day with an eastern wind and low humidity…assuming you are there during the peak season. The greens are very large, and you can expect some three putts. Lastly, the course has history, having hosted two major championships. It is not Pebble Beach, but rates very high on the value scale.

ROUND 4 — Whistling Straits (Irish)

Course Rank: 68

Date Played: July 7, 2010

Starting Time: 9:00 a.m.

Weather: 80 degrees with humidity, rain and thunderstorms

My Score: 90

Number of Lost Balls: 3

Highlights: 10 pars

Lowlights: 4 double bogeys and 2 quadruple bogeys

Excuse for Not Breaking 80: I find thunderstorms on golf courses to be disconcerting. This might have been too much Pete Dye for three consecutive days, especially with all of the walking.

Greens Fee: $170, again purchased as part of a "value" stay-and-play package.

Playing Partners: Scott Rand. A.J. and Tommy from Denver also joined the group. Tommy is a club pro at Meridian Country Club in Denver, and had played with us the previous afternoon at Blackwolf Run during our free replay round.

Practice Facilities: Shared with the Straits course.

My Rating: 7+ for a fun and interesting links design. However, the course is situated away from the lake and is not nearly as dramatic as its more prominent partner.

Absolutely Must Play: Since you are on the Kohler package…yes. If you can only play one or two while in the area, this is the one to skip. Assuming you are playing all three, try and start with Irish. I am sure I would have enjoyed it more with better weather, and had I not played Straits the day before.

Favorite Hole: None of the holes were especially memorable in a positive way. I distinctly remember the two quadruple bogeys. I suppose my favorite was No. 15, a longish par 4 that required a straight drive, and long iron approach shot. There were numerous unique designs and some good tests... especially if you tend to be less accurate off the tee.

Location Characteristics: Situated adjacent to the Straits course, this layout does not have lake frontage. As such, the views are not as spectacular. Like Straits, the property is populated with sheep that nosh on the knee-high heather. There is water on six holes, and it comes into play. Irish is a classic "faux" links design that demands target golf.

Comments: After three straight days of Pete Dye, I was ready for something easier. The course yielded a number of pars, but several holes ate me up. We had Jason on the bag again, and he did a good job of trying to keep me focused; however, it was tough with a one-hour thunderstorm delay to start, and again after No. 3, this time for 90 minutes. At least the clubhouse had a nice bar, where I was able to polish off a very good artichoke cheese dip. As I had started the round with a double and a quadruple bogey, I also needed a beer. Thanks to the alcohol I rallied on the front side, playing the last seven holes in two over par. Carts are available but must stay on the paths, so you might as well walk.

Trip Summary:

Just as I expected, the trip to Wisconsin was a throwback to earlier days, when people were civil and life moved at a slower pace. The Kohler experience, located on the outskirts of Sheboygan, is one of the best golfing values around. For less than $1,000 per person, we had rounds at all three courses, caddies at each of the Whistling Straits layouts, breakfasts, free replays and a decent room. It was also great reconnecting with my childhood friend. As an added bonus, I was able to experience a Fourth of July fireworks show in small-town America.

Dining is unique in this part of the world. I would generally rate the food as pretty average, but I experienced some new and interesting offerings. The fried cheese curds, corn chowder and sausage soup, frozen custard and walleye were generally good. I was stunned to see that cheese is offered with virtually every entrée, either on top or stuffed. It is amazing the average Wisconsonian weighs less than 300 pounds. If the cheese is not enough, one cannot discount the amount of butter utilized in the local eateries, and let us not forget the bratwurst and beer.

Whistling Straits Golf Course is certainly worthy of a top ten ranking. I am still thinking about the course and trying to figure out when I can return. Blackwolf Run is a great golf course in its own right, although I was only able to experience nine of the holes on the rated venue. Whistling Straits Irish course is nice, but pales by comparison to its big brother. Nevertheless, the package is great, and with free replays, is well worth an afternoon. I was also pleasantly surprised by the quality and affordability of the Milwaukee area municipal courses. In particular, Brown Deer and Naga-Waukee were great layouts. For the golf addict, a three-day trip to Kohler is a must.

Bratwurst, Beer and Another Snafu, Part II (*Brainerd, Minnesota*)

Brainerd is a resort community located in the middle of Minnesota, approximately 2.5 hours from Minneapolis. I had previously visited the area for an in-law family reunion, and was happy to go back, given the quality of the golf on my last trip. Although there is only one top 100 course (Deacon's Lodge), once you get past the flies, mosquitoes and humidity, there are numerous other great venues as well. If the family must go along on your vacations, there is plenty to keep non-golfers occupied. Green fees are amazingly affordable, especially if you get the twilight rates, which take effect with at least six hours of remaining light. Because of the generosity of my in-laws, the trip was also a great value. Ultimately, I ditched the extended family on numerous occasions to play courses at Madden's, Cragun's and Grand View Lodge. I was anticipating an intervention, but am not sure they even noticed I was gone. Ultimately, I preferred several of the other local venues, but the top 100 course was enjoyable.

ROUND 5 Deacon's Lodge

Course Rank: 96

Date Played: July 10, 2010

Starting Time: 2:12 p.m.

Weather: 78 degrees, muggy, cloudy, minimal wind

My Score: 80

Number of Lost Balls: 2

Highlights: 12 pars.

Lowlights: 2 double bogeys.

Excuse for Not Breaking 80: Too many flies buzzing around my head on every shot.

Greens Fee: $79 for the twilight rate. It did not get dark until seven hours after our starting time, so this is the only way to go unless you want to be in an air-conditioned, mosquito-free environment by feeding time.

Playing Partners: Charlie Laubach (son) and Tom Longar (long-suffering out-law, for whom I have great sympathy, but that story is for another day), with his son Tommy serving as unofficial caddie.

Practice Facilities: Seemed pretty good, but I was so tired from the Wisconsin boondoggle and driving up from Minneapolis, I did not avail myself of the extra swings.

My Rating: 7, for a decent golfing challenge. Arnold Palmer's design is much less sadistic than Dye's Wisconsin layouts. Ample trees and water make for a scenic afternoon on the links, but this also serves as a breeding ground for all types of bugs, many of which chose to introduce themselves to us and partake of our bodily fluids.

Absolutely Must Play: It is probably not necessary to make the extensive trek to play this course, although a few days in the Brainerd area is well worth the effort, and this is one of several very nice tracks in this locale.

Favorite Hole: No. 17, a par three over a marsh, with water on all sides. I blanketed the flag with a five iron into a moderate wind, from 174 yards.

Location Characteristics: Deacon's Lodge is an attractive, pine-lined course, set along several natural lakes in the Brainerd area of Minnesota (site of much of the movie *Fargo*). This is a resort destination with numerous golf courses and water sports available to visitors. The fairways are relatively wide, but errant shots will find the trees. Favorable bounces are possible, although I did not get any. The water and flora are natural breeding grounds for mosquitoes and flies, so bring along plenty of DEET. Canadian geese are fun to look at but are also quite aggressive, and the natural fertilizer is a distraction at times. Overall, the setting is nice, with natural topography adding to the challenge.

Comments: This is an attractive course set in the Minnesota woods. The greens are large, sloping and tough, although not overly fast. Like most Palmer designs, the course is very playable, even if you are bit off-line (a lot off-line is another story). From the tips, the course plays nearly 7,000 yards and could be quite challenging. I thought the front nine was more exciting, although the finishing holes were very good. The staff at Deacon's Lodge, like those throughout the region, was very attentive.

While visiting Deacon's Lodge, make sure to try out the other local courses. I enjoyed The Pines, The Preserve, Madden's Classic (*Golf Digest* top 100) and Cragun's Legacy. Be prepared for humidity, bugs, thunderstorms and a lack of good red wine. Somehow, the locals believe serving wine at "room temperature" means "warm enough in which to swim." The cuisine in most family-oriented resort communities is usually average, and this was the case in Brainerd.

Unless you are local, or want a family vacation in the Minnesota woods, there are probably better options for the golf fanatic. However, the price is right, and it is a fun experience golfing through the trees. Ultimately, the flies and mosquitoes, as well as rapidly changing weather, can be a challenge. As my son commented, "Better muggy than buggy." Unfortunately, you are likely to have both in this area.

Trip Summary:

A golf marathon to a golf addict is like chocolate to a Labrador retriever; you never know when to stop. During the trip, I played 11.5 rounds in eight days on ten different courses. I took 973 strokes, including 402 putts. I lost 26 balls, but found four. I landed in 14 water hazards and experienced two weather delays. During the trip I consumed a full bottle of DEET and half a tube of sunscreen, as well as 12 ibuprofen tablets and 16 aspirin. The end result was three blisters on my feet, eight mosquito bites, a really sore elbow and an absolutely fantastic time.

It all added up to a great golf vacation, but only 3 top 100 courses were successfully navigated. Despite fighting my driver, the golf was acceptable, with several good iron shots and a couple of critical putts. I even managed to get my annual eagle, with a driver, four iron, and 20-foot putt on No. 10 at Madden's Classic.

Chapter 12

Trumped

Like many metropolitan areas, Los Angeles offers far too few public courses relative to the number of local residents. Other than a smattering of average municipal tracks, the South Bay region offers few golf options. Thanks to Donald Trump, and millions upon millions of dollars, there is now one upscale opportunity. Trump National Golf Club Los Angeles is situated on the Palos Verdes Peninsula, with Pacific Ocean views from all eighteen holes. That is the good news. The bad news is that accessibility is problematic, given the lack of freeway proximity and traffic. This is compounded by the fact that the original design is by Pete Dye, so a round promises to be mentally exhausting before hitting the road for a long commute back to wherever.

I have never been a big Trump fan, but he has had a positive impact on the golf world. This recent acquisition is now a first-class facility, with a totally superfluous, 38,000-square-foot clubhouse—which is one more monument to the man himself. The course has been seen on *Wonderful World of Golf* on the Golf Channel, with Trump hosting. I warmed up for my round by watching Mark Wahlberg and Kevin Dillon duke it out. Of course they edited out all the bad shots, so most of the show was devoted to showing Trump golfing with Arnold Palmer, or meeting with Korean businessmen in the middle of the competition. No doubt, the Donald paid a pretty hefty fee for the course, even before investing another 50 million dollars into the clubhouse and waterfalls, and prior to replacing that portion of the facility that had fallen into the ocean before the turn of the century.

Originally designed by Pete Dye and named Ocean Trails, the course was scheduled to open in 1999. On June 2, 1999, just before the opening, the 18th hole decided to take a dip in the Pacific. For the next several years the course played as a 15-hole facility. In 2002, Trump, or more likely one of the entities in which he has a partial interest, acquired the project. In 2005, after the aforementioned improvements, the course reopened with much fanfare (how surprising for a Trump project), with those involved suggesting the course to be superior to Pebble Beach. Nice try, but NO.

ROUND 6 — Trump National Los Angeles

Course Rank: 31

Date Played: July 21, 2010

Starting Time: 2:30 p.m.

Weather: 70 degrees, cloudy and foggy, light wind

My Score: 77, I shot even par 35 on the back nine.

Number of Lost Balls: 3

Highlights: Two birdies and ten pars

Lowlights: Two double bogeys

Excuse for Not Breaking 80: None needed. I played well with unbelievable putting. I doubt I would break 80 if I played this venue again.

Greens Fee: $174.93 (lots of city taxes on a $160 twilight rate). Regular greens fees are $275.

Playing Partners: Joe Strong. We were joined by Rich (retired finance guy from Raytheon) and Isaac (dentist). Good guys. We spent several hours after the round drinking beer and eating off the bar menu.

Practice Facilities: Very expansive driving range. Short game practice areas seemed a bit limited.

My Rating: 8, for the excellent ocean views. But, perhaps I am rating it so high because I played so well.

Absolutely Must Play: For indexes below 10, yes, and above 10, no. The course is so tricked up, with target golf essential, that the higher handicap players are going to find little to like about the layout. My partners were all frustrated by the time they reached the third hole. On the other hand, if you like Pete Dye designs and want a challenge, this course fits the bill.

Favorite Hole: If you spend most of the round in the fairways, there are a lot of holes to like. No. 1 was my favorite. A short par 4 (314 yards from the blues) offers a sloping green fronted by a lake, with a massive waterfall behind. This gives the illusion of an extremely narrow green, and makes the 100-yard approach shot a real knee-knocker. No. 9 is an unbelievably difficult par 4, with a partially blind tee shot to a 200-yard-plus second shot, with a lake bordering the left side. No. 18 is also a spectacular finishing hole.

Location Characteristics: The property occupies one of the most valuable parcels of land on the West Coast. Trump National is situated on the Palos Verdes Peninsula in Los Angeles County. Terraced above the Pacific Ocean, all of the holes offer views along the coast. On clear days you can see Catalina Island. Most of the holes run parallel to one another. There are environmentally sensitive areas along both sides of most fairways, and barrancas that create challenging forced carries to reach many of the fairways. It is virtually impossible to find balls that are not in the fairway or the adjoining four-inch rough. This rough is extremely penal. I recommend taking your medicine and getting back on the fairway. The environmentally sensitive areas are played like a lateral hazard, so plan on penalty strokes aplenty. Among the local wildlife there are *Homo sapiens* (with their dogs) traversing the coastal land adjoining the property. A city-mandated public access area is heavily used by local residents and is, at times, distracting. On several occasions we were interrupted by talking and shouting from the walkers.

Comments: Only the combination of Pete Dye, Donald Trump and Hollywood could come up with this course. I kept expecting a boat to come out from under the waterfall to the music from "It's a Small World." The co-architect of the course (along with Dye) is listed as the Donald himself, though it struck me as more Duck than Trump. The course was created on a site that typically would be too small for a championship design. As such, there are a number of short holes, and many parallel fairways. From the whites, the distance is only 5,881 yards. To compensate, there is trouble on either side of most fairways, others require 175-plus yards of carry to avoid trouble. The par 5s are extremely narrow, have lots of bunkers and too much protection to reach in two. The greens themselves offer unusually extreme undulation, with most having at least three tiers. If you can play precision golf, and have a strong short game, the course could yield a low score, but I believe most will need several rounds to figure it out. I was very lucky to score well.

Trip Summary:

Ultimately, the experience was a little surreal. The dramatic clubhouse makes little sense, given that there is not a resort attached to the project, nor is there a *Forbes* 400 list of members. Due to the poor access, it is hard to imagine a lot of business activity at the facility. The staff was friendly and competent. The green fees were reasonable by Pacific oceanfront standards. The carts had GPS on board, which was helpful. However, the scorecard feature was not working, and there were no "pro tips"... just the yardages. Some of the sprinkler heads had yardages; however, many were cracked or missing. The waterfall on 17 had been turned off, and the cart path in that area was closed. Golfers received a cheap plastic bag tag, but none of the accoutrements that often distinguish the really high-end facilities. On the whole, my feelings were conflicted. I was thrilled with the views and my scoring, and enjoy really tough designs, but the course struck me as too difficult for the casual player, and I prefer not to have so many parallel fairways. While it is not Pebble Beach by any stretch, the course offers a good day on the links. Go for the view, appreciate the challenging design, and bring lots of golf balls and a good sense of humor.

Chapter 13

Home Cooking

I seldom venture to Torrey Pines for golf, despite being located only 15 miles south of my home. The reasons are twofold. First, I have never quite figured out their reservation system, which provides benefits to city of San Diego residents (I am not in the city limits). Secondly, the courses (North and South) receive very high utilization, such that a five-hour round is not uncommon. This is a tourist-heavy facility, and while many players are not always low handicappers, most feel compelled to play the blue tees anyway.

Parking can be an issue in the area, which necessitates long walks, or bus rides when pro tournaments are played. Nevertheless, it is a great venue to watch the pros play. Further, the annual tournament tends to attract a very strong field. The 2008 U.S. Open was played on the South course, and will long be remembered as the year a one-legged Tiger Woods defeated sentimental favorite Rocco Mediate in a playoff.

Although a municipal facility, the expansive course can be rigged to create sufficient difficulty to host a U.S. Open. The attraction of Torrey Pines is the dramatic Pacific Ocean frontage and surrounding canyons that make this property one of the most desirable on the West Coast. A camera is a must and binoculars if they are active on Blacks Beach (the nude beach situated down the cliffs from the golf course). The course is very playable for amateurs of every level, with only the most wayward of shots resulting in lost balls and penalty strokes. If the rough is up for the professional tournaments, you might consider a forecaddie. Torrey Pines is also attractive because of the high percentage of perfect weather days. Other than the rainy season from January to March, you can almost always count on temperatures between 65 and 80 degrees, with no humidity, and moderate ocean breezes.

ROUND 7 — Torrey Pines South

Course Rank: 20

Date Played: July 30, 2010

Starting Time: 2:00 p.m.

Weather: 65 degrees, overcast, slight wind from the west

My Score: 81

Number of Lost Balls: 0

Highlights: 1 birdie and 9 pars.

Lowlights: 2 double bogeys.

Excuse for Not Breaking 80: Senility. I accidently pulled a nine iron from my bag when the shot called for a six iron, costing me one stroke.

Greens Fee: Gratis. I was treated to the round by Ray Adams, a local commercial real estate agent who had helped us acquire an investment property, and received a decent commission in return. For non-residents, the greens fees are $183 during the week and $229 on Friday to Sunday. Twilight rates are $110 to $137, but the window for completing a twilight round is relatively small most of the year. For those lucky enough to be living in the city of San Diego, the rates are $61 to $76.

Playing Partners: Andy Laubach (brother), Joe Strong and Ray Adams (who treated the group to the round).

Practice Facilities: Below average. The driving range is a long walk from the starter and pro shop. If you need to hit balls, do so before checking in. The balls were poor, reduced distance design, and rock hard. There were not enough stations to accommodate all the golfers. The putting green, however, is quite expansive.

My Rating: 8. Torrey Pines is a municipal golf course. Given the location and notoriety, the facility gets excessive play. To its credit, the maintenance staff does an excellent job keeping the course in good condition. Further, the setting is very attractive. Ocean views abound, as the course meanders along the cliffs and across a variety of arroyos. However, there are few holes that offer a "wow" factor.

Absolutely Must Play: Yes. First, this is a U.S. Open course, and has been the site of PGA events for many years, so you must respect the history. Secondly, San Diego is a terrific vacation destination, and Torrey Pines is the one "must-play" round in America's Finest City. The South course is more difficult and has the history, so be sure to play this one at least once. The North course offers the same physical attributes, but not the same challenge. I would not come to San Diego solely for a golf vacation; however, when visiting, a round here is worth the time and expense.

Favorite Hole: The course has a lot of good but not memorable holes. The signature hole is No. 3, an elevated tee box hitting down to a par 3, with a terrific ocean view in the background. However, there is not much to the hole aside from the view. My favorite is No. 13, a par 5 that goes down into a ravine on the second shot, then requires a precise, largely blind third shot to an elevated, well-bunkered green. The day we played, the pin placement was back right, which is really tough. No. 18 is a par 5 that offers the only lake (more like a pond) on the course, protecting the green.

Location Characteristics: Torrey Pines is situated approximately 10 miles north of downtown San Diego. The location is characterized by views of the Pacific Ocean and is situated amongst coastal canyons. There are a couple of Torrey pines left, but most of the trees are mature eucalyptus. Sea birds are constantly flying over, as are hang gliders and F-18s (or are they 14s?) that take off from the Miramar Marine Corps Air Station to the east. The coastal setting is worth the price of admission.

Comments: Torrey Pines is owned by the city of San Diego. The project was developed in 1957, long before land values would have made the property too expensive for anything but custom home development. As a city course, the facilities are a bit dated, and there is a "bureaucratic" feel to the operation. The course that the public plays is a far cry from that which greets the pros each year, or what Tiger faced when he played on one leg in the 2008 U.S. Open. The black tees (not open to the public generally) play 7,628 yards. Our round was 1,000 yards shorter, with lower rough, wider fairways and slower greens. I have played Torrey Pines after pro events, and can attest that the rough can be ridiculously difficult. The greens have subtle breaks, and at times can be very fast, especially with a downhill putt toward the ocean. Overall, it is a playable layout that should afford most golfers an opportunity for a few pars.

Given the sea level, heavy air, wind, lush fairways, and many uphill shots, the course plays unusually long. I found myself hitting a lot of three woods and hybrids into the greens, after decent drives. The blue tees, if set up correctly, measure 7,051 yards, and are only recommended for 0-5 indexes. I was amazed at how many groups were flailing away from these tees. The whites play plenty long. My playing partners all shot between 95 and 100, despite indexes of 11 to 16. They did this without losing balls or taking penalty strokes. Like so many places, the short game will make the biggest difference in your score. Lagging putts is critical given the large greens.

Trip Summary:

The round at Torrey Pines was enjoyable. The foursome was fun, and the caddies made for a most enjoyable walk, although this is one venue where I would not hire a looper. I was able to get away with a few wayward drives, before finding my game late and shooting 38 on the back side. By the end, I had the greens figured out. As a result, I made a number of mid-range putts following good chips. Amazingly, I had no three-putts on the day; the same could not be said for my playing partners. Despite the overcast weather, the views were great. The facility is not perfect, but it is unlikely you will go away disappointed.

Chapter 14

Dodging a Bullet

Since beginning my quest two months ago, I eagerly have been awaiting *Golf Magazine*'s 2010 "Top 100 Courses You Can Play" edition. Given current economic conditions and the overbuilt nature of golf courses, I was not expecting huge changes, but was worried one or two courses already played would drop off, or my travel plans could get screwed up. Last night, while working on more logistics, I noticed that my bookmark took me to the new 2010 article. My initial trepidation proved unfounded, as this year's list included only seven new venues. Of those that dropped out, at least two have been closed (which was already going to make playing them problematic). I was very pleased to see that all of the courses played or scheduled to date are still on the list. As an added bonus, one of the new courses (checking in at number 10) is Old Macdonald at Bandon Dunes. Since we scheduled a round on that course for our visit in September, it is essentially a "freebie" as I work through the list. Amazingly, Bandon Dunes now boasts numbers 1, 5, 10 and 15. Wow, are my expectations going to be difficult to meet.

The six other new courses include one in the Chicago area, which is no problem, and another one in Hawaii, always a decent place to vacation. Michigan, Arizona and North Carolina should not be difficult, given future trips. The only painful addition will be the trip now required to French Lick, Indiana. Falling off the list were courses in Nevada, Idaho, Maryland (two of them), Mississippi, Massachusetts and South Carolina. Overall, I think it is a net positive.

Chapter 15

Rocky Mountain High

The 2010 U.S. Open at Pebble Beach played havoc with my annual trek to the golfing paradise located within the confines of 17-Mile Drive. I could have scheduled a trip; however, the intense interest in the golf course led the Pebble Beach Company to increase prices and limit their usual specials. Thriftiness would not allow me to pay full freight, so this year my wife and I had to make alternative arrangements. (Ironically, our substitute trip would be cut short by a last-minute opportunity to play Pebble Beach, but more on that later.) With plenty of alternatives, we opted for the rarefied air of Colorado.

I had heard rumors about playing high-altitude golf, but nothing could prepare me for the thrill of hitting a golf ball as far as the pros. The highlight was a 380-yard drive, albeit downhill and downwind. We booked a great deal on a condominium in the Beaver Creek area of Vail that included a golf package at Red Sky Ranch. The location represented a decent base of operations for trekking out to Lakota Canyon (one hour west), and ultimately Redlands Mesa (two-plus hours west). The only negative was the aforementioned greens aeration at Broadmoor East, which was going to necessitate a return trip.

Round 8 Red Sky Ranch (Norman)

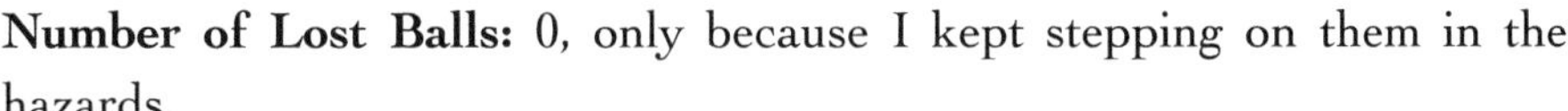

Course Rank: 26

Date Played: August 28, 2010

Starting Time: 1:30 p.m.

Weather: Mostly cloudy, scattered thunderstorms, 65 degrees

My Score: 85

Number of Lost Balls: 0, only because I kept stepping on them in the hazards.

Highlights: 1 birdie, 5 pars

Lowlights: 2 double bogeys

Excuse for Not Breaking 80: Excuses, have I got excuses. It started with the detour trying to get onto I-70, which put me behind schedule so I could not warm up. This was followed by the pro shop attendant directing me to the driving range to check in, at the opposite end of where I was supposed to go, followed by what felt like a 20-minute drive from the guest clubhouse to the first hole. By the time I arrived, the group I was supposed to play with had taken off (early). I was put behind two foursomes, and not matched up, so play was excruciatingly slow. Of course, there was a good deal of wind and some rain, plus my system was not ready for the altitude. Throw in a very poor driving day, no course knowledge, and lightning-fast, tricky greens, and the formula for a high round was in place.

Greens Fee: $175 as part of a stay-and-play package.

Playing Partners: None.

Practice Facilities: They looked pretty decent, but I was too rushed to take advantage.

My Rating: 7+. The course was decent, but lacked any "wow" factor. Many of the holes seemed redundant.

Absolutely Must Play: With outside influences negatively impacting my experience, I would have to say no. I gave the course a second chance two days later, but still was not enamored. However, high altitude golf is good for the ego, and the accommodations were great.

Favorite Hole: Most of the holes are good, and some are very good. I liked No. 18, a 573-yard, downhill dogleg left that would be difficult to reach in two for most golfers, and is protected in front by a creek. However, I think my favorite was 16. This hole is a downhill, 230-yard, par 3, with a left to right sloping green. I put a four iron 15 feet past the hole, and sank the putt.

Location Characteristics: There are great vistas from many holes. This course is situated in the Rocky Mountains at around 8,000 feet. Most of the holes traverse across the mountains, with the most northerly offering great views. The development includes two championship courses, which alternate as the Members or Guest courses every other day. There are also two clubhouses, one exclusively for members. It is a five-minute golf cart ride to No. 1 on the Norman Course from the visitors' clubhouse. The setting is attractive, and, no doubt, accounts for the high rating. The ball carries very well at this altitude.

Comments: In retrospect, I was a bit disappointed with the experience. Granted, the weather was not great. Ultimately, there were few memorable holes and too many were similar. Most of the holes run east/west along the hillside. As a result, balls are prone to significant sideway movement down the hills. What this means is that all tee shots and approaches must be played to the uphill side of the target. For someone with a general left to right ball flight (like me) it often involved even greater uphill lines. Finally, the prevailing wind was generally down the hillside, further exacerbating the movement. It was laughable at times when approach shots would bounce ten yards to the uphill side of the green and would kick back across. Virtually every putt broke in the direction of Interstate 70, below the course. Lightning-quick greens make three-putts inevitable, although they roll true. Ultimately, there were some good holes, but many that were largely forgettable. Holes 11, 13, 14 and 15 seemed to be the same hole, with slightly different yardages. Fortunately, the course is bailed out with a great finish on Nos. 16 to 18. Red Sky Ranch was in excellent condition, with first-class facilities. It is just not a course that suits my eye. I will probably return someday, but for a top 30 layout, I feel you can do better.

Round 9 — The Golf Club at Redlands Mesa

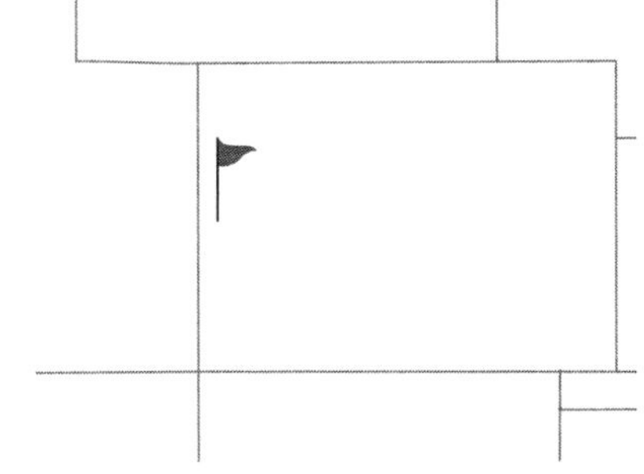

Course Rank: 94

Date Played: August 29, 2010

Starting Time: 1:30 p.m.

Weather: 85 degrees, cloudy skies, some drizzle, and scattered thundershowers with wind gusts to 30 mph.

My Score: 86

Number of Lost Balls: 0

Highlights: 6 pars

Lowlights: 2 double bogeys

Excuse for Not Breaking 80: The wind gusts did not help, but I do not ever recall having putted so poorly (probably selective memory). I had my first four-putt green in at least five years, plus four three-putts.

Greens Fee: $105

Playing Partners: I started solo, but after six holes joined up with a nice couple from Denver.

Practice Facilities: The limited facilities were fairly typical for a municipal facility and range balls were included in the greens fees.

My Rating: 8+. Similar to municipal golf courses, the condition and the facilities were average, but I loved the course layout. Jim Engh did a terrific job designing this course with great elevations and shots through canyons. Hours after the round I could still remember every hole. I think I took more photographs of this course than any other played to date. This one is definitely underrated.

Absolutely Must Play: Yes. If you love elevated tees, and I do, you will truly enjoy this design. Grand Junction is nothing to write home about, but it was worth a two-hour detour to play this one, even with the wind.

Favorite Hole: No. 5, a devilish downhill par 5 that requires an iron off the tee, to avoid going through the fairway on this dogleg right hole. The second shot must be a lay up except for the longest hitters as the pin is elevated above a hazard. The elevated green is on two levels. My shot that rolled back to the bottom level left me with an impossible first putt. Honorable mention goes to No. 17, a 200-yard par 3 from a severely elevated tee box.

Location Characteristics: Grand Junction is situated in the high desert area of western Colorado, near the dramatic mesas that rise above the desert floor (visitors are strongly urged to take the rim drive along the Colorado National Monument). The course is situated just below these landforms. Located about four hours west of Denver, it is not an easy trip, but offers great views along the way. The primary attractions are the dramatic views. Grand Junction is not a place I would want to spend a lot of time, owing to a miserable weather pattern that goes from freezing to hot and back to freezing in the blink of an eye, and let us not forget the difficult accessibility. Nevertheless, a short visit is worthwhile.

Comments: During the summer the temperatures can be warm in this area of the high desert, so be prepared. The views are amazing, and I could not get enough of the elevated tees. I strongly urge hiking up to the black tees on those elevated holes, as the vistas are nothing short of spectacular. The front side offers the highest elevations, with several dramatic holes. The stretch of Nos. 2 through 5 is extraordinary. Overall, the layout reminds me a bit of Wolf Creek in Mesquite, Nevada. Redlands Mesa falls slightly short of that venue, but I really enjoyed the round. The overall facilities are average, but the golf is exceptional. I am not sure I will ever be back in the area, but if I get close you can bet I will give it another shot.

Round 10 — Lakota Canyon Ranch

Course Rank: *73*

Date Played: August 31, 2010

Starting Time: 9:00 a.m.

Weather: 65 degrees, partly cloudy, mild wind

My Score: 82

Number of Lost Balls: 3

Highlights: One birdie, eight pars

Lowlights: Two double bogeys

Excuse for Not Breaking 80: My decision to "Tin Cup" it on 18, as I was convinced I could reach the blind green in two on this par five…wrong.

Greens Fee: $89, with a cart, plus $5 for range balls.

Playing Partners: None.

Practice Facilities: Below average. The condition suggested possible financial problems.

My Rating: *7*. The condition was below average for a top 100 facility, with older carts, scruffy driving range balls and a poorly maintained range. The rating could jump if some money were reinvested in this layout.

Absolutely Must Play: No, but the front nine has some terrific holes.

Favorite Hole: The par 5, No. 4 is a great challenge. An elevated tee shot is followed by a tough lay up before approaching an elevated green.

Location Characteristics: Lakota Canyon is situated high in the Rocky Mountains, just west of Glenwood Springs. The drive through Glenwood Canyon is breathtaking. There are plenty of elevated tees with panoramic views down the mountains. The course includes several water features, tree-lined fairways and large elevation changes, all making for a photogenic setting.

Comments: Lakota Canyon was designed by the same golf course architect as the Golf Club at Redlands Mesa. Jim Engh has a gift for utilizing the natural terrain to create fantastic elevated tees. In particular, the front nine is exceptional, as are the final three holes. This course offers my favorite type of starting hole; a dogleg left, par 5, from an elevated tee box. No. 2 is benign, but then the elevation takes over. The finishing three holes are really tough, especially 18, which requires a precise drive, a strong lay up, and excellent approach. The hole tempts the long hitter to go for it in two, although the visibility of the green is limited, and there are hazards on all sides. The course, built in 2000, appears to have originally been designed as the focal point of a proposed residential community. While some homes have been constructed, it now appears to have come to a standstill. The carts are older and need to be replaced, the clubhouse is a temporary facility, and the grounds show some signs of stress.

Trip Summary:

In addition to the amazing mountain setting and terrific condo, the Vail area is also known for its high-quality cuisine. Ultimately, my favorite meal during the top 100 tour took place at Zino Ristorante, located close to Beaver Creek. The overall quality of our vacation in Colorado was first rate, and attractively priced relative to other resort communities. The golf was good, but not great, although some of the holes were spectacular. The 15-percent distance premium on my golf shots was an added bonus.

The Denver area is easily accessible from most areas of the country, as it serves as a hub for a number of carriers. As such, direct flights are plentiful and the cost is reasonable. Lodging during golf season is great in the Vail area, with plenty of other outdoor activities for the non-golfer. Although, I did not love the golf, I will be returning. Hopefully, Zino will still be serving the seafood cappellini.

The Colorado trip was cut short, as my brother successfully bid on CharityBuzz.com and won a twosome for the pro-am at the First Tee Open, to be held at Pebble Beach. I could not resist the opportunity to leave the Mile High City and make my way to the Monterey Peninsula.

Chapter 16

Back to Reality

Coming off a "golfer's high" in Pebble Beach, it was probably unfair to move so quickly back to the "rat race" of golfing the top 100. After the Colorado whirlwind, coupled with the Pebble Beach First Tee Open, it would be nearly impossible to evaluate another venue fairly. Because we were in the area, however, and had missed the cut on Sunday, my brother and I decided to kill time before our flight back to San Diego. Fortunately, Pasatiempo is situated more or less along the route to the San Jose airport. I had heard great things about this Alister MacKenzie design, which harkens back to the classic golf course architecture of the golden age of 220-yard drives, and non-technologically enhanced equipment. Built in the year of the great stock market crash, it still has a Roaring 20s feel. Because of the age, and changing equipment, the course has undergone several redesigns to lengthen the layout. In fact, according to our playing partner, they are working with Tom Doak on another redesign. I am not sure they need it.

Round 11 — Pasatiempo

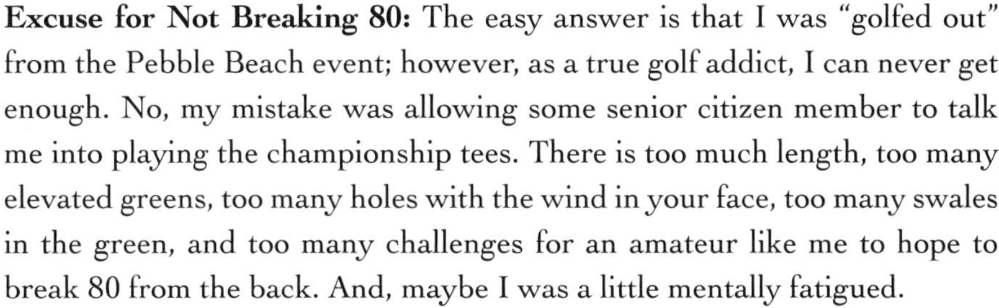

Course Rank: 11

Date Played: September 5, 2010

Starting Time: 11:10 a.m.

Weather: Overcast with some fog, and a mild breeze blowing off the Pacific. Temperature was 65 degrees.

My Score: 89

Number of Lost Balls: 3

Highlights: 5 pars

Lowlights: 4 double bogeys, 1 triple bogey

Excuse for Not Breaking 80: The easy answer is that I was "golfed out" from the Pebble Beach event; however, as a true golf addict, I can never get enough. No, my mistake was allowing some senior citizen member to talk me into playing the championship tees. There is too much length, too many elevated greens, too many holes with the wind in your face, too many swales in the green, and too many challenges for an amateur like me to hope to break 80 from the back. And, maybe I was a little mentally fatigued.

Greens Fee: $220 plus $30 cart fee

Playing Partners: My brother Andy, Dave (member of the board, and unofficial tour guide) and Will (member of the club).

Practice Facilities: Decent putting green and chipping area. The driving range is not located with the rest of the practice facilities, and is accessed via a van that runs back and forth from the clubhouse. We did not have enough time to hit balls.

My Rating: 8. The course did not have the "wow" factor attributable to my favorite venues (of course, I had played Pebble Beach the previous day). While the first hole supposedly offers an ocean view, fog hid this from our foursome. Other surroundings consist of older, single family homes, which detract from the visual appeal. The strength of the course lies in the subtle nature of the design. For high handicappers, it might be difficult to appreciate the value MacKenzie places on every shot. Most holes could yield pars; however, each swing needs to be above average.

Absolutely Must Play: Yes. I think every avid golfer should take advantage of the classic courses. Unlike many of the "tricked up" designs today, this golf course offers a comparable challenge based upon more subtle design features. There are no easy holes. Missing greens virtually assures a bogey. I will need to play the course again so I can see what it looks like from the fairways.

Favorite Hole: I liked No. 16, the number 1 handicap. The blind tee shot I hit was perfect, and my approach was pretty good. The flag, however, was stuck on the left side on a very small shelf, resulting in a three-putt from 25 feet. No. 11 is great as well; however, it was quite expensive as I placed several shots in the ravine. I thought every hole had character, with the opening three—including a 235-yard uphill par 3 to a well-protected green—being brutal. (All the more reason to avoid the championship tees.)

Location Characteristics: Pasatiempo is situated in the hills of Santa Cruz, about 30 miles outside of San Jose, on the way to the Monterey Peninsula. I would have liked to have seen more mature pines, although that would have led to a higher score. There was no significant water on the course, and the surrounding homes seemed uninspired. There are some distant ocean views when it is not overcast.

Comments: The setting of Pasatiempo is not as dramatic as many of the top venues. The strength of the course lies in the inspired design of one of the great golf course architects. MacKenzie loved this course so much he lived for many years in a house bordering the sixth hole. The first three holes are likely to set the stage for a high-scoring day. The first two are long par 4s into the wind, with tricky greens. The third is a crazy par 3 that is virtually impossible to reach in regulation from the championship tees. The par 70 layout gets easier after the start; however, it will bite you again right after you make the turn. Holes 10 and 11 are good for at least one double bogey. The finishing hole is a dramatic downhill par 3. Avoid the front left bunker. For the golf addict, Pasatiempo is well worth the trip. For the golf historian it is a must. While there, I strongly recommend you try the Burger Dog at the drive-through snack bar after the front nine.

Trip Summary:

Pasatiempo is easy to schedule if you are making the trek to the Monterey Peninsula. I recommend adding this course to your itinerary, time permitting. In fact, the CordeValle Resort is also situated within close proximity and can easily be included in a trip with the Monterey triumvirate. This is a great once-in-a-lifetime vacation that should not be missed by any golfing fool. Aside from the cost (and it is pricey), there is nothing to match the Northern California golf experience. While I would have preferred a more pastoral setting for Pasatiempo, you should not miss this MacKenzie golf experience.

Chapter 17

Managing Expectations: The Pea Soup Theory

In Buellton, California, there is a restaurant that is widely known for its pea soup. Few things sound less appealing than a bowl of liquefied peas, yet people drive for miles just to partake of this "treat." I have been to this restaurant on several occasions. The soup looks just as unappetizing as it sounds; yet, when you sample the serving, it is not horrible. Due to the low level of expectation, many actually describe the taste as pretty good. Let's be honest, it is still just pea soup, but reduced expectations often result in an unlikely outcome. Conversely, high expectations often lead to disappointment.

For years I had been regaled with the wonders of golf at Bandon Dunes. With the opening of the new course in 2010, the resort now sports four of *Golf Magazine*'s top 15, including number one: Pacific Dunes. I cannot recall a situation that was riper for a letdown.

My three brothers and I have made regular pilgrimages to golf resorts in the western United States, but had missed the last several years due to... well, let's not point fingers. Anyway, the prospect of Bandon Dunes with the bros was too compelling to let slide. Indicative of the desirability of the facility, we could not get reservations for our preferred *or* back-up dates, despite calling four months in advance. Ultimately, we had to pay premium dollars to reserve a four-bedroom, four-bathroom cabin, and schedule rounds at each of the four courses.

Unfortunately, two days before leaving I contracted a severe head cold. This, combined with the fact that I was still not over the First Tee Open at Pebble Beach, put my mindset at less than perfect.

Getting there created additional stress. Bandon Dunes is the classic location "where you cannot get there from here." What you could call a turbo jet (but it still has a propeller) is the only way, short of a ridiculous drive or private jet, into the area. All flights into North Bend airport (not to be confused with Bend, Oregon, which is located farther north and east) originate in San Francisco or Portland, and require travel on United Airlines. That means paying for checked luggage, which is hard to avoid when you are traveling with golf clubs.

I was not disappointed in the travel given my low expectations for United Airlines. After checking the clubs, and paying for them, my brothers and I joined the TSA line with our carry-on luggage. Moments later, a dictatorial customer service representative with a bad attitude came up to my brother and asked him which airline he was flying. John made the mistake of acknowledging we were flying on United. Despite a carry-on that had made the grade on every other carrier he had flown, the lady insisted he follow her and have the bag measured. Upon rechecking the size, it seems he missed by an inch, and was compelled to ante up another $35. Great customer service has never been a feature of this airline. In truth, United Express, which served North Bend, was a cut above the parent company. (Ironically, we ran into the same woman several weeks later as she was hassling another traveler.)

The TSA also proved a challenge. They decided to test a full body scan machine, and yours truly lucked into being a guinea pig. Not only did this slow the process, but required removal of everything on my person, including such weapons of mass destruction as my handkerchief, Chapstick, etc. I could spend the next ten pages on the TSA, but I will leave that to the stand-up comedians. Thank goodness our family has German blood and had arrived very early.

Ultimately, the plane departed on time and arrived 25 minutes early to San Francisco. (How is it possible to make up 25 minutes on a one-hour flight?) I was loaded up on cold medicine so I hardly noticed the puddle jumper we took into North Bend. This time we were 20 minutes early on a one-hour, fifteen-minute flight. I was not going to complain, as we had a tee time one-hour and twenty minutes after our scheduled landing, and the drive was estimated to take approximately 30 minutes. Our entire luggage arrived, and, after paying a big premium, Hertz rented us a minivan. It took the full 30 minutes before we entered the Bandon Dunes complex. We attempted to check in quickly, but our cabin was not ready, so we raced to Pacific Dunes (number one on the list), for our 2:40 starting time.

Round 12 — Pacific Dunes

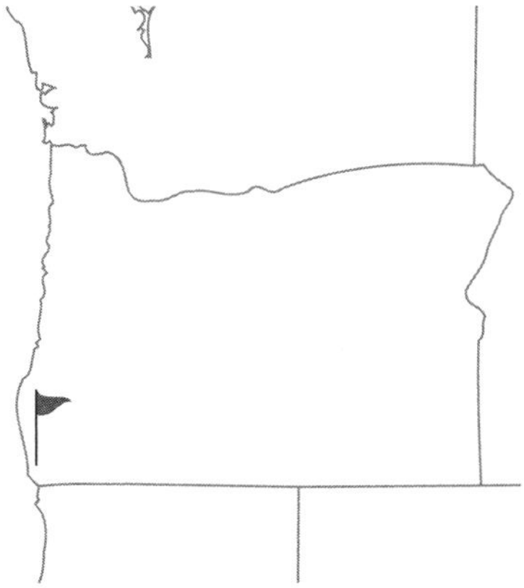

Course Rank: 1

Date Played: September 22, 2010

Starting Time: 2:40 p.m.

Weather: Overcast, mild wind, 60 degrees

My Score: 89

Number of Lost Balls: 0

Highlights: 2 birdies, 5 pars

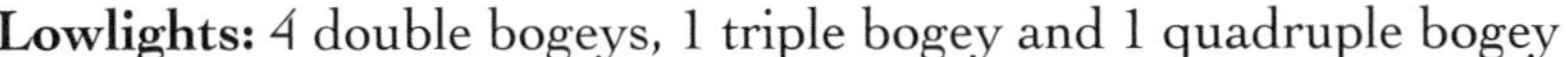

Lowlights: 4 double bogeys, 1 triple bogey and 1 quadruple bogey

Excuse for Not Breaking 80: Jet lag and lack of warm-up did not help. We left San Diego at 6:00 a.m., arrived in North Bend at 1:30 p.m. and went straight to the course for our starting time. After a quadruple bogey on the first, I went eight over on the next four holes, putting me at 12 over after five. I was lucky to break 90.

Greens Fee: $220

Playing Partners: Brothers, John, Chris and Andy. Caddies: Jack (mine) and Tim. Our caddies would stay with us for the entire trip. I felt sorry for Tim, as John was spraying the ball pretty good. No wonder these guys are all so skinny.

Practice Facilities: Expansive. We drove past them before hitting the course.

My Rating: 8+. Perhaps it was the long trip, perhaps the head cold, or perhaps it was the high expectations, but Pacific Dunes did not rock my world, and is certainly not number one. Further, while the setting is terrific, this project lacks history. Lastly, so many of the features that I find less attractive about links golf are emphasized on this layout. I much preferred the design at Whistling Straits. Don't get me wrong, this is terrific golf, but I think the *Golf Magazine* raters need to get real.

Absolutely Must Play: Yes. A trip to Bandon Dunes is a must. Pacific Dunes provides a great environment, and an attractive design that meshes magnificently with the natural surroundings.

Favorite Hole: The overall experience and feel is top-notch, but few of the individual holes were memorable. I liked Nos. 9 and 12 because I made birdie, but these were not exceptional holes. Both Nos. 17 and 18 were enjoyable, with the par 3, No. 17 offering one of the better visuals. The long par 5, No. 18 was probably my favorite, as it created a challenging finish. There are numerous holes along the Pacific Ocean, but the layout was less intimidating/exciting than those holes along Lake Michigan at Whistling Straits, and the views more understated.

Location Characteristics: It is hard to beat the natural surroundings that characterize the Bandon courses, although rugged weather is required to create this environment. All but Bandon Trails have some oceanfront holes, albeit on the cliffs above the water. Unlike Pebble Beach, the water does not come into play. In fact, other than one lake on Bandon Trails there is no water whatsoever. The mandate was to create golf similar to that of the Scottish link courses. To this end they have done a credible job; you can save the airfare across "the pond" and spend a week in Oregon. However, the overall cost may be the same. Aside from the ocean, there are naturally rolling hills and lots of gorse, where deer roam freely. Primarily, however, it is moguls, undulations, hillsides and large greens. They do not allow carts on the course (except two per day for handicapped players, driven by employees). The weather is transient, and heavily impacted by proximity to the coast. Wind, rain and fog are common.

Comments: Pacific Dunes is an interesting golf course that has incorporated the natural surroundings in a way that is almost breathtaking. Everything there is natural. However, the golf did not live up to my expectations, especially for a public course ranked number one. I like to be rewarded for good shots and punished for second-rate efforts. I prefer to have the holes more "shaped" than a classic links design, and I am not a huge fan of tight lies. Normally, I can rely upon a strong short game to keep my score down, but this type of layout requires an entirely new set of shots, with which I am not well-versed. As a result, the round was, at times, frustrating. Fortunately, after the first five holes, I was able to right the ship and begin to appreciate what Tom Doak had accomplished in his architecture. While it may not be my favorite style, it is hard to argue the results.

Round 13 — Bandon Trails

Course Rank: 15

Date Played: September 23, 2010

Starting Time: 7:30 a.m.

Weather: Chilly, 55 degrees, clear morning to start, windy and overcast to finish, with the temperature in the low 60s.

My Score: 86

Number of Lost Balls: 2. I found the only water in the development on No. 11.

Highlights: 7 pars

Lowlights: 2 double bogeys, 1 triple bogey

Excuse for Not Breaking 80: Early putting woes led to a string of bogeys; however, I was hanging in pretty well until a double/triple finish knocked me out of contention.

Greens Fee: $220

Playing Partners: John, Chris and Andy, with our caddies, Jack and Tim.

Practice Facilities: Large putting green at the course. We did not visit the central practice facility. This was partly due to the time, and partly due to the 36 holes scheduled for the day. By the way, they do not have holes cut in the putting green. Rather, you putt at some above-ground plastic flag. This is true of all the Bandon courses and seemed a bit cheesy.

My Rating: 9. The course strayed from the traditional links style, with many of the holes framed by pines, and more dramatic elevation changes enhancing the experience.

Absolutely Must Play: Yes. Just as Blackwolf Run is a good complement to Whistling Straits, so is Bandon Trails to the other three.

Favorite Hole: There were quite a number to choose from, with all but two getting a grade of 8 or higher. I liked No. 11, as it brought water into play on a very long, sloping hole. No. 13, set up against a hillside, is interesting, although I managed to "butcher" it with a poor short iron. No. 16 is a great, elevated par 5, with plenty of trouble. Nevertheless, I found No. 14 to be my favorite. This is a short par 4, but almost impossible to hold the fairway on the left side, due the narrow, sloping design. The pin placement was brutal coming from the right, with almost no green with which to work.

Location Characteristics: Unlike the other three courses, Trails has significant elevation and plays through a forest. As a result, there is more character to the course.

Comments: Having had a good night of sleep, I was more prepared for this round. Although the lies were still tight, the course afforded more good shots. Nearly every hole was a treat, with the trees and elevation changes more suited to my tastes. It could have been a very low round, save for a couple of poor putts, two poor shots, and the last two holes. Regardless, this would prove to be one of my favorite Bandon layouts.

Round 14 — Old Macdonald

Course Rank: 10

Date Played: September 23, 2010

Starting Time: 1:00 p.m.

Weather: 20 to 25 mph winds, overcast, drizzle, high 50s

My Score: 87

Number of Lost Balls: 1

Highlights: 2 birdies and 4 pars

Lowlights: 4 double bogeys and 1 triple bogey

Excuse for Not Breaking 80: Wind, cold, second round of the day, bad attitude. I had a terrible start...*again*...13 over on the front side.

Greens Fee: $110, half price for second round of the day.

Playing Partners: The brothers Laubach, with Jack and Tim on the bags.

Practice Facilities: Same large practice putting green. We did not hit balls beforehand.

My Rating: 7. In order to be a top course, you need a good starting hole. Nos. 1 and 2 were bland and reminded me of a local municipal track. To be fair, everyone else liked the course more than I did. Between the weather and my head congestion I may have been less open to the stark nature of the design, although the finish is much better than the start.

Absolutely Must Play: No. If I return to Bandon, I would probably skip this one. I understand what they were trying to accomplish, and they pulled it off. However, golf course design has advanced in the 200 years since this type of course dominated.

Favorite Hole: No. 16 is a challenging par 4, with a "mini mesa" blocking the left side, and doglegs in that direction. Any tee shot that is short or lands to the left will result in a blind approach. I also found No. 18 interesting, with a couple of large "haystacks" protecting the front. I was underwhelmed with the front nine.

Location Characteristics: Old Macdonald manages to bring modest elevation changes into play and offers some ocean proximity, but is generally fairway, fairway and more fairway, which, at times, is difficult to distinguish from the greens. There is a bit of gorse and some big bunkers, but generally it is quite open. The winds make it punishing, especially on the long par 4s, which cannot be reached in regulation.

Comments: Old Macdonald is an homage to the original Scottish links courses. To that end it succeeds. As an enjoyable test of golf, it leaves something to be desired. The first two holes seem uninspired. A very short, flat par 4, followed by a short, flat par 3 with some modest bunkering, does not get the juices flowing. The blind tee shot on No. 3 helps…unless you clip the tree on the left side of the hill (I did). After that, wind, drizzle and cold made the first nine holes ponderous. I was ready to walk off, in part due to the chills, but was nowhere near the clubhouse. The back nine was more interesting, especially the last four, taking the bitter taste out of my mouth. Still, my first impression was that this was barely a top 100 course, let alone top 10.

While I vowed not to play the course again, I was back two days later, as an opening presented itself before we headed home. Without a caddie, I shot the same score, but had eight more putts, and several really weak chips that could have been avoided with some expert help. Further, although the day was billed as being spectacular weather-wise, as soon as the sun came up, it pulled a thick fog across the course, reducing visibility to 40 to 50 yards for nine holes. On No. 10, my brother lined me up on a long approach. I put it over the recommended line, only to find my ball ten minutes later, 110 yards right of the green. I still found the finishing holes to be fine, but nothing changed my mind regarding the layout. For me, the course was overrated. However, I know people who swear this is the best of the Bandon courses.

Round 15 Bandon Dunes

Course Rank: 5

Date Played: September 24, 2010

Starting Time: 10:50 a.m.

Weather: 65 degrees, partly cloudy, mild wind

My Score: 78

Number of Lost Balls: 1, a ridiculously poor five iron into the ravine along No. 17 that led to a triple bogey.

Highlights: 5 birdies and 6 pars

Lowlights: 2 double bogeys and 1 triple bogey

Excuse for Not Breaking 80: None needed. The score should have been a 75 except for the tragic approach shot on 17.

Greens Fee: $220

Playing Partners: Caddies Jack and Tim once again joined the brothers Laubach.

Practice Facilities: With the later tee time, I finally had an opportunity to hit a few balls (12), which was enough for me to find my game. It is an impressive facility, but I like to walk directly from the range to the tee box, and that is not possible.

My Rating: 9. Yes, it is another links-style design, but, like Whistling Straits, seemed to frame the holes better. In addition, the weather was improved (except for the four holes where the fog rolled in), and my game was better.

Absolutely Must Play: Yes. This is what I had envisioned when making the reservations.

Favorite Hole: Lots to choose from. Nos. 5, 16 and 17 are all challenging, and the par 3s for the most part are good. My favorite was No. 4, a short par 4 that requires a precise tee shot, and then a mid range iron into a fascinating green, with the ocean in the background.

Location Characteristics: The course is adjacent to Pacific Dunes, and offers the same general features. I liked the character of the design on this one a bit better, but both offer expansive ocean vistas, some elevation changes and plenty of native gorse. Bandon Dunes is a classic links design, but the minimalist architecture flows well.

Comments: Despite a double bogey start, and the triple on No. 17, Bandon Dunes was an enjoyable round. The weather was benign, except for the temporary, blindingly dense fog. Although not as picturesque as Bandon Trails, it gets a similar rating due to the extensive ocean views. This is the oldest course at the resort, and seems to be settling in nicely. My brothers noticed that the fairways seemed more receptive, with at least some grass under the ball. This course also had a secondary level of rough that was perfect to play from. The greens putted true. Overall, it was good to play this course last, as it made up for some of the earlier disappointments.

Trip Summary:

The Bandon Dunes golf vacation is the ultimate "back to nature," "man's man" experience. Sure, some players were dragging along their wives/girlfriends, and a few groups of women scattered around the course; however, this was the exception. For those chauvinists who believe a woman's place on the golf course is behind the wheel of a beverage cart (they do not have beverage carts at the Bandon courses), they will enjoy the experience. Perhaps owing to the cost, the isolated location, the "no carts" policy or the intimidation, it seemed that 90 percent of the golfers at Bandon Dunes were professional males between the ages of 35 and 65. Exclusivity is certainly a characteristic of the experience, although I doubt the ownership would acknowledge this fact. One only needs to note the lack of bathtubs in our lodging, no spa and no shopping to know that the developers did not target non-golfers. The feeling is distinctly that of a hunting lodge.

The overriding characteristic of Bandon Dunes is the balance between golf and nature. The buildings at the project are typically understated. For an exclusive set of courses, the pro shops appear as an afterthought. Aside from the maintenance equipment, of which less is required due to the design, there are virtually no powered vehicles on the courses. Snack bars and facilities are hidden or blended into the background. There are no cart paths, no stakes, no utility lines, no water pumps in sight, and very limited, subdued signage. The eye is drawn to the ocean, forests and natural terrain. I suspect the high ratings for these golf courses reflects the judges' appreciation for what the project has been able to accomplish, although my personal opinion is that they went overboard on Old Macdonald.

Expectations being what they were, it is easy to explain why Bandon Dunes was a letdown. Rating Pacific Dunes ahead of Pebble Beach, and placing all four courses in the top 15, created feverish anticipation, upon which the golf could not deliver. The rush to play the first course, my persistent head cold, fog and rain certainly did not help, but the reality is that these courses are not Pebble Beach or even Spyglass Hill. They are generally good, bordering on great, layouts that blend seamlessly with the Oregon Coast. However, everything else being equal, I would rather be on 17-Mile Drive in Monterey.

Chapter 18

Juggling Act

Nobody ever said the logistics of playing 100 golf courses throughout the United States would be easy, but I may have underestimated the challenge. Parents' Weekend at my daughter's college in the Boston area offered an excellent excuse to knock a few more venues from the list. The interactive map at the *Golf Magazine* website suggested I could fly to Syracuse, New York and play the two courses at Turning Stone Resort, drive down to Williamstown, Massachusetts, for a round at Taconic, and finish up in Boston. The initial planning was simple. JetBlue (one free piece of luggage) offered a non-stop flight from San Diego to Boston for the return trip, and one-stop flight into Syracuse. My wife and I booked a flight arriving late Tuesday night, planning to stay at an airport hotel, with a short trek to Turning Stone Wednesday morning and an afternoon round scheduled. A mid-morning round on Thursday would leave plenty of time for the three-hour haul to Williamstown later that day, and an early morning round at Taconic Golf Club on Friday, before the final push to Boston. Arrangements for the trip were simple, or so I thought. One downside was that the Shenandoah course at Turning Stone was being aerated on Wednesday, so the Thursday round would include punched greens. On the positive side, I negotiated a reduced green fee. A significant open issue was the tee time at Taconic, which could not be made until 7 days in advance. No problem; there are only 8,000 residents in Williamstown, nobody goes off first thing and the local college students would be in class…right?

Arriving at my office at 7:15 a.m. on the Friday before the scheduled round, I promptly called the pro shop at Taconic, where a friendly woman on the other end advised me that the first available starting time was 2:00 p.m.

No, there was no tournament, just the normal Friday play, and, anyway, it was 10:30 a.m. back there and "why didn't I call earlier?" This was not going to work. I needed to be in Massachusetts by 7:00 p.m., and that required a three-hour drive. With the course fully booked, I could expect a minimum 4.5-hour round. I took the reservation reluctantly, but knew it would never happen.

After musing over the issue for a few minutes, I called back to see if I could get a later time on Thursday, and was able to secure the same 2:00 p.m. time slot. I then called Turning Stone to see if I could be "first off" on Thursday morning. If I could start at 8:00 a.m., finish in 2.5 hours, and drive the three hours to Williamstown, I would be able to make the second round with 30 minutes to spare. The nice people at Turning Stone again tried to talk me out of playing the aerated course, but allowed that I could be first off. I accepted the 8:10 a.m. starting time with the knowledge I would be the only player on the course before 10:00 a.m. This should have raised a red flag. On the positive side, the leaves would be changing, so there would be some good photo ops.

Round 16 — Atunyote at Turning Stone

Course Rank: 65

Date Played: October 13, 2010

Starting Time: 12:00 p.m.

Weather: 60 degrees clear and calm

My Score: 85

Number of Lost Balls: 1

Highlights: 1 birdie and 5 pars

Lowlights: 2 double bogeys

Excuse for Not Breaking 80: I boarded the "bogey train" early and could not disembark (10 on the day).

Greens Fee: $220

Playing Partners: Solo. There was very little play on the course that day despite terrific weather.

Practice Facilities: Perfect for the setting. Plenty of range set-ups, a putting green that mirrored course conditions and solid short game area were available.

My Rating: 8+. Atunyote proved to be an enjoyable round of golf. Once you locate the main entrance you find yourself in a picturesque, pastoral location only enhanced by the changing of the leaves. On the downside, many of these leaves were falling on the course, which created difficulty in locating several errant shots.

Absolutely Must Play: Yes. This course has been home to a PGA event, is in great condition and offers a series of interesting holes. If not for the golf, you have to play this one just to go through the main entrance. The course provides only a small sign off the main road (I missed it twice). This leads to an amazing, ornate wrought-iron gate, which may be opened only by calling the pro shop. The sense of exclusivity is great, as is the winding road through the forest leading up to the clubhouse.

Favorite Hole: There were a lot of very good holes, though few were extremely memorable. I enjoyed the front side hitting through the forests with the turning leaves. The back side was more open, but included more water. My favorite hole was No. 13, a 395-yard par 4 that requires a long straight drive, and then a precise shot into the green, which is well protected on the right by a lake.

Location Characteristics: You are always taking a chance with an October tee time in this part of the world, but if you are rewarded with good weather and turning leaves, the setting is terrific. I lucked into a great day with plenty of postcard views. The tree-lined fairways were great, but I was surprised by the limited wildlife. I would have expected deer, fox and other animals, but the course was largely untouched by the animal kingdom.

Comments: There was nothing to criticize about Atunyote. The entrance is the one of the most exceptional I have seen. The clubhouse is perfectly proportioned: very classy, with a nice pro shop and grill, but not overkill like a Trump course. The practice facilities are first class, the setting is terrific and the staff friendly. It did not hurt that it was a perfect fall day in New England, or that the course was in pristine condition. There were plenty of fun holes. The "slick" greens made scoring difficult, but the ball rolled true. The course is a little out of the way (nearest airport is Syracuse), but the facility has three golfing venues that are all highly rated, a full casino and numerous restaurants. It is a great vacation for a couple of days. I'll admit, the 24-story hotel tower is a bit much for this agricultural community, but all things considered, I would like to return.

Round 17 — Shenandoah at Turning Stone

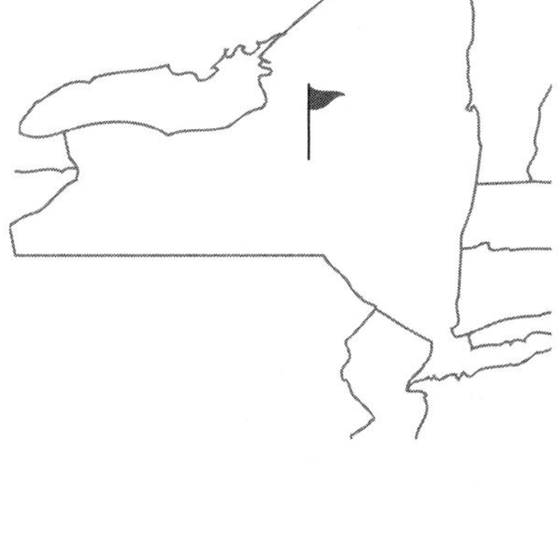

Course Rank: 59

Date Played: October 14, 2010

Starting Time: 8:10 a.m. (scheduled); 9:00 a.m. due to frost delay

Weather: Cold, 45 degrees to start, partly cloudy, light wind

My Score: 80

Number of Lost Balls: 1

Highlights: 11 pars

Lowlights: 1 double bogey

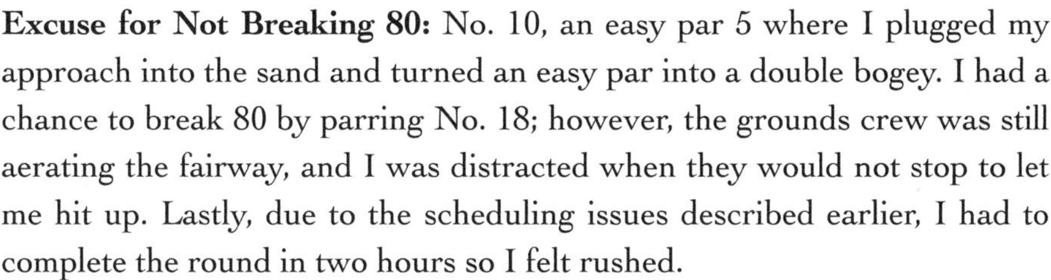

Excuse for Not Breaking 80: No. 10, an easy par 5 where I plugged my approach into the sand and turned an easy par into a double bogey. I had a chance to break 80 by parring No. 18; however, the grounds crew was still aerating the fairway, and I was distracted when they would not stop to let me hit up. Lastly, due to the scheduling issues described earlier, I had to complete the round in two hours so I felt rushed.

Greens Fee: $80; a great rate negotiated because of the aeration.

Playing Partners: There were no other groups scheduled until 10:00 a.m., so I had the course to myself.

Practice Facilities: Very good. The range is shared with another course, and the putting green is of average size, but it is definitely adequate for the recreational golfer.

My Rating: 8. Despite the aeration, cooler weather and rushed round, I really liked this course. This facility is on the grounds of the resort, so it is easily accessible. The setting gets high marks, with the starting hole offering an exceptional view.

Absolutely Must Play: Yes. The Atunyote/Shenandoah combo is a must. In addition, the third venue is in the top 100 in *Golf Digest*. Like Atunyote, Shenandoah was in excellent condition. I am not sure if the greens are as quick when not aerated. If you find yourself in the Syracuse area, Turning Stone is well worth the effort, and quite affordable as compared to other top 100 courses.

Favorite Hole: I gave high ratings to most of the holes, but, without a doubt, I was most impressed with No. 1. The setting amongst the trees is fabulous, with a well-bunkered fairway requiring an accurate drive, followed by a tricky approach shot to an elevated green over a creek. I wish all golf courses could begin with such an exceptional hole. Several of the back nine holes are played through cleared farmland and offer less excitement, but the Rick Smith design finds a way to challenge.

Location Characteristics: Similar to Atunyote, the course is characterized by tree-lined fairways. In addition, there is water on 11 of the holes. Minor elevation changes add to the character.

Comments: I am not a big fan of frost delays, and I am not sure it was warranted in this instance, but otherwise, the course lived up to its reputation. I liked the clubhouse and forested area leading to the first hole. This great starting hole sets the tone for a fun round of golf. It did not hurt that my drives were splitting the fairway all day, and my scoring game was largely on target.

Round 18 — Taconic Golf Club

Course Rank: 41

Date Played: October 14, 2010

Starting Time: 2:00 p.m.

Weather: 60 degrees (and falling), cloudy with gusting wind and rain threatening

My Score: 91

Number of Lost Balls: 1

Highlights: 4 pars. (Are you kidding me?)

Lowlights: 4 double bogeys and 1 triple bogey

Excuse for Not Breaking 80: Mental exhaustion, too much sand, tricky greens, wind, cold and the long drive from New York.

Greens Fee: $145 with cart

Playing Partners: Cory for 11 holes, and Jim for the last five. Always fun to meet new people.

Practice Facilities: Minimal. Like Pasatiempo, this is a classic club that became functionally obsolete as the equipment improved, and needed to be lengthened. As a result, there is no driving range on the grounds. There is a modest putting green just outside the pro shop.

My Rating: 8. Taconic includes a number of interesting holes, and, as a result of recent renovations, offered more than sufficient challenge. Apparently, the redesign architect knew exactly where I would hit all of my drives, and most of my approaches, and placed bunkers in these locations. This is very much a classic design, occupying a spectacular, small-town New England setting.

Absolutely Must Play: No, unless you can find your way to Williamstown, which is easily accessible from nowhere. Also, you will need to wait until the last minute before getting a reservation. Taconic is a neat little course that certainly warrants top 100-consideration. The course is walkable, although there is some modest topography.

Favorite Hole: I liked most of the holes. Each had a subtle (and in some cases, not-so-subtle) challenge. My favorite hole was No. 4, a relatively short par 4 that plays from an elevated tee. There is a creek running along the left side that cuts across the middle of the fairway. I later learned that most people hit an iron or utility club off the tee, as there is little margin for error. I almost put my drive in the creek cutting across the fairway. Because I was short, the approach shot was a wedge to an elevated green that had a severe back to front slope. This may not have been the most difficult hole, but it was characteristic of this classic design.

Location Characteristics: Taconic Golf Club is situated in the college town of Williamstown, Massachusetts, in the far northwestern portion of the state, not far from Albany, New York. Located in the Berkshire Mountains, this small town is a favored destination for "Leafers." The setting is magnificent, including the proximity to Williams College, a prestigious liberal arts school founded in the late 1700s. A fall golf round, weather permitting, affords tree-lined fairways of varying hues. The course was in excellent condition. Modest elevation changes make the holes more interesting and lend themselves to devilish downhill putts. Ultimately, the location is picture-postcard material.

Comments: Without question, Taconic Golf Club is out of the way. However, the golf is excellent. The majority of those players on the course are regulars, as this is not a destination resort. I was impressed by the design and condition, although it clearly does not pander to outsiders. The clubhouse is old and the facilities minimal. My only two objections were the lack of a proximate driving range and the inability to make tee times further in advance. This makes a trek to Taconic more challenging. I recommend keeping a flexible schedule and spending a night in town. Playing during the week is probably easier than on Friday or Saturday. The course is reasonably affordable and offers a good golf challenge. The greens were lightning fast and more problematic because of the slope. This is a good location to take the non-golfer, but probably not young kids. If you are lucky, your child will get accepted to Williams College and you can play when you visit.

Trip Summary:

This was my first opportunity to plan a trip that required significant travel between venues. A review of the top 100 list indicates that it will not be the last. Despite the reservation difficulty at Taconic and weather issues, I was able to complete my mission. Ironically, it would not have been possible, but for the failure to get a morning tee time at Taconic on Friday. A Nor'easter blew into Williamstown the prior evening, and the course was closed. It was fortuitous that I moved the time to Thursday afternoon, even though it meant waiting out a frost delay, then playing 18 holes in less than two hours, and experiencing a hectic drive to western Massachusetts. The poor weather on Friday underscored the risks I was taking in booking this trip so late in the year. Given the isolated nature of Williamstown, I feel I dodged a bullet. Ultimately, the Turning Stone courses were a pleasant surprise and the quaint town of Williamstown offered a great diversion.

Chapter 19

Sometimes You Get What You Pay For, or Blame It on the Gopher Hole

When perusing the list of top 100 courses, I was surprised to see an unfamiliar Southern California golf course listed. This was especially true since I had grown up in the San Fernando Valley, not far from the City of Moorpark, and home to Rustic Canyon Golf Course. The San Fernando Valley is part of the Los Angeles metropolitan area, characterized by too many people, too many cars, too much smog, too many wildfires, too many earthquakes and too many plus-100-degree days. What the Valley does not have are too many public golf facilities. We used to make the trek west to Ventura County, over the foothills, where there were some decent options. Moorpark is one of those growing communities situated within easy driving distance of my old stomping grounds in Woodland Hills. Located adjacent to Simi Valley, this sleepy "'burb" was not easily accessible in the days of my youth. However, thanks to the Ronald Reagan Freeway, it now offers an option for local residents who are not interested in joining a private facility.

I had no trouble booking a late morning round on a Friday. My only problem with the website is that the listed greens fee seemed to be missing a digit. According to our reservation, the round was $32 per person. After paying as much as $500 to play the Wynn course in Las Vegas, I knew this had to be a typo. Nevertheless, the course was on the list, and I would have to take my chances.

Unfortunately, playing the course in winter (fewer hours of daylight), and its location on the opposite side of Los Angeles created a unique access problem for a day trip. According to Google Maps, the expected travel time with no traffic was 2 hours and 20 minutes from my San Diego location. Of course, anyone who travels the route regularly knows that there is always traffic. Google's time estimate with traffic on the day we played was 3 hours and 40 minutes. Great. There is nothing like arriving at a golf course after nearly four hours of bumper-to-bumper traffic.

My brother Chris still lives in the area, so I arranged to meet up with him, as well as drag along my other brother Andy, with a quick stop to pick up Joe Strong in Orange County. Fortified with bagels and coffee, we set out at 7:30 a.m. with the hopes of making our 11:00 starting time. Thanks to the carpool lane we were able to complete the trek in just about three hours, allowing us time to hit a few balls and down a hotdog before setting out on the round.

We checked into the pro shop, and much to my "cheap" nature, were pleasantly surprised to learn that the quoted greens fee was, in fact, correct. This was like playing for free. We did have to pay for a golf cart ($13 per person) and range balls (overpriced at $7.00 for a medium bucket), but overall the cost was less than the round-trip gas.

Round 19 — Rustic Canyon Golf Course

Course Rank: 93

Date Played: January 14, 2010

Starting Time: 11:00 a.m.

Weather: Sunny, 70 degrees, with 35 mph wind gusts

My Score: 90

Number of Lost Balls: 1, on my first shot of the day. Given the open space, I am convinced it disappeared down a gopher hole. There was no reason for this ball to be lost, so immediately, I felt some negative energy.

Highlights: 5 pars

Lowlights: 5 double bogeys

Excuse for Not Breaking 80: Losing the ball on my first shot killed my mojo. Tight lies, undulating greens, my chronic bad elbow and wind gusts all contributed to atrocious scoring.

Greens Fee: $32 was the mid-day rate, plus another $13 for the cart makes this easily one of the most affordable courses in Southern California, although the range balls were expensive.

Playing Partners: Brothers Chris and Andy, and Joe Strong.

Practice Facilities: Lush practice mats on the driving range give a completely false sense of course conditions. There is a chipping green and a putting green. Overall, the facilities were adequate but not exceptional.

My Rating: 5, for below-average course condition and generally mundane surroundings.

Absolutely Must Play: No. I was very surprised this course made the list. Unless you want a cheap round and live in the West San Fernando Valley or Ventura County, I would skip this one.

Favorite Hole: No. 16. This hole has an elevated tee box, hitting downwind, downhill. As such, the 466 yards are easily navigable. I caught one flush and had only 100 yards to the green. I liked Nos. 11 and 14 as well, but generally the holes were pedestrian. The front side seemed particularly uninspired.

Location Characteristics: Natural setting in a canyon, but with surprisingly minimal elevation changes. The area seemed best suited to feeding wildfires. The flora is minimal, with few plants or trees other than some natural scrub.

Comments: This was the least enjoyable round to date. Even without the wind, I would have little interest in playing this course again. The design is "faux" links, with limited character. The fairways and greens are very hard, which makes for a lot of roll. One cannot deny the terrific price, however, be advised you may get what you pay for. The course had dropped 10 spots in the rankings between 2008 and 2010. I suspect by the time I finish this exercise it will no longer be honored as a top 100 course.

Trip Summary:

Playing Rustic Canyon proved to be an all-day affair, with substantial time spent on the L.A. freeway system. Personally, I feel there are at least half-dozen courses I would prefer to play in the Los Angeles area, but it is hard to argue the price. Having now completed 20 percent of the rated courses, it has become clear that there is a bias amongst the judges toward "minimalist" designs (see Old Macdonald). My own preference is for lush fairways, manicured greens, lakes and ponds and pristine bunkers. Unless you live in the area or are visiting the Ronald Reagan Museum (actually pretty cool), save the gas or head out to Palm Desert. The highlight of the trip was nearly running over actor Dennis Franz in the parking lot before the round. By the end of this experience I was on the shelf for several weeks, as making contact with the rock hard fairways had irritated my elbow.

Chapter 20

The South Will Rise Again

Pick one:

When I golf I least like to play when it is ______?

windy
cold
rainy
all of the above.

As a native Southern Californian and self-proclaimed lightweight, the answer is a resounding D. Having said that, I am also obsessive, so I have played in all three weather conditions, although seldom at the same time. It is my understanding that the Irish did not leave the home country because of a potato famine, but rather due to the climactic conditions that those prescient individuals knew would play havoc with their future ball flight.

When I booked my trip to South Carolina/Georgia, I made sure to inquire about the weather in late March. "No need to worry," I was told. "The average temperature is over 70 degrees, and while a bit of rain may blow through, it never lasts long." It was the week before the Masters, and I seemed to recall usually good weather for that little outing. As such, it was with dismay that I received the following wakeup call on the day of my scheduled round at the Ocean Course at Kiawah Island.

"Good Morning Mr. Laubach, this is your 6:30 wake up call (3:30 in SoCal), the temperature outside is 43 degrees, we expect a high of 52 degrees (it did not even get close to expectations), the wind is a gentle 15-20 mph (gentle to whom?), with rain and thunderstorms. Is there anything else I can do for you?"

Now, you might think any normal person would cancel and reschedule for another time. In fact, I was told that all but six other idiots had done just that by the time I got to the course. However, there was a silver lining (aside from the obvious lack of slow foursomes in front of me). Jeff, my caddie, informed me that alligators were less likely to intrude upon my round....too cold.

Jeff looked like an Eskimo when he met me at the driving range, a state of dress I quickly emulated with my three layers of clothes, including rain gear. The driving range faced south and had a crosswind from the west, which did nothing to impress my caddie as I hit shot after shot with a monster slice, well aided by the "gentle" breeze. I could see Jeff's mind racing as he tried to figure out how to convince me to play the ladies' tees, having already failed to encourage me to go back to the hotel. "Don't worry," I informed my reluctant caddie, "I will hit much better downwind." To which he replied, "That would be great, but there are no downwind holes...O.K., maybe one." It turns out Pete Dye likes courses that go only two directions. Similar to Whistling Straits, this one went partway south, all the way back north, and then south again to the clubhouse. In this manner the course is able to maximize the ocean views. Ordinarily, that would have been great, but between the rain misting up my glasses and the water in my eyes from the cold, it was hard to spend much time taking in the scenery, other than marching through the native grasses in search of my errant tee shots.

Thus, my introduction to Low Country golf was less than ideal. Too bad, as the Ocean Course is really great. Unfortunately, the weather would prove to be challenging throughout the trip. The forecast was so bad for Wednesday that I had to cancel a time at May River on Tuesday afternoon, and move over to Harbour Town. This was the smartest thing I did all week, as I was able to complete a round on Hilton Head before the skies opened up, washing out any chance of golf on Wednesday. The cold returned on Thursday, with some drizzle as well, but I was able to sneak in my round that morning at May River before making a beeline to Sea Island. The final round at the Seaside Course was the first of the day, and again was characterized by low temperatures and wind gusts.

Round 20 — Kiawah Island Ocean Course

Course Rank: 4

Date Played: March 28, 2011

Starting Time: 8:30 a.m.

Weather: Cold!!!! 43 degrees to start, 46 degrees at the finish. Showers, thundershowers and prevailing 15 to 20 mph winds.

My Score: 92

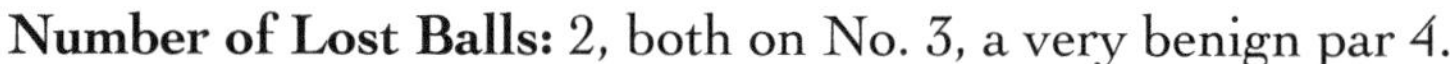

Number of Lost Balls: 2, both on No. 3, a very benign par 4.

Highlights: 4 pars (felt like birdies)

Lowlights: 4 double bogeys and a triple bogey

Excuse for Not Breaking 80: See weather above

Greens Fee: $271.

Playing Partners: Are you kidding? Everyone else canceled due to the weather. I had the course to myself, along with Jeff, my poor caddie. I think he drew the short straw and had to hang around.

Practice Facilities: I was too cold to notice, although I think the setting was near the ocean. The crosswind killed my confidence.

My Rating: 9. Weather aside, the layout appeared to be exceptional. There were the typical "Dyeabolical" design features, which, in the absence of arctic conditions, would have made for a challenging round. The setting is great and is probably a wonderful course to walk in golfing weather.

Absolutely Must Play: Yes, but try to schedule a tee time when you can feel your hands. The course is not forgiving, so it is imperative you bring your "A" game.

Favorite Hole: There were a lot of great holes. I especially liked No. 13, a very narrow, driving hole, and No. 17, a par 3 with major water issues, but my favorite hole was No. 2, a very challenging par 5 that, despite its moderate length, is generally a three-shot hole to the green.

Location Characteristics: The Ocean Course meanders along the dunes adjacent to the Atlantic Ocean, with views of the water from most holes. (I understand the views to be spectacular, but with all of the shivering going on, I really didn't notice.) Situated on exclusive Kiawah Island, I had a modicum of déjà vu driving through the gates that reminded me, to some extent, of the entrance to 17-Mile Drive. The island is lushly landscaped with native pines and palms, although the Ocean Course is largely exposed, with a links feel. On the previous day I had run across the requisite alligators sunning themselves on the Turtle Point layout. Next time (and I assume there will be a next time) I hope to take advantage of the terrific setting with much improved weather.

Comments: The Ocean Course is highly ranked, deservedly so. My experience was marred by the weather, but even suffering through the cold, wind and rain I could appreciate the terrific nature of the design. The staff was very accommodating but took little pity on the idiot from California who decided to brave the elements. Kiawah itself is a wonderful destination location, with plenty of activities for the kids and wife, but would also be a great place for your favorite foursome to spend a few days. There are five courses on the island, all of which are reportedly quite nice. Ultimately, it is an expensive golf vacation, but one that is bound to yield fond long-term memories. I will certainly get mileage out of my weather complaints.

Round 21 Harbour Town

Course Rank: 14

Date Played: March 29, 2011 (changed from March 30 due to pending major storm)

Starting Time: 1:21 p.m.

Weather: 58 degrees, cloudy, rain threatening.

My Score: 82, with a 37 on the back side.

Number of Lost Balls: 1, a ridiculously poorly pulled shot on No. 8 that led to a triple bogey.

Highlights: 1 birdie and 7 pars

Lowlights: 1 triple bogey

Excuse for Not Breaking 80: That stupid pull hook on No. 8.

Greens Fee: $260, plus $100 for the caddie.

Playing Partners: Shane, Jason and Connor, a trio from Wisconsin. My caddie was Don (Double D) a jovial, enthusiastic looper who kept the banter active throughout the round. He did a great job reading greens, and kept me on my game despite a challenging front nine.

Practice Facilities: Attractive, adequate stations, plus chipping green, with trap and putting green.

My Rating: 9. The course was in great condition in anticipation of the PGA event in two weeks. The par 3s are terrific. Visually, Harbour Town is a very attractive course, although you need to be hitting the ball down the middle to score. I was told by another golf shop pro that conditions are worse when it is not tournament time, but for me this was definitely a top-ten experience.

Absolutely Must Play: Yes, if not just for the history. I thought there would be more holes along the sound, but the forests were visually appealing, and water came into play constantly.

Favorite Hole: All of the par 3s were fantastic, and I rated Nos. 1, 4, 13 and 15 as nine out of ten. The best hole, however, has to be No. 18 (the lighthouse hole). This is the picturesque, par 4, signature hole that graces the airwaves when the tournament is being played.

Location Characteristics: Despite the name and famous lighthouse on the sound, the course is primarily forest, with rivers intertwined throughout. Like most of the Southeast, there is plenty of wildlife, including alligators, deer, a variety of birds, and a fantastic array of trees and other flora. The course is comparatively flat (my caddie referred to a three-foot mogul as a mountain). Harbour Town is situated on Hilton Head Island, and access is via a toll road and an additional private entrance (the $5 entry fee seemed to be quite the rip-off). The finishing holes bring the sound into play.

Comments: It would have been nice with better weather, but I have no complaints about anything related directly to the round. My caddie was excellent. Each par 3 was picturesque and required precise shots. There were classic Pete Dye design features, which keep you on your toes. The alligators (at a distance) are a nice addition. It is not the easiest place to access, but a vacation to Hilton Head, or nearby, should definitely include a round at Harbour Town.

Round 22 May River Golf Club at Palmetto Bluff

Course Rank: 62

Date Played: March 31, 2011
(rescheduled from March 29)

Starting Time: 9:00 a.m.

Weather: 57 degrees, cloudy, showers, scattered thunderstorms

My Score: 86

Number of Lost Balls: 1; should have been 0, but I decided not to reach into the water alongside No. 11 after my caddie told me the story of an 85-year-old guy who lost his arm to a resident alligator doing the same thing.

Highlights: 7 pars

Lowlights: 3 double bogeys

Excuse for Not Breaking 80: My teaching pro caddie attempted to integrate a few "minor" swing changes that, combined with the sloppy conditions, did not work out for the best.

Greens Fee: $175, included caddie (not gratuity). One day later and it would have been "in season" and the rate would have increased to $250.

Playing Partners: Solo round with caddie Mike on the bag. I like having teaching pros along for a round even though it tends to mess with my swing. Mike played at Florida State on a scholarship and counts Matt Kuchar among his friends. I doubt he thought I was "pro" material.

Practice Facilities: Very good, expansive driving range and adequate putting green. They provided quality range balls, and the grass was in good shape before I butchered a couple of practice shots.

My Rating: 7+. It might have been higher had the course been dry and weather better. Also, I would have liked to have played at high tide, as the rivers apparently rise such that it is more visually appealing. This is a typical Nicklaus design but with wider fairways. The tee boxes were up, which made many of the holes a bit short for my taste.

Absolutely Must Play: No, but if you are in the Savannah/Kiawah area it is well worth the effort, especially when you book into the Inn at Palmetto Bluffs Resort, which is a terrific, well-run operation and rated number one by my wife.

Favorite Hole: Because I was playing the forward tees, I am not sure I had the benefit of really seeing some of the holes. As such, none rated 9 or higher on my scale. At the same time, I did not rate any of the holes below a 7. No. 10 is an interesting par 5 that could have been exceptional if the yardage had been longer. The green on No. 7 is worth some attention if you are lucky enough to play this course. I guess my favorite hole was No. 11, the short par 3, where I lost my ball and where my round turned from pretty good to not so good. That is because my tee shot hit the green on the fly, but spun down the side hill and into the pond. We could see my ball sitting just inside the water, but had a difficult time navigating the steep slope to the water's edge. The story about the guy losing his arm started nagging at me. Although we could not see any alligators, Mike pulled the flag out of the hole and carried it to the edge of the water to poke/pierce any gator that should show itself while we attempted to retrieve my Pro V1. As it turned out, we found several other Titleists that more astute golfers had left, but could not recover mine from the edge. O.K., maybe it was not a great golf hole, but the image of my caddy holding the flagstick as a weapon will be forever etched in my mind.

Location Characteristics: The course is set in a magnificent nature preserve on the site of a former plantation. A variety of pines, and an occasional palmetto palm, line the fairways. At low tide there are numerous marshes and dry, or semi-dry riverbeds, which fill at high tide. I saw snapping turtles and am sure alligators abound. (I am still thinking about those alligators.) I hate to be redundant, but the setting is marvelous and will provide a welcome distraction from the inevitable "blow up" holes. On the other hand, the region is known for bugs. While it was a bit cool, and early in the season,

I knew it could be an issue when I saw a bottle of bug spray on every hitting station on the driving range and another in each golf cart. As it turned out, I got warm during the round and reduced from a jacket to a vest. I had not sprayed my arms, which, a day later, were inundated with bite marks.

Comments: Once you get inside the gate at Palmetto Bluffs it is well worth the 10-minute drive...better yet, stay at the resort. Hank Haney reportedly has a house, as do the former Atlanta Braves pitching aces (Maddux, Smoltz and Glavine). The quaint little village of Wilson is a great throwback. I will probably go back, as my wife liked the resort more than any other at which we stayed. Try to time the round to a high tide, and be ready with the camera and bug spray. The wider-than-normal fairways offer the potential to score well and should result in fewer lost balls. The summer season is likely to be characterized by high humidity...best to avoid. My caddy was already complaining about the upcoming weather despite the low temperatures.

Round 23 — Sea Island Seaside Course

Course Rank: 25

Date Played: April 1, 2011

Starting Time: 7:30 a.m.

Weather: 48 degrees warmed to 56 degrees by the time I finished, 10-15 mph winds with gusts to 30 mph.

My Score: 82

Number of Lost Balls: 0

Highlights: 8 pars

Lowlights: 2 double bogeys

Excuse for Not Breaking 80: What type of idiot starts a round in the dark? This type of idiot.

Greens Fee: $350

Playing Partners: I had to make a flight out of Jacksonville at 12:55 p.m. (a 75-minute trip from the course) so I booked the first tee time, and asked for a caddie who could complete the round in 2.5 hours. Rodney proved to be the perfect partner, able to keep pace while regaling me with the history of the course, the area, the old pros (and new ones) and the general state of golf. I think he was dismayed when I elected to play the middle tees, but after the previous day at May River I felt I needed more of a challenge. I did not endear myself when I double bogeyed the first after putting a ball in the lateral hazard. Nevertheless, I recovered nicely and shot an acceptable round.

Practice Facilities: Most impressive to date. Too bad it was dark outside. The driving range abuts the local bay, offering a great setting for a range. I never did get to the putting green as I was pressed for time. Regardless, the range was unforgettable, at least what I could see.

My Rating: 8. I liked Harbour Town more but really enjoyed this layout. It was great for walking.

Absolutely Must Play: Yes. The Sea Island area is magnificent, and the water orientation offers spectacular views. Saltwater rivers meander throughout this links-style design. Fazio did an excellent job of renovating the old course making it playable, while remaining a great challenge. I would prefer to have had more par 5s (there are only 2), but that increases the challenge. The course is close enough to Jacksonville that you could play this course in the morning and TPC Sawgrass in the afternoon.

Favorite Hole: I enjoyed No. 2, a challenging par 4 with a marsh protecting the left side on the drive, and additional water impacting the approach shot on the right side of the hole with the prevailing wind pushing the ball in that direction. Nevertheless, my vote is for No. 4, a brutally tough par 4, into the wind, with water issues that proved a great number 1 handicap.

Location Characteristics: The Seaside Course is heavily influenced by the bay, with the links design and water proximity yielding regular, steady winds. It was too early for alligators, but I had already seen my share. The entrance to the course is lushly landscaped, but the course itself is wide open with a sprinkling of palms and other native trees.

Comments: Overall it is not perfect, but definitely a top 50 layout. The course is home to an annual PGA event (McGladrey Classic). There are too many par 4s (12), with eight being between 385 and 411 yards. As a result, there is less variation, although the winds can certainly alter the club selection. Get a caddie and walk the course. There is limited topography other than on the undulating greens, and it is a comfortable stroll. The clubhouse is terrific, with an excellent pro shop. I am told the second course (Plantation) is terrific as well and is also less expensive, so I would recommend a couple of days in the area. The Cloister at Sea Island is a great resort, and well set up for families. According to my wife, the bartender pours a great (albeit strong) Mai Tai.

Trip Summary:

Apart from the weather issues, my visit to Charleston, Savannah and Sea Island was exceptional. During the many storms I was able to take "covered tours" of the historic districts in these Civil War towns. Having slept through history in high school and college, I was pleased to learn we had won the Civil War, although the locals assured me it is still undecided. In addition, I stayed at some of the more spectacular resorts in the country. The American Express Fine Hotels and Resorts program not only covered breakfasts and got me a resort credit, but also enabled us to secure some amazing room upgrades. It started at The Sanctuary Hotel at Kiawah Island, where we received an enormous, oceanview (when the rain was not falling) suite. Not to be outdone, once we found our way to the Inn at Palmetto Bluffs at May River, we were given a freestanding 1,000-plus square foot cottage with a large enclosed patio overlooking the river. My wife informed me this was a great place to watch the lightning crack against the sky...*Yay!* (Sarcastic from a gloomy golfer wannabe.) The drive into Palmetto Bluffs from the main gate is so long they give you a CD to listen to while you make the trek. This is a very exclusive, somewhat isolated former plantation turned wildlife preserve, which would have been exceptional had we been able to enjoy the outdoor amenities. Even the dolphins, which purportedly play in the river, took the two days off to remain below the waterline. Lastly, in a mad rush, we got to Sea Island for one short day. We received a suite with two bathrooms, two patios, full kitchen and too many amenities to enjoy given our limited time.

Another highlight of the trip was the food. Although not very adventuresome, my wife and I sampled many of the Low Country dishes and were quite pleased. Neither of us opted for the gator, but grits were part of many meals, as were the local seafood dishes. Pour Richard's in Bluffton, South Carolina, was a real treat, and the shrimp and grits was exceptional. Too many breakfast buffets at the resorts, however, put a severe crimp in my Hawaii wardrobe...scheduled for two weeks after our return.

The four courses I played represent some of the best in the country, with three hosting PGA tour events. If you are prepared to pay the big bucks, this

Southeastern swing is a must. If I can afford it after my quest is complete I will definitely return—just as long as the weather is guaranteed. By the way, it must be really brutal in the summer. Each of the four caddies I used, without prompting, was already griping about the heat and humidity that was on the way. By comparison, my cold, windy and wet rounds were viewed as "walks in the park."

Entr'acte

As I near the first-year anniversary of my quest, and having recently been inspired by the 2011 Masters, I feel compelled to take a break, as no doubt you have been hoping. By the time June 1 rolls around, I will have completed 31 of the top 100 courses, putting me ahead of schedule with respect to my five-year plan, albeit somewhat behind schedule on my retirement savings. Before the one-year mark I have a week scheduled in Hawaii and then a random romp through Minnesota, Illinois and Wisconsin. This assumes the snow is off the ground in the upper Midwest. Thus far the journey has been fabulous, although my own top 100 list will differ significantly from that of the erstwhile editors of *Golf Magazine*. Rather than reflect upon the efforts to date, I feel compelled to provide a bit of editorializing on the state of golf. If you care nothing about my opinions, and really who should, skip this chapter and move directly to our 50th state in the next chapter.

The best golf tournament in the world is the Masters. This is not an opinion. The tournament benefits from being the first of the majors, when everyone still has a shot at the elusive Grand Slam, and the promotion of the event is the most intensive. However, what makes the Masters number one is that it is the only major tournament played at the same venue every year. By now, we are all familiar with Amen Corner, Rae's Creek, the reachable par 5s at Nos. 13 and 15, the Sunday placement on No. 16, and other features of the course that makes for the most recognizable back nine in the world. Lastly, one cannot discount the amazing history of the event. The best golf event may be the Ryder Cup, but for a pure tournament, nothing can match the action staged every April in Augusta, Georgia. Hats off to the gentlemen who run the event, as it truly is a "tradition unlike any other." No other tournament comes close. Now you may think I am just pandering to the powers that be at Augusta in the hopes of one day wrangling an invitation to play those hallowed grounds. O.K., maybe there rings some truth in that, but that does not alter that fact that few golfers I know covet playing any course more than this one. That is not to say it is the best golf course in the world. I will not be able to answer that question until I have had the opportunity to stroll the fairways and challenge Rae's Creek (hint, hint), but no true golf aficionado could fail to grasp the enormity of the aura surrounding the course.

The tournament itself fully captures all that is great and not so great about golf. As I write this, Charl Schwartzel has miraculously birdied the final four holes to capture the green jacket. Australia acquitted itself well, as Adam Scott and Jason Day were brilliant down the stretch, with Geoff Ogilvy at one time tied for the lead in the clubhouse. It marked the meltdown by Rory McIlroy on the 10th hole. The golfing leprechaun from Northern Ireland, a mere 21-year-old phenom, had been brilliant to that point. (Between you and me, once Phil Mickelson had dropped out of contention, I found myself cheering for the wide-eyed Irishman.) The final round 80 was no doubt a disappointment to McIlroy, but he "feels" like the best player in the world right now, and I suspect will get his share of major victories. His poise during and after the round speaks volumes about his character.

The same could not be said for America's face on this tournament, one Eldrick Woods.

Once again, the networks, and most reporters, were fawning all over Tiger. Many declared he was relevant again following a 31 on the front side that brought him from "also ran" status to contender. With the pressure mounting on the back side, his putter disappeared...again, and he was relegated to a tie for fourth. Does that mean he is back? All I know is that following the unfortunate Thanksgiving 2009 meeting between his Escalade and a nearby fire hydrant, he has still not won, and his finish in the 2011 Masters was exactly the same as his finish in 2010. His overall score of 10 under was about the same as his 11 under in 2010. To be fair, however, he is starting to put the ball in the fairway. For what it is worth, I do not believe the personal issues led to Tiger's fall, but rather the improbable comeback by Y. E. Yang in the 2009 PGA that burst the invincibility that previously surrounded him.

Tiger's snippy comments following the round, contrasted with Rory McIlroy's gracious attitude after finishing his dismal final round, causes me to be concerned about this country. No wonder the world sees us as the ugly Americans. Of course, had it been Mickelson representing this country, we would not be having this conversation. For what it is worth I would love to play a round with Phil at The Bridges (or anywhere), with McIlroy being a close second for a preferred golfing partner.

Chapter 21

Aloha and Mahalo

I believe these may be the only two words in the Hawaiian language. For example, "Which way to the nearest beach?" is loosely translated as "Dude, aloha, aloha, mahalo aloha," followed by some hand gesture in which the thumb and little finger are extended. Seriously, Hawaii may be a great place, but it makes no sense as one of the fifty. To begin with, it is 2,500 miles from the mainland, nearly the distance between the east and west coasts of the continental United States. Second, and more importantly, there is a uniquely local, laid-back attitude that can be frustrating to a type-A personality such as myself. To be fair, however, one certainly feels on vacation when on the islands.

This trip, like many before, did not come off without a hitch. We successfully booked a great package deal through Costco Travel well in advance—so much so that I was unable to secure tee times at all of the venues. Not to worry, everyone said, it would be no problem. Well, problem. When I called Princeville to book my time exactly 60 days in advance, I was informed that they had made the decision to renovate the greens and would be closed for several months. This resulted in the forfeiture of my non-refundable airline tickets from Maui to Kauai for the one-day golf visit. Further, it necessitates a return trip at some future date.

Round 24 — Kapalua (Plantation)

Course Rank: 23

Date Played: April 19, 2011

Starting Time: 1:00 p.m.

Weather: 82 degrees, with 20 mph trade winds

My Score: 85 (par 73)

Number of Lost Balls: 3

Highlights: 10 pars

Lowlights: 2 double bogeys and 1 triple bogey

Excuse for Not Breaking 80: I could blame the trade winds, punched greens and blind tee shots, but it was probably also equal parts POG juice and Captain Morgan (the night before).

Greens Fee: $158 (twilight rate)

Playing Partners: Joe Strong.

Practice Facilities: The drive up to the range was really cool, through the jungle and a couple of tunnels. The facility was fine, although we hit into the wind, effectively screwing up my swing.

My Rating: 8+, based largely upon the fabulous views and elevations.

Absolutely Must Play: Yes. The Tournament of Champions is the first event of the PGA season, and Nos. 17 and 18 are two of the most photogenic. You should play the course multiple times as there are several blind tee shots.

Favorite Hole: There were plenty of good holes, but No. 17 was the most exceptional—a 500-yard par 4 down an enormous hill that allows you to "top" a ball 300 yards. My drive measured 327 yards.

Location Characteristics: The course is situated in the hills at the north end of Maui. As a result, there is substantial topography that must be navigated. Many of the holes offer expansive views of the ocean. Trade winds are common and make this very long course even longer. Blind tee shots create an added challenge, with the first round on this venue likely to play several strokes tougher than your replay.

Comments: The greens had been aerated two weeks earlier and were not fully recovered. This pushed several putts off line and made for slower speed. On the other hand, I believe at normal speed, three-putts would be much more common. The setting is terrific, and the topography makes for excitement, as well as feelings of invincibility on those long downhill holes. Expect trade winds unless you play early. Of course, this makes twilight play out of the question, and I was too cheap to pay for calm conditions. Without the wind and the blind tee shots, the course would be much more receptive. All in all, however, it is well worth the trip.

Round 25 Challenge at Manele (The Experience at Koele)

Course Rank: 50

Date Played: April 20, 2011

Starting Time: 1:50 p.m.

Weather: 85 degrees with mild Kona wind, no clouds

My Score: 81

Number of Lost Balls: 1 (stupid shot as usual)

Highlights: 12 pars

Lowlights: 1 double bogey and 1 triple bogey

Excuse for Not Breaking 80: Second round of the day (shot 78 at The Experience in the morning), combined with hot conditions.

Greens Fee: $175

Playing Partners: Joe Strong. Our wives (Pat and Greta) came along for the ride, and to serve as camera crew, but mostly they just heckled us.

Practice Facilities: I was too exhausted to check them out.

My Rating: 8. (I would give The Experience a 9, even though it is not part of the top 100.)

Absolutely Must Play: Yes, to get an opportunity to visit Lanai (ferry from Maui), and to play The Experience as part of a 36-hole excursion. Combined, it was a great golf getaway, even if it used up a full vacation day.

Favorite Hole: No. 5 offers a blind tee shot that, if hit too long, will funnel down a steep incline into trouble. The fairway is significantly elevated above the green. The two most dramatic holes are Nos. 12 and 17, which both require a forced carry over cliffs lined with lava rocks above the bay. On the day, however, my favorite hole was No. 17 at The Experience. This hole may be the most elevated I have ever played. A lake comes into play on the right, with most balls pushed in that direction by the local wind and slope. The green is guarded on the right side by a large tree. I hit a spectacular drive, only to be blocked by the tree on the approach to a deep right flag. I played safe left to the fringe, and sank a thirty-foot putt for birdie.

Location Characteristics: The Challenge is characterized by rolling desert terrain with expansive bay and ocean views. Much of the back nine is played along the cliffs above the ocean. Without wind or trees it was difficult to stay cool. The great views serve as a distraction. The Experience is situated at elevation, and offers a pseudo-alpine feel. The course reminded me of Colorado with large pines lining the fairways. There was plenty of water to help keep you focused.

Comments: The Challenge course was immaculately maintained with pristine fairways and greens. The cliffs and the ocean provide a great backdrop for the typical Nicklaus design. Good shots yielded numerous pars, but a couple of errors kept my score in the 80s. Forced carries were required on a number of holes, with some waste areas and canyons coming into play on second and third shots. By the time I finished I was overcooked, and would have preferred some breeze or trees. Nevertheless, I found the trip worthwhile. The day would not have been as much fun if the guys at Maui Golf had not suggested the two rounds. (They offered a significant discount, with the ferry included.) The Experience definitely offered a "wow" factor; with No. 17 being one of few holes I have ever rated a 10. In addition, they had an exceptional par 4 hole with an island green (No. 8). The Experience was a memorable round, even if it did not embody the traditional Hawaiian design.

Round 26 — Mauna Kea

Course Rank: 19

Date Played: April 21, 2011

Starting Time: 11:36 a.m.

Weather: 90 degrees, calm and sunny

My Score: 84

Number of Lost Balls: 3

Highlights: 1 birdie and 10 pars

Lowlights: 3 triple bogeys

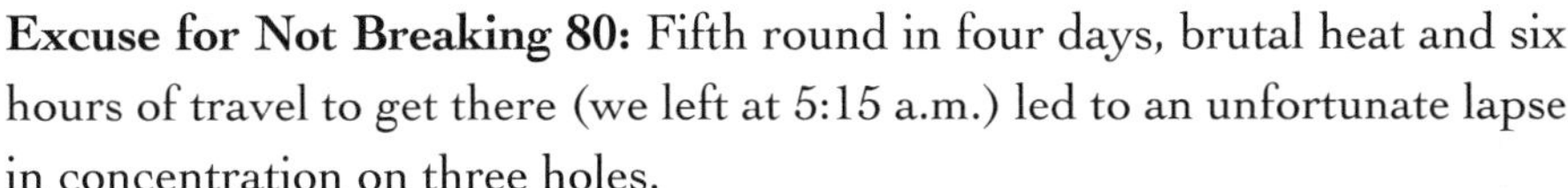

Excuse for Not Breaking 80: Fifth round in four days, brutal heat and six hours of travel to get there (we left at 5:15 a.m.) led to an unfortunate lapse in concentration on three holes.

Greens Fee: $175

Playing Partners: Joe Strong.

Practice Facilities: Definitely adequate, but not overwhelming. The range and putting green were conveniently located near the first tee.

My Rating: 8. Despite being completely exhausted and overheated, I appreciated the Robert Trent Jones, Sr. and Rees Jones redesign.

Absolutely Must Play: Yes. This is a challenging course with numerous well-placed bunkers, ocean-view holes, and a preponderance of elevated greens that make club selection challenging. In addition, the greens were very quick (and very true), which caused a great deal of difficulty early, after slow and/or recently aerated greens at Makena, Kapalua and The Experience. Mauna Kea offers a classic Hawaiian golf experience.

Favorite Hole: No. 11 is a difficult par 3 into the wind, somewhat reminiscent of No. 17 at Pebble Beach. However, No. 3 was my favorite. This 179-yard hole requires all carry over the ocean. From the tips, this hole is 272 yards. Unfortunately, this was one of my triples, as I put my tee shot in the rocks adjacent to the ocean. I then hit a great third shot from the tee box, only to three-putt.

Location Characteristics: Mauna Kea is isolated, approximately 25 miles north of the Kona airport. The course is situated in the hills above the Pacific with plenty of topography, most of which seemed uphill. Palm trees, Bermuda grass, lava rock, hibiscus and typical Hawaiian flora and fauna fill the course.

Comments: I am not sure why the PGA Tour does not hold an event at Mauna Kea. From the tips the course is 7,370 yards, and plays longer due to the presence of elevated greens. The course rating of 77.2 says all you need to know. The setting is great, and, despite the hot weather, I was shocked by the limited play. This is an older, traditional course that has benefitted from a semi-sadistic Rees Jones redesign. I wish I had not been so exhausted before arriving, and that the weather had been more accommodating, as I believe this course may have rated higher. There are plenty of challenging holes, but like most good courses, there are plenty of pars to be had if well played. The three triple bogeys are testament to the risk/reward nature of the design. This is a definite must for those with the opportunity to play, but I am not sure it is worth the 18-hour day.

Trip Summary:

The irony of flying Alaska Airlines to Hawaii was not lost on me when I boarded in San Diego. While on the subject, I am not sure if it is Alaska Airlines or Delta (with whom we booked the flight), but they may have surpassed United in poor customer service. Despite getting a seat assignment when booking originally, the operator elected to ignore this information and cleared our seats. This did not prove to be a problem going, but on the way back I was incredibly frustrated, having arrived at the airport three hours early and unable to reserve a seat. The less than pleasant counter person, who was engrossed in conversation with a security guard, indicated she would not be able to help me until 15 minutes before boarding. The idiocy of the seating situation is enough to cause me to boycott both airlines going forward. I may be running out of acceptable carriers.

No doubt Hawaii is at the top of the list for many vacationers. Balmy weather, fancy resorts, volcanoes, beaches and that mellow island atmosphere can be intoxicating (as can the Mai Tais). But an intense golf vacation runs counter to the laid-back character of the place. The wallet also will take a beating, especially if you need to island hop to other courses. It is probably best to stay on Maui if golf is your thing. Excellent courses await at Kapalua, Wailea and Makena, to name a few. It is also worthwhile to take the ferry over to Lanai for 36 holes. (By the way, this is not the old leper colony.) My favorite course during the trip may have been The Experience at Koele, although friends have had less than perfect weather when they have played.

I began to OD on the complimentary Mai Tais, and eventually switched to Blue Hawaiians which, if watered down enough, are a real thirst quencher. Even if not watered down they quench the thirst, but can lead to a big hangover the next day (I speak from experience). My final thought is, go to Hawaii to vacation, with golf as an added bonus if time permits. There are better, cheaper and more convenient places to test your skills on the fairway. I will return to the islands because Princeville chose an inopportune time to renovate their greens, and because I have a compulsive urge to complete each of the top 100.

Chapter 22

Cheers

Two trips to Minnesota in less than twelve months are bound to send one to the local watering hole. Fortunately, this is no problem in a state where there is at least one bar or tavern for every lake; which, if the license plates are correct, would be 10,000. The urban areas may have a reduced per capita number of alcohol serving establishments, but it seems they make up for it in the rural communities, which comprise most of the state. Of course, what would you expect from a people that drill holes in the ice in order to fish?

My brother-in-law and I, who are jointly referred to as the "outlaws" by my wife's family, were dragged to the hinterlands in May to attend my nephew's wedding. Actually, I was dragged; Tom has made a conscious decision to live there, so shame on him. Despite my best efforts, I could not convince the happy couple to have the wedding moved to a later date, say sometime after winter in Minnesota, which ends about Independence Day. Since I did not get the chance to play The Quarry at Granite Ridge last year, I figured it was a good opportunity to complete the most remote course on the list. I was somewhat consoled that the owners indicated the course was scheduled to open by the end of April—weather permitting—when I made the reservation. Tom was eager to join me as he grew up in the Iron Range, not far from Biwabik (pronounced *bye-wah-bic*). As the date grew closer it became apparent that I would not have to golf in snow, but frigid, sub-50 degree weather was likely.

Tom picked me up at Terminal 2 in Minneapolis on Wednesday afternoon, after another successful Southwest flight. We then made a four-hour trek, in the dark, to the metropolis of Biwabik; population 954, number of bars/

taverns 12 (approximately one of every two commercial establishments in town). To be fair, while no one lives in Biwabik (and who can blame them), it is a popular ski area. The local economy is based upon the alcohol consumption of skiers, fishermen and summer golfers. I had booked a room at the Lodge at Giant's Ridge, a facility that offers excellent swing season deals.

The next morning it was obvious why the lodge offered such a great rate. Peering out my second floor window, I could see a sizable snow bank. Not enough for skiing, but not conducive to great golf either. At least there was no snow on the course. In fact, by the time we got to The Quarry, just down the hill, the temperature had risen to a balmy 46 degrees. We decided to eat breakfast before heading out, with the hopes that the weather would improve into the 50s. Because we planned to play 36 holes, however, we were unable to wait for our hands to thaw. Needless to say, the weather proved a scoring challenge.

Round 27 — The Quarry at Giant's Ridge

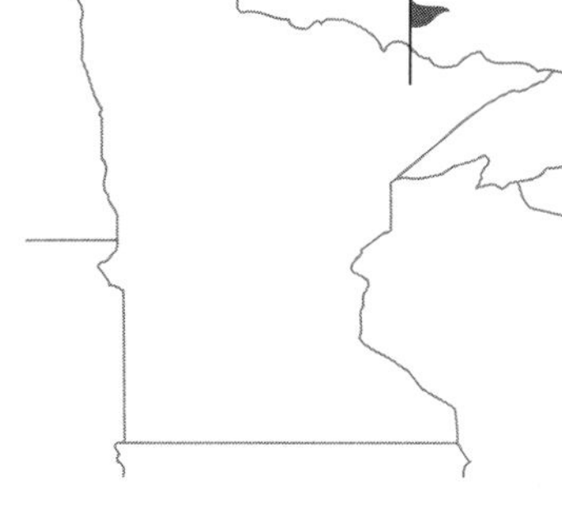

Course Rank: 54

Date Played: May 12, 2011

Starting Time: 9:00 a.m.

Weather: 48 degrees, with 10 mph winds, cloudy. By No. 18, the temperature was still only 52 degrees. The chill factor made for tough "sledding."

My Score: 84

Number of Lost Balls: None, although I put five shots in hazards.

Highlights: 1 birdie and 8 pars

Lowlights: 2 double bogeys and 1 triple bogey

Excuse for Not Breaking 80: I was mentally unable to recover from the sight of snow outside my window that morning.

Greens Fee: $52, swing season rate.

Playing Partners: Tom Longar, brother-in-law, and comrade "outlaw" at my nephew's wedding scheduled for the weekend. We did not see any other idiots stupid enough to brave the cold weather.

Practice Facilities: More than adequate. I only hit a few practice balls, as I wanted to stay out of the cold.

My Rating: Solid 8, with plenty of elevation changes, attractive tree-lined fairways and a plethora of interesting holes.

Absolutely Must Play: No, but if you find yourself anywhere near southern Ontario, Canada, it is worth the detour. I am not sure I would travel out of my way, given other options, but if you play the course, you will not be disappointed.

Favorite Hole: No. 2 is a terrific, 558-yard, uphill par 5, which requires a forced carry on the tee shot, a precise second shot and a well-executed approach. Once this is accomplished, you must navigate a large, heavily contoured green.

Location Characteristics: The Quarry is situated in the heart of the Iron Range in northern Minnesota. There are large rock formations throughout the golf course that can do major damage to a Pro V1. The golf course is cut into the hillside, through thick forests, with plenty of elevation changes. Granted, there are only six perfect golf days a year this far north. I am not sure of the elevation, but the cold weather offsets any benefit that might be derived from thin air.

Comments: The Quarry is rated 54 on the top 100 list. This is no small accomplishment given the outlying location. The course is a terrific challenge, situated in a pristine setting in the forests of northern Minnesota. This is a well-designed track that requires excellent shot making and command of all parts of the game if you are going to score well. Even when the score balloons there is plenty to enjoy about the course. One of the great advantages of my quest to play the top 100 is the opportunity to enjoy a layout like The Quarry. The second course at Giant's Ridge (The Legend) is also worth the effort. This course is more "resort" oriented, with wider fairways, but still offers a stout challenge. The Lodge at Giant's Ridge provides excellent, affordable accommodations during the non-ski season. We also were able to play the Wilderness Course at Fortune Bay, which is about 30 minutes away. This course appears on *Golf Digest*'s top 100 and is also an excellent track. Thus, a visit to the region provides numerous possibilities, and could be combined with a Brainerd, Minnesota, stop to create a decent, low-priced golf vacation. I understand the fishing is excellent in this region as well. Weather and isolation aside, The Quarry is worthy of the top 100.

Trip Summary:

While growing up, I recall weather reports that often listed International Falls as the coldest place on the mainland USA. Biwabik could well be a suburb and suffers the same weather issues. It is tough when mid-May weather is too cold for golf. It is little wonder the pro tour is not littered with native Minnesotans. If you have to go to Minnesota, and do not mind the extra travel, a diversion to the Iron Range may be in order, but only if you are a golf junkie like myself. Too bad the area is so isolated, because there are plenty of good golf venues. By the way, this far north, the sun could stay up until midnight. In late June, a 54-hole day may be possible, and you will not have any trouble finding a local watering hole.

Chapter 23

The Sun Will Come Out Tomorrow

In addition to being a confirmed golf addict, I am also an optimist with respect to weather. Of course, I live in San Diego, so how could I possibly maintain a realistic perspective? The wedding in Minnesota in May drove my decision on this trip, albeit with much trepidation. The weather reports before leaving for Minnesota were not encouraging, but they did suggest some improvement was coming. (Not so.)

After the quick detour to my nephew's wedding, I had to rise at 6:00 a.m. in order to catch a 45-minute flight to Chicago, where I would meet up with my official Midwestern golf partner, Dr. Scott Rand, for a late morning round at Cog Hill. I usually do not recommend early morning flights or long travel before playing golf, but we had limited time, with eight rounds scheduled in five days. This intense level of play ran contrary to the recommendations of my sports chiropractor, who was now threatening to drop me as a patient. Every time he made progress on my aching elbow, I would run off on another golf junket. *Addicted to golf? Moi?*

Our first challenge was a tight time frame. Our tee-time was looming and we still had to pick up my luggage before making the trek over to Cog Hill. As it turned out, we had the course to ourselves, because no one else was crazy enough to challenge the cold, wet and windy conditions. We did not have the luxury of delaying our round, so Scott and I proceeded to make fools of ourselves by trying to beat the elements (we lost).

Round 28 Cog Hill Golf Club (Number 4–Dubsdread)

Course Rank: 16

Date Played: May 15, 2011

Starting Time: 11:10 a.m.

Weather: 45 degrees, rainy, 25 mph winds, with gusts to 40 mph

My Score: 89

Number of Lost Balls: 1

Highlights: 6 pars

Lowlights: 5 double bogeys

Excuse for Not Breaking 80: See weather above, combined with sleep deprivation.

Greens Fee: $155

Playing Partners: Dr. Scott Rand, designated Midwest partner and golf junkie.

Practice Facilities: Expansive facilities, with overhead covers at the range. This proved especially useful given the conditions. Unfortunately, the wind was in our face and the water kept blowing onto my glasses. I was only able to hit a few knock down shots before we headed to the course.

My Rating: 7+, although it was tough to derive any definitive opinion given the weather.

Absolutely Must Play: Not necessarily, but most people will eventually make the Chicago pilgrimage, and you will not be disappointed (unless you have my weather). Given the proximity, the Chicago courses may easily be added to a Wisconsin itinerary.

Favorite Hole: Most of the holes were fun, although none were especially memorable, perhaps because I could not see in the driving rain. No. 9 was a narrow, winding par 5 that I found to be a good challenge.

Location Characteristics: Located west of downtown Chicago, the venue is influenced by its "Windy City" proximity. Lemont is a suburban area of Chicago that provides a nice setting. This is an older course with mature trees and a couple of ponds.

Comments: Once I had donned my cold weather gear and covered it with my rain gear, I was able to begin appreciating the course. Cog Hill (Dubsdread) is an older, mature layout that experienced a major renovation during the past several years. The course has hosted numerous PGA events including the Western Open and BMW Championship. The clubhouse is older, as are most of the facilities, with none of the pretentiousness of the more exclusive resorts. The topography is comparatively flat, and you could probably walk the course quite easily. There are wide, ample fairways. Most of the greens are well-bunkered and elevated. As such, an extra club is often required. Ultimately, we had miserable weather that kept all sane people away. In fact, I was told only one group had gone out ahead of us, and I did not notice any afterward. I cannot blame the course for the weather conditions, but it made it difficult to appreciate the experience and to analyze the design. The condition appeared to be very good, and the greens were in good condition, even if they had not been mowed. The layout was straightforward with no real "tricks." Overall, it was a good time, albeit one cold, wet and windy afternoon.

Round 29 — The Glen Club

Course Rank: *72*

Date Played: May 16, 2011

Starting Time: 8:30 a.m.

Weather: 48 degrees, 15-20 mph winds with gusts to 30 mph. At least there was no rain.

My Score: 92

Number of Lost Balls: 1

Highlights: 6 pars

Lowlights: 4 double bogeys and 2 triple bogeys

Excuse for Not Breaking 80: I could blame it on the excessive drinking the night before, but it could have been the very cold, windy conditions. I was too hung-over to notice.

Greens Fee: $148 (with cart)

Playing Partners: Scott Rand.

Practice Facilities: Very good.

My Rating: *7+*, for very good condition, some interesting holes and the Illinois Golf Hall of Fame on site.

Absolutely Must Play: Maybe, if you are in the Chicago area. This Fazio design offers a great setting. The Glen Club offers several hotel rooms above the pro shop and the Hall of Fame, which were terrific.

Favorite Hole: Both Nos. 5 and 18 are long challenging par 5s that I found very well designed, with precision shots required. Unfortunately, in the wind, I was not precise, earning triple bogeys on each.

Location Characteristics: The Glen Club is situated in Glenview, Illinois, a suburb north of Chicago. Northwestern University uses these facilities. This suburb appears to be relatively affluent, with many high-priced homes lining portions of the course. Despite a general links design, there were many added elements, including lakes and large bunkers. The rough was irregular, with many opportunities to lose stray shots. Because of the weather, this rough was regularly in play. This is a comparatively new course, constructed on an old military facility. Most of the flora is newer and not fully mature.

Comments: After a wet Cog Hill the day before, I was cautiously optimistic about my round. It was dry, so the rain gear was stowed; however, the low temperatures and high winds created a chill factor that was not conducive to scoring. I felt I played well, but my score said otherwise. The Glen Club is a challenging design, even though Tom Fazio typically creates a very playable layout. I may need to return to see how we would have fared under warmer, less windy conditions.

Round 30 — Erin Hills

Course Rank: 35

Date Played: May 17, 2011

Starting Time: 7:48 a.m.

Weather: Overcast, 52 degrees, 10 to 20 mph winds, with gusts to 30 mph

My Score: 84

Number of Lost Balls: 0

Highlights: 9 pars

Lowlights: 3 double bogeys

Excuse for Not Breaking 80: You must walk the course, and there are significant topographical changes. I was five over par through 13, putting for an eagle on 14. I three-putted from 20 feet, never got my legs back, and ran off three straight double bogeys. I was exhausted by the time we finished, which did not serve me well for the afternoon round at Blackwolf Run. I should probably start working out…nah; that would take away from golf time.

Greens Fee: $250, includes $50 for caddie.

Playing Partners: Scott Rand, along with our caddie, John.

Practice Facilities: More than adequate to work on all parts of the game. The condition was good.

My Rating: 9. I increased this rating upon further rumination.

Absolutely Must Play: Yes. Aside from being in the U.S. Open rotation (2017) and hosting the 2011 U.S. Amateur, Erin Hills provides an extremely challenging, but fair, test of links-style golf. Every hole offered a unique challenge, with well-placed bunkers and a variety of greens. The course plays long, and the walk may not be appropriate for some. If you cannot hit a reasonably long ball off the tee, the course may be too much.

Favorite Hole: I gave unusually high ratings to six holes. The par 5s were all exceptional, and I liked the challenge of the 450-yard, uphill, wind in the face No. 10. However, the downhill, par 3 No. 9, at only 143 yards, was the best, given all of the trouble surrounding the green and the precision required.

Location Characteristics: Situated on farm land, Erin Hills is located in a rural area north of Milwaukee. This is a classic links design with few trees and limited water features. Erin Hills retains its farming roots with many of the out buildings being farm structures (i.e. the cart barn is really a barn). The course is not quite as exceptional as its neighbor to the north (Whistling Straits), but is not far behind.

Comments: I would have preferred more docile weather, but I really enjoyed this round. Virtually every hole was memorable, and you needed to have all parts of your game working. The setting is pastoral, and the staff friendly. Our caddie was knowledgeable and survived the trek. Despite my lack of physical conditioning, I do not usually have much trouble walking a course with a caddie. Nevertheless, this all-walking course had me exhausted by the time I returned to the clubhouse. The property is somewhat isolated, but since you will be playing the Kohler courses (Whistling Straits and Blackwolf Run) you should make the one-hour detour to Erin Hills. I will be interested to see how the pros deal with the 7,920-yard layout in 2017.

Round 31 Blackwolf Run (River Course)

Course Rank: 12

Date Played: May 17, 2011

Starting Time: 2:30 p.m.

Weather: 53 degrees, 25 mph winds

My Score: 90

Number of Lost Balls: 4

Highlights: 7 pars

Lowlights: 3 double bogeys and 1 quintuple bogey

Excuse for Not Breaking 80: Weather, too tired, too difficult, and the 10 strokes on No. 11 did not help.

Greens Fee: $248, but as part of the package is effectively much lower.

Playing Partners: Scott Rand.

Practice Facilities: Very good.

My Rating: 9, for the "wow" factor that awaits you as you reach the river portion of the course in the backwoods. A playable start leads to a sadistic middle of the round, beginning with No. 5.

Absolutely Must Play: Yes, unless you have a particular aversion to Pete Dye courses. This one is memorable, especially after you get past the fourth hole.

Favorite Hole: There are so many interesting holes. I might have preferred No. 11, a horseshoe-shaped par 5, but I lost two balls and carded a 10. My favorite was No. 5, a ridiculously tough par 4 into the breeze that includes a river on the right, an elevated tee box, trouble left, and a tricky elevated green with a front bunker to catch wimpy approaches. Honorable mention to No. 13, a ridiculous 192-yard par 3 that requires you to work your ball right to left, over the river. There is no bail-out area. I suspect many people find this hole annoying.

Location Characteristics: Blackwolf Run River Course is situated in the woods, with several lakes and a massive river that comes into play constantly. Water messes with your mind on 13 of the holes, eight of which are on the back side. This was my second visit to Blackwolf Run, but I had not been able to play Nos. 5 to 14 previously. This is a very picturesque course, which is good because it takes your mind off the fact that your score is ballooning out of control with every mishit.

Comments: I was pleased that I had the opportunity to play that portion of the course that was closed the prior year, even if I was 15 over par on those nine (with two pars). As a lover of sadistic designs, and those that appeal to my need for constant stimulation, Blackwolf Run proved to be just the ticket. I'm not sure what Pete Dye was smoking when he designed the course (or maybe it was Alice), but there is a carnival atmosphere to some of the holes. Any golf trip that includes this course along with Whistling Straits will be a sure winner. Of course, if you aren't a fan of Dye, you might as well skip the whole thing. In combination, the two courses are a testament to the brilliance (my opinion) of this architect. Bring lots of balls and a good attitude, because the first time through you are likely to be frustrated.

Trip Summary:

Weather proved to be an issue for most of the trip, with improvement not occurring until I was in the car on the way back to the Milwaukee airport. Despite the elements, we had a great time, especially once we pulled back into Kohler, Wisconsin, after a fun morning round at Erin Hills. We were able to visit the Illinois Golf Hall of Fame at the Glen View Club. This facility also offered some very interesting accommodations. A "not so quick" round at Lake Geneva's The Brute course provided a good diversion during our travels. This course could easily have been on the top 100 list, although excruciatingly slow play on the back nine was annoying.

The daily double of Erin Hills and the River Course at Blackwolf Run was more than my aged and achy body could handle, but made for a great day, especially getting to enjoy another bowl of corn chowder and sausage soup at the Blackwolf Run restaurant.

The last two days included another visit to Whistling Straits (Straits Course). This is a perfect example of the goofiness in Wisconsin. The Whistling Straits complex has two courses. One is called Straits and the other is Irish. So, when you tell someone you played there you say I played Whistling Straits Straits. Confusing huh? I think they were sitting in the back room after developing the second course and realized each had to have a name. Once they had used up Irish, they ran out of names and started over. It would be like giving your kid the same middle and first name. Aside from this oddity, I love Whistling Straits Straits.

I avoided the quintuple bogey at No. 4 this time, and brought my score down to 85. This was pretty good considering the blustery conditions. It was so windy that I hit a driver at No. 7, a 176-yard par 3, and ended up pin high, but only because I caught it flush. Whistling Straits Straits is still not Pebble Beach (see my comment on last year's round) but it is easily top ten. I found Whistling Straits Irish more enjoyable this year. This may be because it was the first day the wind dipped below 20 mph, and the sun came out. We also snuck in a round at The Bull at Pinehurst Farms, in the Kohler area. This is a nice Nicklaus design, but suffers by comparison to the Kohler courses and Erin Hills.

Chapter 24

The World's Most Frugal Golfer, or Nothing Succeeds Like Excess

I am sure you all know a "thrifty" golfer, but I think my son Charlie could give them a run for their money (literally). I love the kid dearly, but getting him to part with his hard-earned income (he is a very well-paid engineer) can be a challenge. He is amazingly thoughtful, honest and would never take advantage of anyone or any situation. It is just that he really does not like to part with his savings. He comes by such stinginess honestly (I am not exactly a huge spender). The kid shoots 90+/- on the course, but has never spent a cent on clubs, balls, hats, attire, green fees, lessons, etc. Most of the golf balls he plays have spent quality time in a lake or other water hazard.

Anyway, Charlie was having his 24th birthday, so I figured I would drag him along on my next golf junket. I gave him a few choices, and, despite his dislike of heat, he chose Las Vegas in June. He has always been fascinated by Sin City, even though he does not gamble...imagine that.

Before hitting the glitz and glamour of Vegas, we packed up our shorts and sunscreen and headed to Mesquite, Nevada, to play one of my favorite courses: Wolf Creek Golf Club. Given the timing, it was no surprise that it felt like a blast furnace when we exited the car. On the positive side, the average temperature for my recent Midwestern trip and the Nevada boondoggle was about 75 degrees; unfortunately, I got there by playing in 53 degrees and 97 degrees, respectively.

Round 32 — Wolf Creek Golf Club

Course Rank: 60

Date Played: June 12, 2011

Starting Time: 10:00 a.m.

Weather: Sunny, 86 degrees to start, 97 degrees at finish

My Score: 88

Number of Lost Balls: 2

Highlights: 7 pars

Lowlights: 5 double bogeys

Excuse for Not Breaking 80: Too busy taking pictures.

Greens Fee: $125, off-season rate. We booked a package deal with the Casablanca Hotel and Casino.

Playing Partners: Son Charlie, Michael, a club pro from The Ledges in St George, Utah, and McKella, his girlfriend.

Practice Facilities: Nice view, but not very extensive. We could only hit irons given the restricted area.

My Rating: 9, for some of the "coolest" golf holes you will ever play. The elevation changes, doglegs, water and contrasting desert bordering the course are fantastic.

Absolutely Must Play: Yes. This was one of my favorite courses when I played it five years earlier, and it did not disappoint. There are at least a half dozen signature holes. It is out of the way, and I am not a big fan of Mesquite, but it is worth a day trip from Las Vegas.

Favorite Hole: There are so many unique holes it is difficult to select just one. No. 2 offers a huge elevated tee and severe dogleg left, with waste areas

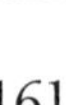

on the left and a creek running across the fairway. Selecting the line of flight on the tee shot is challenging. No. 3 is a blind uphill, long par 3 that is like nothing I can remember (the purists probably hate this one). No. 8 may be the most spectacular hole. An elevated tee box with all carry to a green, surrounded by a creek, 217 yards away. My favorite hole, however, is No. 1. The tee shot is elevated, with trouble on the left. The view is breathtaking, with pristine white sand traps and deep green fairways offering a stark contrast to the surrounding desert, from which you must abandon your ball. (These "environmentally" sensitive areas are littered with pristine golf balls, which provide a strong allure to the cheap golfer. I could have picked up at least a year's worth of Pro VIs had I dared to violate the course rules and make my way into the sand and dirt.) The view is just a sampling of things to come. The second shot is to a narrow fairway, with a large three-tiered green awaiting the third shot. What a great way to start.

Location Characteristics: Wolf Creek is situated in the high desert area of eastern Nevada, not far from Utah, by way of a slice of Arizona. High temperatures are not uncommon. There is little flora, aside from the typical desert growth providing a great contrast with the lush fairways. The course does not permit entering the "environmentally sensitive" areas to retrieve wayward shots. I cannot imagine how you could damage sand, but rules are rules. I suppose the owners subsidize the operation by collecting these balls, of which there are many. Despite being desert, there are numerous water features on the course, further adding to the beauty. Monstrous elevations add excitement to many of the tee shots. Aside from the golf (there are a couple of other nice courses in town), Mesquite does not have a lot to offer…unless you like second-rate casinos and older hotels. Personally, I would stay in Vegas, but would definitely make my way out to Wolf Creek for a round.

Comments: Wolf Creek is the classic "love it or hate it" course. Those who hate it include low handicappers who cannot stand the number of blind shots that lead to scores above their expectations, and high handicappers who lose more money on golf balls, than at the tables. The majority, however, love the course. I would not recommend going out there with the idea of breaking the course record, as course knowledge is required. Rather, one should appreciate the fascinating backdrop and the twisted mind of the architect who created such interesting golf holes. A second option is to schedule 36 holes and use the newfound course knowledge of the first round to "score" the second time through. This course was one of my all-time favorites before I started this journey, and remains in that category. Wolf Creek is not as pristine as some of the big budget Vegas venues, but is worth the 90-minute trip from the Strip.

Round 33 Cascata

Course Rank: 55

Date Played: June 13, 2011

Starting Time: 11:30 a.m.

Weather: 91 degrees to start, sunny, light winds, 100 degrees at the finish

My Score: 86

Number of Lost Balls: 2

Highlights: 1 birdie and 7 pars

Lowlights: 5 double bogeys

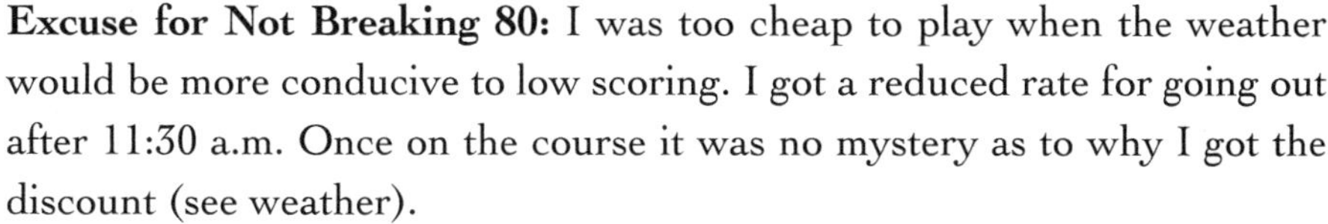

Excuse for Not Breaking 80: I was too cheap to play when the weather would be more conducive to low scoring. I got a reduced rate for going out after 11:30 a.m. Once on the course it was no mystery as to why I got the discount (see weather).

Greens Fee: $275, plus fee for forecaddie ($70 with tip each)

Playing Partners: Son Charlie, and Drew, the forecaddie.

Practice Facilities: Very nice. The driving range offers a dramatic waterfall as a backdrop. There are ample hitting stations, and an expansive putting green. Like everything else at Cascata, it was first class.

My Rating: 9 for a great golf course and great operation.

Absolutely Must Play: Yes. If you want to see how a course should be run, Cascata is the place. From the entrance, to check-in, to the lockers, to the forecaddies and design, the operation is first class, and the course is great as well.

Favorite Hole: All of the holes were very good, but after Wolf Creek, did not seem as dramatic. No. 14, is a challenging par 4, with an elevated tee, and a fairway that pushes the balls right, into a creek. I hit a perfect drive, only to get wet.

Location Characteristics: Cascata is a desert course, as are most in the Vegas area. Visually, the course is similar to Wolf Creek, with prominent elevation changes, dark green fairways with plenty of sand and water features, set against a backdrop of barren desert. They are more accommodating on retrieving your balls from the environmentally sensitive areas…so long as you do not mind battling the rattlesnakes. It is a fascinating environment, especially for residents of more forested regions.

Comments: Cascata is a hidden gem, located about 30 minutes from the Strip. The greens fees are steep, but if you do not mind the swing season in the middle of the day (i.e. really hot), there are deals available. After Shadow Creek and Wynn, the greens fee will seem like a bargain. Alternatively, you could lose big at Caesars Palace and receive a complimentary round as a consolation prize. The facilities are first rate, the service impeccable, and the course is a lot of fun. A particularly interesting feature of the round is the entrance to the course from the cart "barn," which is reminiscent of Mr. Toad's Wild Ride at Disneyland, as the two-door gate opens before your eyes as you embark on your journey. If given a choice I might recommend you play Cascata before venturing to Wolf Creek, as I believe the dramatic elevated desert shots will seem more impressive before the Mesquite round. Lastly, if you like pristine conditions, you will love the course. Despite the limited play they do not scrimp on the maintenance. There are a number of good choices in the Las Vegas area, but if you can swallow the cost, this is a definite must.

Round 34 — Shadow Creek

Course Rank: 17

Date Played: June 14, 2011

Starting Time: 10:30 a.m.

Weather: 88 degrees to start, 97 degrees to end, minimal wind

My Score: 80

Number of Lost Balls: None, as we were able to fetch my drive on No. 18 out of the water.

Highlights: 10 pars

Lowlights: None

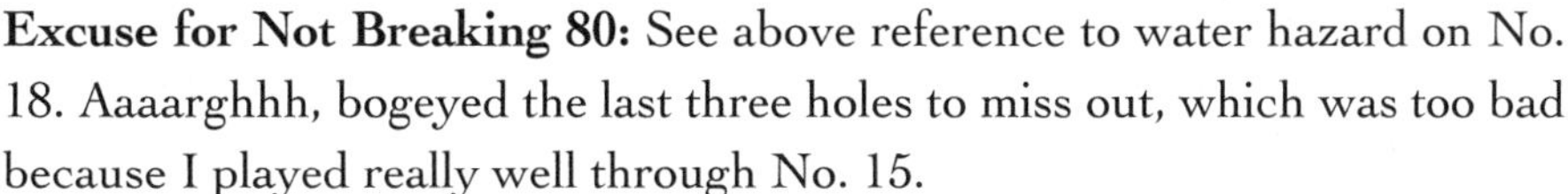

Excuse for Not Breaking 80: See above reference to water hazard on No. 18. Aaaarghhh, bogeyed the last three holes to miss out, which was too bad because I played really well through No. 15.

Greens Fee: $500 (gulp) per person

Playing Partners: Son Charlie, and Craig, the forecaddie.

Practice Facilities: Like everything else at Shadow Creek, the practice facilities are exceptional. Despite severe restrictions on the amount of play, the range is large with multiple hitting stations. The range balls were in great shape. In addition, the landing area included many mature trees.

My Rating: 9, for the total experience.

Absolutely Must Play: Yes, once you have mortgaged the house to cover the green fee, or, alternatively, gambled six figures in the casino, the Shadow Creek experience is like nothing else. From the limousine that picks you up at an MGM Hotel, to the secluded location (tough to do in the desert), the

locker room, the clubhouse, forecaddies, range and impeccable condition, this is a must. Ultimately, you do not play Shadow Creek; you experience it.

Favorite Hole: There are a lot of good to very good holes. My favorite was No. 15, a relatively long par 4 that requires an accurate drive and more accurate second shot to navigate the creek that runs along the left side of the fairway before cutting in front of the green. A high score awaits the golfer that fails to respect this one.

Location Characteristics: Shadow Creek is located in a barren, industrial district of northern Las Vegas. The surrounding properties are flat with limited character. In fact, before the limousine pulls into the hidden driveway, there are moments when you feel you are being kidnapped to some God-forsaken desert lair. Behind the guardhouse and a thick oleander screen, you enter an ersatz alpine wonderland. It takes several minutes to become immersed in pine trees, creeks, rolling hills and lush fairways. I fully expected the temperature to drop by 20 degrees once I exited the car…it did not. The clubhouse is large, but not Donald Trump over-the-top. Rather, the place exudes understated class. The locker room is impressive, with a "who's who" of luminaries identified as members. Steve Wynn, Kirk Kerkorian, President Clinton and President Bush occupy the first four lockers. Locker 99 belongs to Wayne Gretzky. In between, there are lockers belonging to the most famous names in sports, politics and entertainment. There is more staff than players, making sure no need goes unmet. Shadow Creek formerly housed Steve Wynn's private zoo; however, most of those animals are gone. Nevertheless, we were regaled by numerous unique birds during the round. Apparently, three coyotes have been thinning the ranks of the exotica, although our forecaddie assured us that two of the coyotes were no longer an issue. The flora is equally impressive given that it is growing in this barren environment. Creating elevated tee boxes would seem to be impossible in this area, but there are many on the course. Ultimately, it could hardly be described as desert golf, except for the hot weather.

Comments: There are really no words to describe Shadow Creek. The place is über-exclusive, without being pretentious. The facility guards its privacy so much so that they have only recently begun allowing golfers to take photographs. They still will not allow the USGA access to rate the course. I was told only four paying groups are allowed each day, with only six groups of "comped" players. As such, overcrowding is not a concern. It must be tough to lose money all night and then get up early, borrow clubs and play well. The round is something of a consolation prize for those individuals willing to gamble six figures in the casino. The greens fee is tied for the highest on *Golf Magazine*'s top 100 list, and there is no such thing as a twilight rate. You pay $500 or nothing. Is the golf as dramatic as Pebble Beach? Probably not, but you really cannot compare the two. If you have the money, give Shadow Creek a try.

Trip Summary:

The three courses we played represent some of the highest quality, most entertaining venues I have encountered. And, despite the extreme temperatures, I loved all of the facilities. The biggest downside is the cost. Although Las Vegas is known to offer some of the best deals around, it can also be a very expensive place to vacation. This does not even count the casino contributions you might make. Contrasting the high costs with my son's fiscal conservatism was quite amusing. I noticed one evening he was playing with his calculator. When queried as to what he was doing, he responded that he was figuring out how long a vacation he could have in Las Vegas for the cost of our three-day extravaganza. With green fees, caddies, hotels, meals and shows, we spent a combined $2,800 (funded entirely by the patriarch). With cheap hotels offered as low as $20 per night, daily all-you-can-eat buffets for $30 per person and four hours a day of nickel slots (approximately 1,000 pulls), with a 95-percent payout ($2.50 losses per person per day), he calculated we could have stayed in Vegas for a month. There are free shows in many of the casinos, pools everywhere and people-watching to fill the time. I love the way his mind works, but a month in Sin City would be too much to handle.

Fiscal issues aside, I think the Vegas golf vacation is one of the best available, with overall pricing a bit less than Pebble Beach. This trip also can include another $500 round at Wynn (discussed later) if you really want to blow your annual budget. Las Vegas is easy to get to, and hotel rooms are comparatively cheap. In order to play Shadow Creek you will need to stay at an MGM resort. If you are willing to brave the heat, you can generally find some good deals. Be forewarned, however, when you venture out during the day, you will see Las Vegas without its makeup—and it is not a pretty picture.

Chapter 25

Comme Ci, Comme Ca

I believe that Idaho is the Indian term for *ambivalent*. I cannot ever recall a trip for which I had so few words. I liked the golf, the food was good, the hotel rooms fine, the weather was terrific, the setting pristine and the people friendly. I was not disappointed, nor was I pleasantly surprised with my sojourn to Idaho. Would I go back? Yes, probably, maybe. There are places I prefer, but I could also see myself residing in the "white bread" communities of Northern Idaho for several months (summer) each year. The natives seem to love it, although I would go stir crazy during the off-season. Coeur d'Alene is a nice resort course, but not one I would want to play all the time. More on that later. The complex at Circling Raven was great, but beyond the grounds there was not much.

At the end of the day, I was glad I went, but am not ready to book a return trip. Although an opinionated individual, I have no opinion on Idaho; nor do I have strong opinions on the golf either.

Round 35 — Circling Raven Golf Club

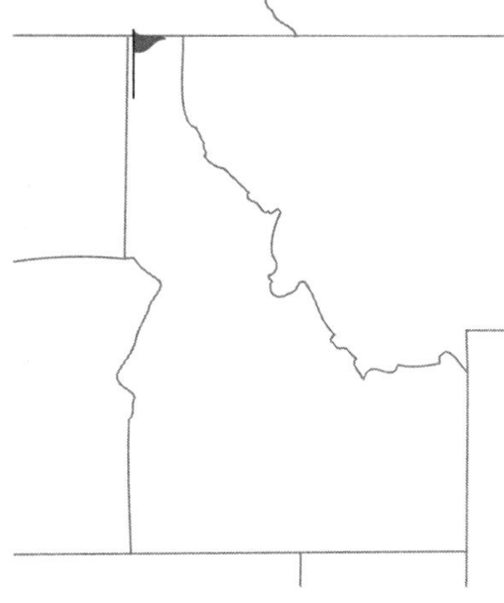

Course Rank: 92

Date Played: July 10, 2011

Starting Time: 9:30 a.m.

Weather: 62 degrees to start, 78 degrees at finish, light wind…just about perfect

My Score: 79

Number of Lost Balls: 1, I was not permitted to enter the environmentally sensitive area to retrieve my Titleist, which was tantalizingly just out of reach.

Highlights: 2 birdies and 10 pars

Lowlights: 3 double bogeys

Excuse for Not Breaking 80: None, but could have been 75 if not for a couple of brain cramps.

Greens Fee: $95 (comped by Bob, my hero)

Playing Partners: Bob, Director of Public Relations for the hotel and resort. Certainly one of the more interesting and entertaining partners to date. It is always great to get the behind-the-scenes stories on the local course.

Practice Facilities: Very expansive, with a short game area and putting green. Not exceptional but adequate.

My Rating: 8, as the overall experience was very enjoyable.

Absolutely Must Play: No, Yes, I don't know. Everything was very well done. The course was in excellent condition, the challenge was definitely there, the setting was spiritual. I remembered every hole the day after the round. Ultimately, while all the holes were memorable, few were signature level. I would definitely play this course again, but getting there is not easy. Ultimately, I do not feel strongly one way or the other.

Favorite Hole: The most dramatic hole is No. 13, a long (218-yard) downhill par 3 with wetlands on the right side. The back right pin placement is almost impossible. For fun, I hit a driver from the gold tees (253 yards) and just missed the front of the green. There were many good and very good holes, but few great ones.

Location Characteristics: Circling Raven is located in the Palouse area of upstate Idaho. This is fertile, rolling country that is well suited to farming. The course is situated over 600 acres making it one of the least dense layouts in the country. There are no homes along the fairways, and, on the back side, you cannot see any other holes from the one you are playing. The tribe that runs the facility has worked hard to retain the native flavor of the land, and, have succeeded very well. Ultimately, the location is beautiful and serene.

Comments: You seldom have the opportunity to spend four hours with one of the local staff. I had two opportunities to play with Bob, whose enthusiasm for the course, the hotel/casino and the tribe was unequivocal. He may have overstated his case a bit, but there was plenty to be proud of, and I was impressed with what they had accomplished on this outlying parcel. The resort itself, and all of the related activities, dining, gaming, spa, etc. were top-notch. Further, they had an exceptional pro shop. A great deal of thought had gone into the planning of the facilities. In addition, this may have been the best bargain to date. Certainly, this was the best course I have played for under $100. The Circling Raven Resort is still developing. Walking trails are in the process of being completed. My wife was hugely impressed with the facilities and the treatment we received, and Chinook Steak, Pasta & Spirits was a great restaurant. I think we both agreed that the value far exceeded that of the world-renowned Coeur d'Alene Resort one half hour to the north.

Overall, the finishing holes are less inspired than the earlier holes, with an easy par 3, short par 5 and average par 4 to end the round. Accuracy is important, as environmentally sensitive areas grab the wayward drive and must be played with a penalty. The greens were hard and did not hold shots. These greens were swift but true, and in great shape. Bottom line, like everything else in Idaho, there was a lot to like, but other venues have a stronger draw.

Round 36 — Coeur d'Alene Resort

Course Rank: 81

Date Played: July 11, 2011

Starting Time: 9:30 a.m.

Weather: 68 degrees to start, 84 degrees at finish, clear skies, minimal wind

My Score: 78

Number of Lost Balls: 0

Highlights: 11 pars

Lowlights: None

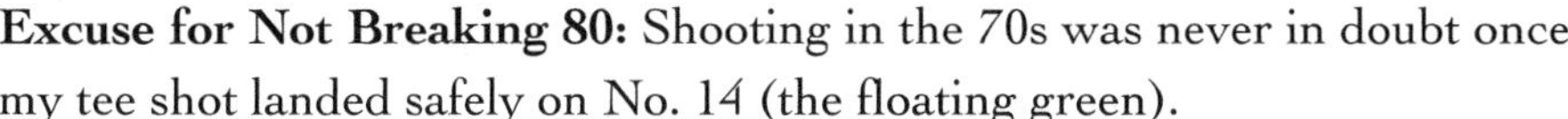

Excuse for Not Breaking 80: Shooting in the 70s was never in doubt once my tee shot landed safely on No. 14 (the floating green).

Greens Fee: $225, but my cost was $180 with the stay-and-play package.

Playing Partners: Dale (Canadian), Fran and Neil (Phoenix senior citizens), Forecaddie for the other three was Don; my walking caddie was Brendan. It was an odd pairing without much synergy.

Practice Facilities: Range balls are hit into a cordoned off area of the lake. The floating golf balls are brought back in by the tide. These are reduced distance balls, and you have no idea how far they are traveling. If this makes you tense, no problem, as they have a masseuse on-site to get you ready for the round. The short game area is good, and the putting green acceptable as it prepares you for what is to come.

My Rating: 9, or 8, or 9, or 8. Tough call. This is a classic resort course, with lots of signature holes, some terrific views and neat gimmicks. However, the challenge falls a bit short, as the course is designed with the idea of keeping 30 handicappers moving at the suggested pace of 4 hours 30 minutes. There

is definitely a "wow" factor on some of the holes, and the novelty of the floating green is worth the visit.

Absolutely Must Play: Probably, if for no other reason than to challenge the floating green. Nos. 3 to 6 and 11 to 14 are really terrific. The others largely seem to fill out the 18. The finishing holes and the par 5s are a little below average. For the recreational golfer, however, there are plenty of oohs and ahhs.

Favorite Hole: I liked Nos. 3 through 6, with plenty of elevation change and really tough greens, but you cannot ignore the unique 14th hole with the floating green, where you are shuttled by boat after hitting your tee shot. This hole is extremely picturesque, and, if you play the blue tees, requires a stout 160 to 180 yards depending on the day. I parred this one on day one, and birdied it on the second day.

Location Characteristics: Situated along Lake Coeur d'Alene, the course is heavily forested, making this one of the more picturesque settings in golf. Reportedly all holes have some water views; however, many are obstructed by trees that line most of the fairways. In season, the location is often characterized by perfect summer weather, although the lake is comparatively cold if you decide to recreate in the water. Access to the golf course is generally via a boat that offers a ten-minute ride from the resort, although you can also enter from a road on the backside of the facility. Ultimately, this is an idyllic setting that enhances the golf experience.

Comments: Coeur d'Alene is clearly a different experience. The floating green is one of several novelty holes that keep things interesting. The par 3s are second only to Harbour Town in terms of the "wow" factor. The setting is exceptional and the staff terrific. I was surprised how close the resort is to Spokane, meaning that Southwest Airlines can get you there. My only complaint is that the challenge may be insufficient for low handicap golfers. A second round played from the gold tee boxes was still less difficult than most of the other courses on the list. This helps the recreational/resort golfer enjoy the experience more than some of the more sadistic layouts. It also helps pace of play. I was impressed that the forecaddies are graded on meeting specific time guidelines, and are required to check in after nine holes to make sure the speed is acceptable. Bottom line: Do not miss the opportunity to play the course if given the chance. Just check the spelling of your name on the certificate you are given for playing the island hole in par or better.

Trip Summary:

I have absolutely no complaints about my Idaho golf trip. The courses were interesting; Circling Raven provided a very good challenge, while the setting of Coeur d'Alene was terrific, and I had the opportunity to play the island hole. Circling Raven represented a great value, although there was not much remarkable beyond the grounds of the hotel and casino. Coeur d'Alene offers a "touristy" lake experience, although I felt the hotel and golf package was a bit costly for the location and quality. We had a number of good meals on the trip, although the selection of dining establishments was limited. The Idaho experience would not rank as a top five relative to the best golf vacations, but it is certainly far from the bottom. My final word on the Idaho trip? I do not really have one.

Chapter 26

Nickel and Diming

There are few things more irritating to the frugal minded than planning vacations, creating a budget, and then getting hit with a series of add-ons. Generally, these annoying costs take the form of baggage surcharges, resort fees and local taxes. I will often fly Southwest Airlines just to avoid the baggage surcharge, even if the total cost is similar. Resort fees drive me crazy, as they seldom provide anything of interest to me. Under this category you might find pool access, free parking, free Internet and a free newspaper, all at the bargain basement price of $25 per night. These fees are especially odious at large resorts. As a result, I generally eschew the already overpriced fancy hotels for the utilitarian Hampton Inns or Country Inn & Suites, where they include breakfast. I sleep just as well in these rooms. Unfortunately, many of the top 100 courses require a stay at a particular resort.

Of particular frustration are local fees and taxes. Most municipalities have found the local populace more accepting of higher taxes on visitors to their city, rather than paying themselves. Thus, hotel taxes are uniformly high. Those taxes on rental cars can get downright onerous. On several occasions, I have found the taxes and fees to be nearly as much as the car rental. The worst of these taxes appear to be in Denver, Colorado, which is still paying for its airport fiasco decades after opening. You would think the marijuana tax would help them reduce the cost to visitors.

Given my hatred of these add-ons, you can imagine my chagrin when I tried to reserve a car in Denver and return it in Albuquerque, New Mexico. I thought it would be an interesting drive and provide some flexibility in playing The Broadmoor, which had shut me out the previous year, and following up with the two New Mexico courses. When booking the reservation, I was floored to learn the drop-off fee would be $400, or about three times the cost of renting the car. Fortunately, while I was blowing off steam regarding this affront, my practical son suggested we fly from Denver to Albuquerque. This proved to be an excellent solution, saving over $250 on two tickets as well as hours of driving. By the time I was winging my way to Denver, I had briefly overcome my annoyance. That is, at least, until I started getting hit with the taxes and resort fees at The Broadmoor, which is not that affordable to begin with.

Round 37 — The Broadmoor (East)

Course Rank: *75*

Date Played: August 19, 2011

Starting Time: 11:30 a.m.

Weather: 85 degrees, partly cloudy

My Score: 85

Number of Lost Balls: 0, although I pulled one out of the water on No. 18.

Highlights: 1 birdie and 7 pars

Lowlights: 4 double bogeys

Excuse for Not Breaking 80: The greens are very fast and the rough is... rough. The four putts on No. 4 did not help. By the way, that is a crazy green.

Greens Fee: $235, as part of the package.

Playing Partners: Ed and Betsy from Houston, and Ed, Jr. from Denver. Betsy had a classic country club swing, but not enough clubhead speed to get through the rough, or she might have beaten me. They were a fun group to play with, which was good given the generally slow play.

Practice Facilities: Very nice. I had some time to kill so I was able to break in a new driver. The putting green is highly recommended, as the greens are slick. I did not use their short game facility. The practice area serves several courses, so there is a lot of activity.

My Rating: *7+*. Broadmoor East is a picturesque, classic Donald Ross design. There are, however, numerous parallel fairways that provide for a crowded feeling. The green speed is too fast and the rough is too tough for a resort course, which results in five-hour rounds, despite spending little time looking for balls.

Absolutely Must Play: No, but if you are in the area, I would definitely give it a try. The main attraction is probably The Broadmoor facility itself, which is a first-class operation...albeit a bit on the pricey side for us cheapskates.

Favorite Hole: There were few distinguished holes typical of the older, classic architecture, although all provided subtle challenges. No. 3, a par five, was interesting with a risk/reward second shot over water. However, No. 18, a par 4 that also offers water, was my favorite. The creek along the right side, adjacent to the hotel cottages, adds to the challenge.

Location Characteristics: Located at 6,100 feet at the base of the Rockies, there are dramatic views into Colorado Springs. For those wishing to hit 300-yard drives but can only go 240 at sea level (like myself), there are opportunities. I hit two of the par 5s with irons on my second shot. The elevation changes allow for a number of up and downhill shots, and the putts are heavily impacted by the natural slope. Access is more difficult than I would have preferred. Colorado Springs is approximately 90 minutes south of the Denver airport. The resort itself is dramatic and worth an extra day. Garden of the Gods is good for a bit of sightseeing, but my wife claims it falls short of the National Monument in Grand Junction.

Comments: Broadmoor East is a classic golf course for the purist. There are effectively only two tee boxes for men (ignoring the 5,840 yard gold tees, which would play under 5,500 at sea level), with the blues being too much at 7,355 and the whites being a bit short given the elevation. The challenge of the course is the small, quick greens that lead to multiple three-putts. The rough is difficult. In particular, you do not want to be in the greenside rough, short-sided and downhill. If you are hitting straight and putting well, a low score is possible. Because this is a heavily played resort course, the fast greens and difficult rough result in slow play. We waited on nearly every shot. The setting, however, is great and will likely distract from the pace. Bring your camera, your "A" game, and your wallet, and stay for a couple of days at the resort.

Round 38 — Black Mesa Golf Club

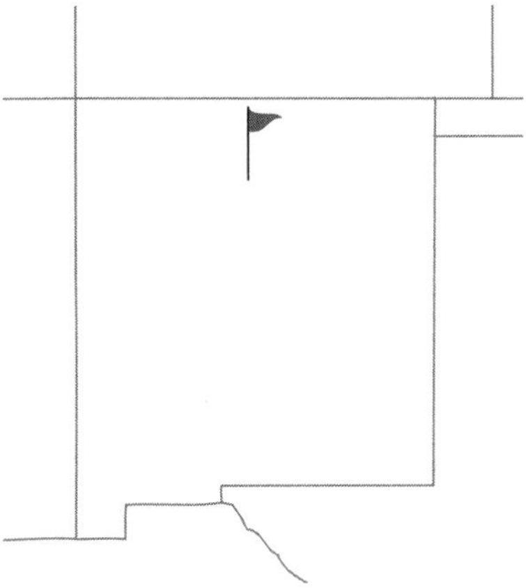

Course Rank: 40

Date Played: August 20, 2011

Starting Time: 11:30 a.m.

Weather: 78 degrees, light wind, overcast, threatening.

My Score: 83

Number of Lost Balls: 2, both on No. 13

Highlights: 4 birdies and 4 pars

Lowlights: 5 double bogeys

Excuse for Not Breaking 80: Humidity, which caused my glove to get slick, resulting in errant tee shots on Nos. 13 through 17, which included 4 double bogeys. I finally got smart and switched gloves on 18 (too late to save the day). I had been one over par through 11.

Greens Fee: $87, but we got a great deal on a stay and play at Santa Claran Hotel/Casino, with an out-the-door cost of $187.59 for everything. Once you get there, Black Mesa is a terrific bargain.

Playing Partners: Started solo, but joined up with duo Joe and Jim on No. 6, where I impressed them with a "ho hum" birdie.

Practice Facilities: Average. The driving range was expansive, but was in average condition. The putting green was decent.

My Rating: 7+, with some interesting holes. The Baxter Spann layout provided a good warm up for the next day at Paa-Ko Ridge. The desert backdrop was less inspired than other comparable venues.

Absolutely Must Play: No, but the course should be included on any New Mexico trip. Although, is anybody really going to find themselves in New Mexico? The location north of Santa Fe is somewhat isolated.

Favorite Hole: No hole was able to garner a nine rating, but most were solid eights. My favorite was No. 16, a 494-yard par 5. The hole is played directly uphill, with a great drive and well-placed second shot still no guarantee of a low score, as the hole plays close to 600 yards.

Location Characteristics: Black Mesa is situated in the high desert area of central New Mexico, about 30 minutes north of Santa Fe. The area has been developed on part of a local Indian reservation. This is an outlying location, with not much to recommend a long stay; however, there are those who will enjoy a trip into historic Santa Fe. The course offers plenty of elevation changes and typical desert flora. There are several dramatic views, and the course is spread out in such a way that nearly every hole is independent, with no parallel fairways. Miss the primary cut and you are in environmentally sensitive areas, so bring a few extra balls. Because of the elevation, the yardage plays shorter, although compensation in the form of elevated greens will require playing virtually every shot in the bag well.

Comments: I liked Black Mesa and would play there again. The outlying location is the greatest impediment, with surrounding amenities being limited. Local accommodations are nothing exciting, so a day trip from Albuquerque may be the best way to experience the course. Since you will be heading to Paa-Ko Ridge at some point, you should consider Black Mesa part of the golfing package. The holes are challenging, but low scores can be had with well-placed shots, as evidenced by my four birdies on the first 11 holes. Unfortunately, double bogeys, or worse, are likely with any errant shot. If you like playing at elevation in a desert environment where the green grass contrasts with the sterile surrounding desert, then you will enjoy a day at Black Mesa.

Round 39 Paa-Ko Ridge Golf Club

Course Rank: 29

Date Played: August 21, 2011

Starting Time: 8:30 a.m.

Weather: 65 degrees, partly cloudy, finished at 80 degrees. Light breeze.

My Score: 85

Number of Lost Balls: 0, although I caught a lucky break on No. 18 after hitting my worst shot of the day.

Highlights: 1 birdie and 6 pars

Lowlights: 3 double bogeys

Excuse for Not Breaking 80: I'm just not that good. This is a tough course from the blue tees.

Greens Fee: $117.50, which included a $10 pre-booking fee.

Playing Partners: I joined up with Brandon from New Jersey, a solid ball striker who shared my affinity for fast play, at least to the extent you can play fast given the difficulty. We breezed through the round in just over three hours, which afforded me the 47 minutes to play the third nine before an afternoon shotgun.

Practice Facilities: Above average. The range was in good shape, although the balls needed upgrading. There was a short game area and putting green that I forsook in order to jump ahead of a potentially snail-like foursome.

My Rating: 9. This Ken Dye design was an unexpected pleasure. The staff was great, the condition exceptional, the views dramatic and the course more challenging than I could handle. I raised the quality of my game, but still the course was humbling. Perhaps I should have played from the closer tees.

Absolutely Must Play: Yes. I enjoyed the Black Mesa course the prior day, but this one was a cut above. There were no boring holes. Paa-Ko Ridge demands great shot making and will reward you for the well-struck ball, while penalizing the stray shot.

Favorite Hole: There were so many great holes. Fully half received a rating of a 9. The remaining holes were all solid 8s. The most impressive were Nos. 16 and 17, two holes with elevated tee boxes. I should note that Brandon and I eschewed the lower-placed blue tee boxes and sought out the maximum elevation. I was able to par both holes despite increasing the difficulty. I suppose I liked No. 17 better, because after the difficult elevated tee shot there remained a long iron approach to the green. On the other hand, No. 16 had such great elevation that I was able to hit the par 3 green from over 200 yards with a six iron. I strongly recommend making the trek to the upper tee boxes, if only for the photo.

Location Characteristics: Paa-Ko Ridge is situated in the suburb of Sandia Park, east of Albuquerque, at an elevation of nearly 6,000 feet. As such, you get extra carry. The area is best described as high desert; however, the course is lined with a variety of vegetation as opposed to the open desert that dominates Black Mesa. This frames the course very well. There are several forced carries required over arroyos and creeks. This is a rolling golf course with plenty of elevation change that makes the shots interesting and provides excellent views. Neighboring homes are situated within an upscale residential community.

Comments: Paa-Ko Ridge definitely is an experience worth going out of your way to enjoy. I understand there are other great courses in the region, including Sandia Park and the University of New Mexico course, as well as the aforementioned Black Mesa. Once I have completed my mission, I will try and put together a foursome to return. Perhaps it was the low expectations, the great weather or good tempo to the round, but I cannot say enough good things about the facility. Lastly, *Golf Magazine* did not identify which of the three nines comprised the top 100 layout. I presume 1 and 2, because they are older, however, there was no drop off in quality on the third nine. Of course, I was playing at Mach speed, so maybe I missed something.

Trip Summary:

The facilities at The Broadmoor are impressive, but were difficult on my wallet. The course was fine, although it seemed a bit tough for a resort layout. In addition, the location is not easy to access for a quick one-night stay. New Mexico is a unique experience, with Paa-Ko Ridge being a very pleasant surprise. Black Mesa proved to be a good test of golf, but occupied an outlying location. If the spouse is anxious to visit Santa Fe, you can easily sneak off to this facility.

Chapter 27

From Blackouts to Bethpage Black

The rest of the country may have missed it, but allegedly a maintenance employee was able to botch things up such that the entire county of San Diego, parts of Orange County, a portion of Arizona and much of Tijuana was without power for approximately 12 hours. While a blackout in Tijuana may improve the atmosphere, it creates havoc for airports. I spent much of the previous evening seeking information from the media. This was complicated by the lack of electricity. I finally hopped in my car for a respite from the heat and to get some news. The first thing I learned was that I should not be driving. Of course, I could not get that information without driving so, alas, I risked the wrath of the local gendarmes by cruising the abandoned and pitch-black streets doing my best not to look like a looter. The blackout knocked out television service for President Obama's job speech (not a problem), as well as the opening day of NFL football with Green Bay hosting New Orleans (big problem). The prospect of a flight cancellation seemed very high at 8:45 p.m. when the local news conference by San Diego Gas & Electric indicated power might be restored by sometime late afternoon the next day. This was not going to work for a 1:40 p.m. flight and seriously put my round at Belgrade Lakes (Maine) in jeopardy. Having allocated only 30 hours for a round trip from Boston, two rounds of golf (the second in Sunday River, about 1.5 hours from Belgrade Lakes), meals and a night on the road, my trip was looking to be another incomplete effort. I was not happy about a potentially expensive return trip to New England. Further, the window to play golf in Maine is only slightly longer than in Biwabik, Minnesota.

My concerns were resolved at 1:24 a.m. when power was restored and every appliance known to man turned on, waking me from a fitful sleep. By morning the airport was operating and our flight was reported to be on schedule.

This was going to be a crazy trip, not unlike some of the previous fire drills in which I have partaken this year (e.g. the race to Mauna Kea, Charleston to Jacksonville with 4 courses in four days, and the recent Denver/Albuquerque weekend). Aside from the golf, the main purpose of this excursion was to abuse my favorite daughter, as she constantly has done to us over the years. It was our plan to make her pick us up at the airport that evening (missing some important college party), say hi for five minutes, steal her car and use it for the next week (saving on a rental) before making her drive us back to the airport. Our itinerary included one night in Boston, one in Maine, another in Boston, three on Long Island, and one in Connecticut. Interspersed would be five rounds of golf, three nights in Manhattan (maybe not so smart on the 10-year anniversary of 9/11), and meetings with several acquaintances from our days on the East Coast.

On the positive side, my wife's long-lost high school friend was able to secure us a starting time at Bethpage Black on Wednesday. This may not sound that impressive until you try to get a starting time on Long Island's top public course. As a Type "A" personality, I like to have my travel plans firmly set well in advance of my trips. Unfortunately, Bethpage is a New York state park. Like most public operations, make everything as difficult as possible. First, out-of-state residents can only make reservations two days in advance. For a course like the Black, the likelihood of securing a decent tee time is about as likely as calling Augusta National and having them say, "Sure, c'mon out and play anytime." They do not book times between 7 and 8 in the morning, and they keep one slot per hour open for walk-ups. If you want get there at 5:00 a.m. you might be O.K., but I have heard horror stories. As such, I had months earlier contacted my old fraternity brothers, whom I assumed landed jobs in New York. Surely one would be living in the city. While it was great catching up with my old contacts, it turns out no one actually lives in New York. Connecticut, New Jersey, sure, but no luck in the Empire State. Fortunately, the aforementioned high school friend of my wife had stayed in Brooklyn, and her husband just happens to play golf. They were up for the challenge...anything to try and beat the system.

For the uninitiated, the reservation process at Bethpage goes something like this:

1. You get vetted for a registration card by faxing a copy of your driver's license, contact information, email address, etc.

2. You wait for the public employees to contact you with your approval as an in-state or out-of-state individual.

3. They do not contact you, so you fax them the information again.

4. They still do not contact you, so you call a bitter public employee who tells you to "just go online and see if you are there."

5. You are surprised when, in fact, you actually are registered.

6. As a local resident, you call seven days in advance only to find that all of the tee times are taken up for the day you want to play and realize you should have called earlier as reservations start promptly at, but not before, 7:00 a.m.

7. You get through at 7:01 a.m. the next day and secure a starting time just one hour later than it will take in order to finish before dark.

8. You create a phone bank with multiple calls going to the reservation number so that you hit at exactly 7:00 a.m., and voilà, you are in business. Was that really so difficult? If you are an out-of-state resident, do not waste your time.

Round 40 — Belgrade Lakes

Course Rank: 84

Date Played: September 10, 2011

Starting Time: 12:24 p.m.

Weather: 65 degrees, sunny, 10-15 mph wind

My Score: 78

Number of Lost Balls: 2

Highlights: 1 birdie, 11 pars

Lowlights: 1 double bogey

Excuse for Not Breaking 80: None needed; putting was good and I managed to stay in the fairways.

Greens Fee: $100 (prime weekend rate). This is an affordable golf course.

Playing Partners: I played my first nine (the back) with Jamie from New York.

Practice Facilities: Driving range was a net with 5 beat-up old balls. The putting green was extensive and had great lake views.

My Rating: 7. Lots of good holes, fine condition, some great views, but a long way to travel.

Absolutely Must Play: No, but the views are great, and there are plenty of very good golf holes.

Favorite Hole: No. 16 is a brutally difficult par 5 that requires a great drive, an excellent second shot and a well-placed approach. The hole affords lots of trouble. I also enjoyed No. 1 as a starting hole with an elevated tee box and view of the lake. Nos. 9 and 18 share a very large green.

Location Characteristics: The course meanders through tree-lined fairways in the hills above the Belgrade Lakes recreational area. Elevated tees and greens make for a picturesque round. During the warmer months there is a lot of boating nearby, so the place is family friendly. The overall facilities are minimal, and the lack of a driving range puts some of us at a disadvantage, although I birdied my first hole. The visual effect compensates for many of the shortfalls, but there are better facilities if you are traveling.

Comments: If you are in New England, by all means play the course; you will not be disappointed. In addition, there are plenty of local purveyors selling Maine lobsters (unfortunately, my schedule precluded partaking of such), with other excellent seafood options to choose from. The recreational area provides activities besides golf (although who really cares). I enjoyed the terrain, trees and course design. The facility is a bit off the beaten path, so I would not go out of my way to play the course again, but certainly would stop in if my travels took me to the region. The course benefits the straight hitter, as it is not too long. I probably could have posted a decent score from the tips (6,723 yards). From my tees I had numerous short wedges into the greens. Bring a camera, as there are plenty of great photo opportunities.

Round 41 — Sunday River Golf Club

Course Rank: 85

Date Played: September 11, 2011

Starting Time: 7:00 a.m. (big mistake)

Weather: 46 degrees, cold, calm, clear, eventually warming to 60 degrees

My Score: 84

Number of Lost Balls: 1, but three recovered from the hazards.

Highlights: 10 pars

Lowlights: 2 double bogeys and 1 triple bogey

Excuse for Not Breaking 80: It is too tough to score well with no feeling in your hands for five holes.

Greens Fee: $120, as part of the stay-and-play package.

Playing Partners: Rick from Rhode Island, a fun guy with lots of stories.

Practice Facilities: Average. The driving range was small and not recently mown. You had to pay extra for the balls. Putting green was fine.

My Rating: 7. Very similar to Belgrade Lakes, with great views, lots of elevation changes, and similar tree-lined fairways. The course is much more difficult, however, and not recommended for the casual golfer. Because of the difficulty you can expect a slow round. We teed off first as a twosome, and it still took us over four hours.

Absolutely Must Play: No; see Belgrade Lakes. However, if you really like tough courses, this one should fit the bill.

Favorite Hole: It is hard to argue with No. 1, a challenging par 5 that requires a precision drive and well-placed second shot that must compensate for the side hill slope. The approach is downhill to a small green. The course also ends strong with No. 18 being a difficult par 4.

Location Characteristics: Sunday River is similar to Belgrade Lakes, with lots of trees, views, elevation changes and separation between holes, making each a unique experience. I was so busy trying to figure out where to hit the ball, I missed much of the atmosphere. The big advantage of going off first is that you might avoid the 5+ hour round; however, the disadvantage was that we spent the first five holes just trying to stay warm.

Comments: I love challenging courses, and Sunday River certainly met that criteria. I personally feel the layout (Robert Trent Jones II) was too difficult for most hackers. Short hitters need not spend the money. My partner, who was clearly a good golfer, had trouble breaking 100. Missed shots will lead to doubles and triples—if you have a good recovery game. This slows play, which is an issue for us Type "A" personalities. The most disappointing part of this visit was the selection of hats in the pro shop. Granted, they were probably closing for the season, but the only available was a boring red option. As with Belgrade Lakes, this property is a bit off the grid. Nevertheless, if you live in or visit New England, and you have some extra balls, give this course a shot.

Round 42 Bethpage Black

Course Rank: 6

Date Played: September 14, 2011

Starting Time: 10:18 a.m.

Weather: 80 degrees, humid, calm

My Score: 83

Number of Lost Balls: 0

Highlights: 2 birdies and 7 pars

Lowlights: 2 double bogeys and 1 quadruple bogey

Excuse for Not Breaking 80: The heat and humidity wore me down, resulting in 8 over on Nos. 15 to 17.

Greens Fee: $135 for non-residents; better deal if you are from New York State.

Playing Partners: Jim Markowski, my new best friend who got us the reservation; Joe Strong, who happened to be in town from California; and Billy, a local fireman who had the opportunity to join us. We had Vincent as a caddie.

Favorite Story: The most memorable part of the day was getting from Bethpage to Jersey City to meet with our wives for dinner. Jim insisted on ignoring the GPS and trying to circumvent traffic by going north instead of taking the direct route. This resulted in a few significant delays and numerous moving violations, which Jim (as an attorney) pointed out, are not really violations in New York. Among the many transgressions included making a U-turn on a freeway on ramp, turning right against red when it was posted as illegal, and making a left turn from a through lane that necessitated blocking traffic behind us. This did not go over well with the New York cabbies. Oh, yes, we also tailgated a bicyclist who was traveling a narrow street. Hey, but we got there, and Jim did a great job on the reservations.

Practice Facilities: The driving range is operated separately, and you pay at that facility. The range is nothing special. There are a number of putting greens near the five different courses that comprise the complex; however, they do not cut any holes into the turf. Instead, you just push a ball along a tightly mown lawn.

My Rating: 9. The Tillinghast layout, updated by Rees Jones, offers many great golf holes. It demands the ability to play all shots, and punishes the wayward effort. I am not usually fond of older, municipal courses, but there was something special about this track, once permission was obtained to enter the facility.

Absolutely Must Play: Yes, if you are afforded the opportunity. Start updating your friendships with New York residents so you have a chance at the tee times.

Favorite Hole: There are a lot of great holes, but Nos. 15 and 16 kicked my butt, so I will go with No. 4. This is not a difficult par 5, but there is a premium on the drive, and usually a good lay up required on the second shot, before hitting an approach to a tough, well-bunkered green that does not hold your ball. I also enjoyed No. 18, a challenging uphill par 4 back to the clubhouse. This final walk uphill will sap any remaining strength.

Location Characteristics: The Black Course is part of Bethpage State Park, which, among other things, includes four other layouts. There are a great many features of a links design; however, trees line the fairways, the rough is thick and the sand traps devilish. In fact, I had two unplayable lies when my ball plugged under the lips of the traps. Despite the level nature of Long Island, there is significant topography, most of which confronts the golfer over the final four holes. There are no carts allowed, so be prepared to put in a solid six miles. The setting is attractive, although not as picturesque as many courses in New England. There are several elevated "blind" greens that require precision approach shots. The landing areas are wide so you should not lose many balls.

Comments: Perhaps the reason I liked Bethpage Black so much was the sheer relief experienced that I was able to clear all the hurdles necessary to play this sadistic monster. I enjoyed how the course would yield up pars and birdies if you hit great shots, but would punish you for any small errors. Getting up and down is difficult from the huge, sloping bunkers, or from the gnarly rough around the greens. Keep it on the short stuff and you are rewarded, but beware of everything else. You will need a lot of clubhead speed to navigate out of the fairway rough.

Bethpage Black is the only course I know that actively tries to discourage all golfers from playing. Warnings that the course is extremely difficult are posted everywhere…kind of like the warnings you see at amusement parks about pregnant women, those with motion sickness, etc. Because there are no electric carts allowed, they also eliminate the casual golfer. One round with the rough and sand, and most mid-range players will vow not to come back. Lastly, the red tape hurdles are likely to discourage many others. Despite all their efforts, the course is fully subscribed most days. Hope springs eternal for the faithful who wade through the bureaucratic morass to take on the challenge. Oh, and by the way, the average round takes in excess of five hours, so plan accordingly. Despite all of these issues, this venue, home to the 2002 and 2009 U.S. Opens, is an enjoyable, must-play course.

Round 43 — Lake of Isles

Course Rank: 83

Date Played: September 16, 2011

Starting Time: 7:15 a.m.

Weather: 55 degrees, sunny, mild breeze, warming to 65 degrees

My Score: 81

Number of Lost Balls: 1

Highlights: 3 birdies and 6 pars

Lowlights: 1 double bogey and 1 triple bogey

Excuse for Not Breaking 80: Hole No. 9! What was I thinking? The only bad shots I hit all day.

Greens Fee: $199, but was part of a package at the MGM Grand.

Playing Partners: Rob, from Barrie, Ontario, Canada. Rob had come down for a weeklong golf vacation when his playing partner broke his leg on the first day. He was scheduled for 8:00 a.m. and had to rush to the tee, which is never good for scoring.

Practice Facilities: Very nice, albeit a long haul from the clubhouse. Lake of Isles has two courses. One is private and shares these facilities. Everything about the course was in great shape and well run. Overall, it was a cut below Cascata in Nevada, but definitely top ten in operations.

My Rating: 8+. I believe *Golf Magazine* has underrated this facility. I liked everything about the golf experience, from the friendly, helpful staff, to the well-stocked pro-shop, to the excellent condition of the course and greens. The setting was terrific with plenty of great photo ops. The New England location offers reasonable access to both New York and Boston.

Absolutely Must Play: Yes. I will make another trek next time I visit the region. I may play from the longer tees, although there was plenty of challenge the day I played. If the weather holds, I would suggest trying the course as the leaves turn.

Favorite Hole: Nos. 1 and 18 are great starting and finishing holes, but I liked the par 3 No. 11 best of all. Only 154 yards, the hole provides a very long, narrow green. On either side of this green is water ready to snare the errant shot.

Location Characteristics: Lake of Isles is situated in a forested area of southwestern Connecticut. The course weaves around a lake, with water coming into play throughout. I suspect the local mosquito population takes over at some time. Expansive bridges are needed to cross portions of the lake. The pastoral setting and pristine condition provide the backdrop for many great holes. Although not immediately adjacent to any major cities (avoid New London unless you have a reason to be down by the water), the resort/casino is monstrous, with plenty of excellent hotels, restaurants and activities. Situated about halfway between Boston and New York City (two hours either way), you can spend a couple of days and play the course several times. This is a difficult track, and, I suspect, plays relatively slow. We were first off as a twosome and played quickly, yet it still took four hours to navigate.

Comments: Lake of Isles was a pleasant surprise. The condition of the course was impeccable and the setting ideal. There are plenty of tee options for all levels of golfer, with a real challenge for those who are willing to take on the test. In some respects, this course was the antithesis of Bethpage Black, providing the exclusivity and condition frequently associated with private courses. I truly enjoyed both, but for entirely different reasons. Although probably not a top ten on my all-time list, Lake of Isles might be close to cracking my top 25. From a golfing standpoint everything was first rate. Book a package with one of the local hotels and the cost is reasonable. My only warning is that you should book early. Despite two months' advance planning, I had a difficult time getting a tee time due to a plethora of local tournaments. This, on top of the Bethpage fiasco, made planning this trip problematic.

Trip Summary:

I would be remiss not to again mention the bureaucracy associated with playing Bethpage Black, which makes the California DMV look efficient. Here are a few of the rules:

- New York state residents can make reservations seven days in advance (but are usually sold out within minutes).
- A reservation may be made by non-residents two days in advance…no point in wasting your time on the toll call.
- The first hour is for walk-ups only, with one foursome per hour reserved for walk-ups as well.
- You can only make one reservation per month.
- You must check in one hour before your starting time or risk losing your spot.
- All members of your group must be there when you check in.
- Only a New York driver's license will get you the in-state rate.
- You check in at a series of windows, manned (or should I say womanned) by three bureaucrats who tell you what you cannot do, but eventually take your money and attach a plastic wrist band.
- You then go to the pro shop to reserve a caddie (you must give them $75 in cash, which is held until you return the caddie rating sheet). You can also buy hats, shirts, etc. and pay for rental clubs.
- You go to the driving range to pick up the rental clubs and pull carts… most players choose to eschew the caddies.
- You arrive at the starter's window 20 minutes early to sign in, after which you can mill around or use the putting greens without holes. The

caddie is supposed to meet you at the starters shack when you get there. Hope that he makes it, because the starter has no authority over the caddies, and cannot contact the caddy master to determine where the looper may be.

- After the group in front of you has moved off the tee box, the starter will announce your starting time and will cut off the wrist band as you pass into the teeing area. He will also shout at you if you put your bag anywhere near the teeing area.

The completion of this trip marked the end of my required journeys to New England. The Maine side trip added significantly to the travel time, but the setting was nice. The golf courses were good, if not great, with the masochist in me wanting to take another crack at Sunday River. I would play these courses again if I find myself in Maine, but I do not see that as a likely scenario. As for Bethpage Black, what more is there to say? I will be retelling stories about the experience for years to come. Although a municipal layout, I have to admit it was intriguing. If you have a friend in New York to make the reservation, you should definitely make the effort. I am not sure if the other courses at the facility would warrant a prolonged stay on Long Island, but there is always the city. Further, you can take the ferry across Long Island Sound and play Lake of Isles, which proved to be a pleasant surprise. The Foxwoods Casino complex is vastly superior to many of the others I have visited, although it is more institutional. Other than the expensive, average-quality meal, there was plenty to like about this resort.

Chapter 28

Fast and Furious

The largest concentration of top 100 golf courses is in the Phoenix area. Ironically, despite having seven entries, my favorite Arizona course (TPC Scottsdale) was not one of them. Although Phoenix is a large metropolitan area, there are not a huge number of things to do other than golf. (A statement that the local Chamber of Commerce will undoubtedly correct if they ever read this book.) There are some good restaurants in Scottsdale, and to some, the shopping could fill a few hours, but the place has always struck me as devoid of culture and history. Therefore, a golfing sojourn is best made with a foursome of golf junkies. My brothers do not generally fall into this category, although our annual trips are usually marathon sessions that leave John and/or Chris with some form of physical discomfort. After Bandon Dunes last year, we decided to up the temperature and play in the desert.

Phoenix is one of the easier logistical trips. The big challenge is finding a time to play when the days are long enough to complete two rounds in a day and cool enough to survive eight to ten hours in the sun. We were assisted in the scheduling as Arizona remains on Daylight Savings Time year round. September is usually too hot, and they over-seed the courses at the end of that month, continuing into October. We booked the trip for the end of October, skirting the course closures by using one of the many booking services. They were also able to get us a great deal on two two-bedroom condominiums. I highly recommend these experts when planning your Phoenix golf trip.

Round 44 — Grayhawk Talon

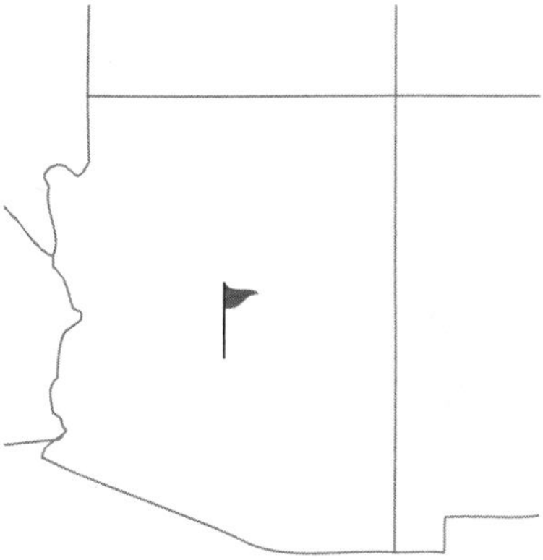

Course Rank: 99

Date Played: October 26, 2011

Starting Time: 7:42 a.m.

Weather: A bit chilly to start, low 60s, finished around 70 degrees, with light winds

My Score: 80

Number of Lost Balls: 0

Highlights: 4 birdies and 6 pars

Lowlights: 4 double bogeys

Excuse for Not Breaking 80: Four double bogeys doomed me. The course played much longer because of the recent over-seeding, and the fairways were not tightly cut, resulting in little or no roll.

Greens Fee: $145

Playing Partners: Brothers, John, Chris and Andy.

Practice Facilities: Above average. The driving range was ample, and the balls in good condition. The short game and putting green areas were also good; however, it was too early and too cold to take advantage.

My Rating: 7, for an attractive course, but one that did not offer many exceptional holes.

Absolutely Must Play: No. That said, Grayhawk is a classic desert course and more convenient to Scottsdale than many. There is a second course (Raptor) as well, so it would be an easy 36 holes. The promise of the first hole did not carry through the round.

Favorite Hole: Although all of the holes seemed well designed, none really stood out as exceptional. My favorite was No. 12—"Double Cross," a 405-yard par 4 bisected by a waste area. With the course playing long, it required a great drive and excellent 5 wood to reach the green in regulation. Grayhawk also has an island green (No. 17) which was an interesting novelty, but at 114 yards could have used a little more distance to get the heart racing.

Location Characteristics: Desert scrub and cacti line the fairways, making chasing your errant shots a bit dicey. My "cheap" brothers kept making forays into the desert in search of lost balls. They succeeded in collecting many, but paid the price in blood (literally). Both John and Chris had large cuts and scrapes after the first several days. The terrain is relatively flat, with fewer panoramas than available at other area layouts. There are several housing tracts near the course, although they should not come into play (alas, our foursome did have a few wayward swings that struck tile).

Comments: I had previously played Grayhawk, but did not remember any of the holes. In fact, a day after playing I could remember only one or two. The par 4s seemed uninspired, with most differing only in their distance. I had a constant feeling of déjà vu. It took awhile to figure out the speed... maybe seven on the stimpmeter. But overall, the experience was good. The facilities are nice, but the holes need more imagination to rate a higher score in my book. I would not hesitate to play Grayhawk again, but there are other good options in the area.

Round 45 — Boulders South

Course Rank: 90

Date Played: October 26, 2011

Starting Time: 1:20 p.m.

Weather: 75 degrees, a bit overcast, with 10-15 mph winds.

My Score: 81

Number of Lost Balls: 0

Highlights: 10 pars

Lowlights: 1 triple bogey

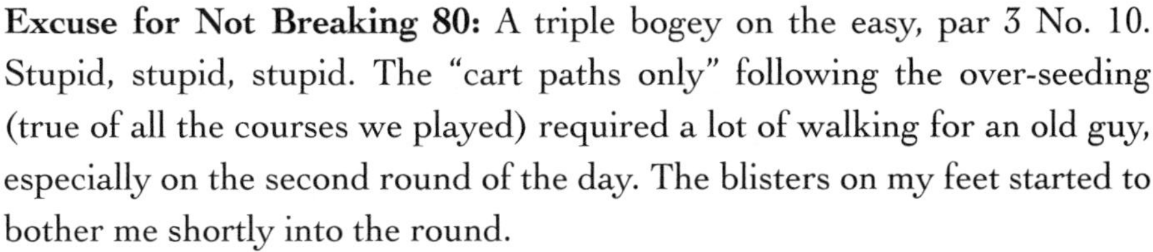

Excuse for Not Breaking 80: A triple bogey on the easy, par 3 No. 10. Stupid, stupid, stupid. The "cart paths only" following the over-seeding (true of all the courses we played) required a lot of walking for an old guy, especially on the second round of the day. The blisters on my feet started to bother me shortly into the round.

Greens Fee: $136

Playing Partners: The brothers Laubach.

Practice Facilities: Decent driving range, decent short game area and putting green. Nothing special, but we were already warmed up from the earlier round.

My Rating: 8+. The design was very inspired, and the use of rock formations and desert flora was superb.

Absolutely Must Play: Yes. If I were to play one course in the Phoenix area, this would be the one (in a close contest with TPC Scottsdale). The South Course, where members alternate with guests between the two courses, offered many great views. The number of photo ops exceeded any of the other places we visited on this trip.

Favorite Hole: The entire front nine was terrific. My favorite was No. 5, a 525-yard par 5 that winds uphill, with the fairway narrowing as you approach the green. The hole offers plenty of trouble, but the exceptional feature is the elevated green set at the base of a massive boulder. This one takes three excellent shots to have a chance at birdie.

Location Characteristics: Again, this is a classic desert design, but with a twist. True to the name, The Boulders has numerous unique rock formations interspersed throughout the course. They have created enough elevation change to keep things interesting, and provide dramatic views. The native plants are a bit pricklier than the other courses, so keep the ball in play, or watch your step. The Boulders is situated in Carefree, well north of the Phoenix metropolitan area, so leave a little extra time to get there.

Comments: I found the front nine of The Boulders South Course to be as good as any I have played. Based on this alone, the rating for The Boulders would be higher. While the back nine loses some of the pizzazz, it is, nevertheless, a lot of fun. The condition was great, and the fairways and greens were reasonably quick. This design offered at least a half-dozen great golf holes, and the incorporation of the rock formations added immensely to the experience. Play this one last if you visit, as none of the other courses, nice as they may be, will provide the same "wow" factor.

Round 46 Troon North (Monument)

Course Rank: 44

Date Played: October 27, 2011

Starting Time: 7:50 a.m.

Weather: Cool 63 degrees to start, with 10-15 mph winds. Near 80 degrees by the time we finished.

My Score: 81

Number of Lost Balls: 2, both on the simple par 3 No. 13.

Highlights: 2 birdies and 9 pars

Lowlights: 2 double bogeys and 1 triple bogey

Excuse for Not Breaking 80: I need to learn to play par 3s. I was five over on Nos. 2 and 13.

Greens Fee: $150

Playing Partners: Brothers Laubach.

Practice Facilities: Good, although we had to drive to the back of the range as the front was closed. In the cold, this was a pain. No time for the short game or putting green, but they looked O.K.

My Rating: 7+, a little better than Grayhawk, but not particularly special. The par 5s were too short from our tees. Nevertheless, there were some interesting holes, and they have worked with the local topography to create some variation.

Absolutely Must Play: No, unless you want 36 holes at one location. There was nothing wrong with the layout. The condition, other than the recently aerated greens, was good. I never have figured out why they punch the greens midway through the over-seeding. Had they aerated them just before closing the course they would have been in great shape when we arrived. None of the other venues seemed to have the same problem.

Favorite Hole: Not much jumped out. The promise of No. 1 was generally not fulfilled. My favorite was No. 16, a long (222-yard) par 3 from an elevated tee box. However, the hole did not offer any exceptional features beyond the length.

Location Characteristics: Troon North is located in the North Scottsdale area, wrapping around the Pinnacle Monument, an interesting rock formation in the middle of the desert. The course has some elevation, which is incorporated into the layout. Typical desert scrub lines the course, with plenty of opportunities to wound yourself if you go searching for stray balls. John and Chris decided to do so (once again) and were rewarded with several new cuts and scrapes.

Comments: As I write this one week after the round, I have virtually no recollection of the holes. A trip to their website jogged my memory, but most of the round was a blur. Monument is not as spectacular as the front 9 at The Boulders, but it has more character than Grayhawk. The aerated greens were a distraction and made it difficult to scramble. Ultimately, the golf is good, and provides a typical desert experience, but the *Golf Magazine* rating is too high on this one.

Round 47 Troon North (Pinnacle)

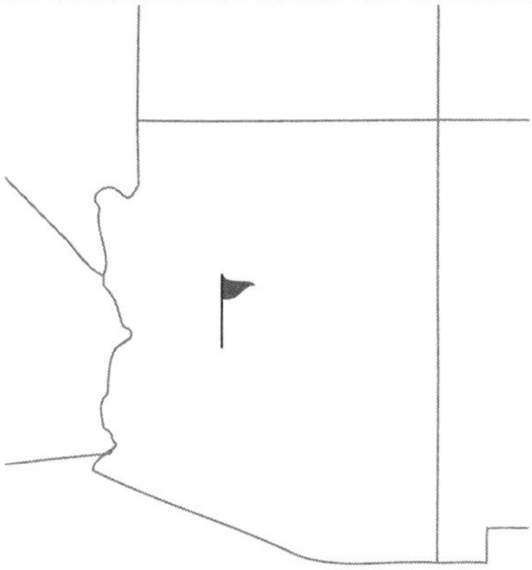

Course Rank: 21

Date Played: October 27, 2011

Starting Time: 1:15 p.m.

Weather: 80 degrees and calm to start, dark and cold at the finish, with some wind.

My Score: 85

Number of Lost Balls: 1, despite knocking seven in the scrub.

Highlights: 7 pars

Lowlights: 3 double bogeys (the last two in the dark)

Excuse for Not Breaking 80: Very slow play, and darkness on the last three holes. I have a tough time hitting a ball I cannot see.

Greens Fee: $150

Playing Partners: Brothers Laubach

Practice Facilities: See Troon North Monument. After 36 holes the prior day (no driving to your ball) and another 18 in the morning, we did not need to warm up. I hit a few putts while waiting for our tee time.

My Rating: 8. It might have been better had it not been for the slow play. I absolutely hate to wait on every shot, and they were not marshalling an earlier group that had booked five tee times. As such, we played the last three holes in the dark. Conversely, the rating might have been lower had the surrounding foothills not been dotted with some of the greatest desert retreats I have seen. Some of these estates almost had me convinced it would be worth putting up with 115-degree summer days to live here.

Absolutely Must Play: Maybe, so long as they can keep things moving. The number of wayward shots into the scrub, and the time it takes to look for them, makes the design poor for "casual" golfers, at least those trying to finish in a reasonable time.

Favorite Hole: There were several very good holes, starting with No. 1. My favorite was No. 10, a seemingly innocuous 378-yard, par 4. This is a visually appealing hole, with a long carry required off the tee, and a huge bunker and waste area running across the fairway and an interesting green.

Location Characteristics: See Troon North Monument, with the additional benefit of the spectacular surrounding residential real estate.

Comments: The experience at Troon North was marred by the slow play and inability to finish before dark due to a 5+ hour round. These greens had been punched earlier than the Monument Course, but were still not fully recovered. It was also surprising that this course seemed to be the least organized, as it is one of the crown jewels in the Troon collection. I have played numerous other Troon golf courses (recently Lake of Isles in Connecticut) and assumed everything would be first class. I could get past the poor selection of hats, but was shocked when checking in for both rounds that the staff had a difficult time with our golf vouchers. This was especially odd since the trip had been booked through a Troon travel agency. The lack of marshalling on the course was directly responsible for our inability to finish in the light. Overall, the Pinnacle Course was not that impressive for a Course Ranked 21 on the list. To be fair, my brother, Andy, the attorney, spoke to the director of golf following the round and was given hats for each of us, and a $50 credit against the round. I appreciate that someone on site was able to address our concerns. I will probably go back someday if I can get an early starting time.

Round 48 We-Ko-Pa (Saguaro)

Course Rank: 43

Date Played: October 28, 2011

Starting Time: 7:40 a.m.

Weather: 60 degrees to start, calm, finished about 78 degrees

My Score: 88

Number of Lost Balls: 1

Highlights: 1 birdie and 4 pars

Lowlights: 3 double bogeys and 1 triple bogey

Excuse for Not Breaking 80: Ten penalty strokes hitting into hazards, although I retrieved all but one ball.

Greens Fee: $85

Playing Partners: Brothers Laubach, who were starting to fade.

Practice Facilities: Pretty good, with an expansive driving range, and good short game area.

My Rating: 7. I had high expectations, but it turned out to be just another desert track: nice, but not that memorable.

Absolutely Must Play: No, but you get two top 100s at an affordable price, in a golfing mecca. The facility is a bit of a drive from Scottsdale, so you might as well play 36 while you are there.

Favorite Hole: For the most part, I found the holes very pedestrian. Generally long but wide-open fairways, with limited character. No. 8 was a decent par 5, but, far and away, my favorite hole was No. 14, a 527-yard, par 5, with a split fairway. Hitting down the middle may result in your ball being buried in a scraggly waste area, with an unplayable lie. Having navigated most of the fairway, there is an elevated shot to a well-bunkered, multi-tiered green. The saguaro cactus lining the fairway is an added bonus.

Location Characteristics: Located east of the metro Phoenix/Scottsdale area, the facility is associated with a casino. The typical desert flora and fauna provide a comparable backdrop to most of the other courses in the region. The lateral hazards came into play often, and I managed to find several.

Comments: I had high expectations for We-Ko-Pa, especially as I usually like Coore & Crenshaw-designed layouts. Ultimately, there was nothing unique enough about the terrain, surroundings or design to make the round memorable. Of course, on the third day of marathon golf, everything was starting to look the same. If you are a fan of desert golf, it is certainly worth the effort. Given the adjoining facility, you might as well make a day of it, and play both of the courses.

Round 49 — We-Ko-Pa (Cholla)

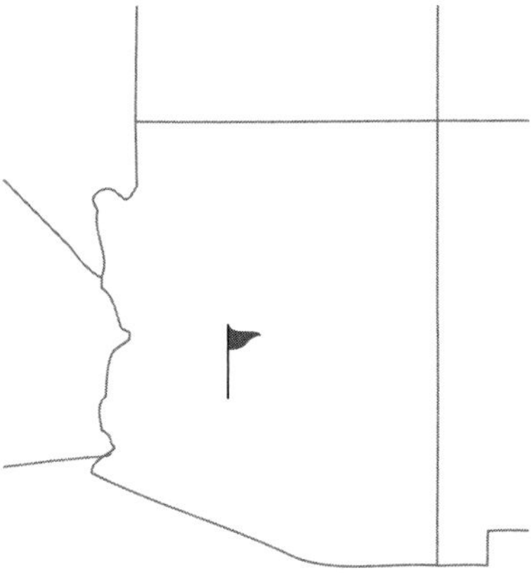

Course Rank: 34

Date Played: October 28, 2011

Starting Time: 1:00 p.m.

Weather: 81 degrees, light wind

My Score: 83

Number of Lost Balls: 1

Highlights: 9 pars

Lowlights: 2 double bogeys

Excuse for Not Breaking 80: Mental fatigue. Could it be possible that even I needed a golf break?

Greens Fee: $85

Playing Partners: Brothers Laubach.

Practice Facilities: Shared facilities with the Saguaro Course.

My Rating: 8, for several interesting holes, but lacking the "wow" factor.

Absolutely Must Play: I am not sure about "absolutely," but I did enjoy the layout. I thought the course started very strong and finished well. As long as you are in the Phoenix area, this should be one of the courses you play.

Favorite Hole: I liked most of the holes, with Nos. 1, 5 and 16 being standouts; however, *numero uno* on my list was No. 8, a long, 587-yard, par 5. The hole has a big dogleg right, a risk/reward second shot, and an approach to a narrow downhill green, with trouble right and left. It is easy to see why this is the number 1 handicap.

Location Characteristics: See Saguaro review above. In addition, the world's largest fountain shoots off in the distance every hour and makes for a very interesting backdrop. There are better views from this course, especially on the back nine.

Comments: I liked this golf course. Despite playing with too little sleep, too many rounds in too few days and the recent aerating of the fairways, the Cholla course was one of the better venues in the Phoenix area.

Round 50 — Southern Dunes

Course Rank: 87

Date Played: October 29, 2011

Starting Time: 10:00 a.m.

Weather: 75 degrees and calm

My Score: 84

Number of Lost Balls: 0

Highlights: 2 birdies and 7 pars

Lowlights: 5 double bogeys

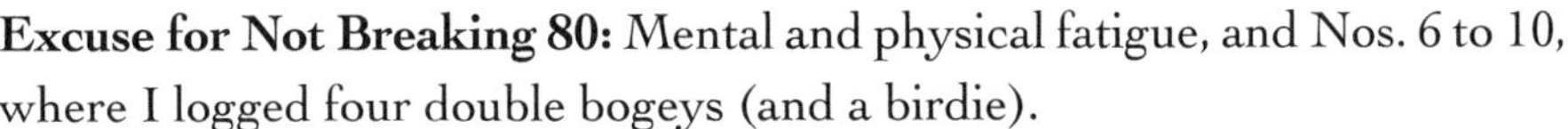

Excuse for Not Breaking 80: Mental and physical fatigue, and Nos. 6 to 10, where I logged four double bogeys (and a birdie).

Greens Fee: $129

Playing Partners: Last of seven consecutive rounds with the Laubach brothers.

Practice Facilities: Adequate, but nothing spectacular.

My Rating: 7, as the setting was fairly neutral and infested with flies. Southern Dunes provided more sand traps than the average facility.

Absolutely Must Play: No, although the Fred Couples design is fun. This is not really desert golf, aside from the weather, and is too far out of town. There are better options.

Favorite Hole: Southern Dunes offers a variety of interesting holes, usually involving doglegs and plenty of sand. In fact, several of the holes place bunkers in the middle of the fairway. My favorite hole was Number 17, a 170-yard par 3, with the tee shot to a blind, elevated green, with lots of sand in front for those of us who fail to adjust for the elevation. The back right pin placement is very tough.

Location Characteristics: The course is situated on Native American land nearly an hour from where we stayed, albeit closer to the airport, so we had a quick getaway. Rather than traditional desert surroundings, the property is constructed around farmland. The Maricopa location is not very interesting, and there is nothing for the nature lovers...unless you have a fascination with sand.

Comments: Although the location was lacking, the course design was pretty good. Ample sand traps provide the second greatest hazard, with the flies being number one. The course is playable and is advertised as a links design. There are plenty of undulations, and did I mention the vast sand traps? Water comes into play on Nos. 10 and 18. If you are traveling with a spouse who is a casino junkie and does not play golf, you can drop them off and give Southern Dunes a shot. While I suspect it may have a limited shelf life on the top 100 list, it is, nevertheless, a relaxing round of golf. You could almost say it is like a day at the beach...given all of the sand you will have in your shoes by the end of the round.

Trip Summary:

If you like a lot of golf in a short period, Phoenix is the place for you. Plan on staying in the Scottsdale area, as it is more proximate to the courses. Use one of the booking services and you can find a perfect condominium, so you do not have to sleep with a snoring partner. For convenience and fun, I would add TPC Scottsdale to the rotation. This course is home to the Waste Management PGA event, which draws the biggest attendance on tour. Definitely hit Boulders South (remember it is only available for outside play every other day). Try and get an early time at Troon North Pinnacle. In addition, I would look at booking in the spring, although you might get hit with higher in-season rates. I will definitely return to Phoenix, as it offers easy access and there are plenty of golf options.

Chapter 29

Mr. Kite, Mind if We Play Through?

I am in Las Vegas waiting for a connection to Jacksonville for my second attempt at playing the top 100 courses across northern Florida. My first attempt conflicted with the Florida swing on the PGA tour, which employs three of the top 100 venues, including TPC Sawgrass, Bay Hill and the Copperhead course at Innisbrook. In addition, the golf booking company I contacted one year earlier informed me that the challenges of booking this trip would be too difficult, and I would not enjoy the effort. Fortunately, Tee Times USA had a better attitude, and was able to create a package for me.

The trip was scheduled for six days, including nine rounds of golf. There are five top 100 courses and another PGA tour stop (Magnolia Course at Disney World). We have two nights in Jacksonville, two in Orlando and two in Tampa. Although Phoenix has more courses in close proximity to one another, the Jacksonville to Tampa swing brings more renowned courses into play. Level terrain and plenty of water should characterize the trip. I never have been a huge Florida golf fan, but I am looking forward to this schedule. My only concern is that the weather looks to be a factor...again.

Round 51 Ocean Course at Hammock Beach

Course Rank: *78*

Date Played: February 12, 2012

Starting Time: 7:30 a. m. (scheduled). Frost delay until 8:50 a.m.

Weather: Bitterly cold and windy. Temperature at the start was 38 degrees with 20 mph winds. It warmed up to the mid 40s, but still required three layers of clothes.

My Score: 86

Number of Lost Balls: 1

Highlights: 1 birdie and 7 pars

Lowlights: 3 double bogeys and one triple bogey

Excuse for Not Breaking 80: Cold, cold, cold!!! I was seven over on Nos. 2 through 4.

Greens Fee: $200, part of a stay-and-play package

Playing Partners: Brother Andy.

Practice Facilities: Good. However, because of the cold, my hands stung on every shot.

My Rating: *7*, perhaps influenced by the arctic weather. The layout seemed fine, but despite the name, there were limited ocean views.

Absolutely Must Play: No. The project has a desirable resort feel, but there were few memorable holes.

Favorite Hole: No. 6, a short par 5 with water along the left side. The hole requires precise shot making.

Location Characteristics: Reportedly, six holes border the Atlantic Ocean, however, due to various flora and topographical features this is not obvious. The project is situated adjacent to the Hammock Beach Resort, which is a great place to spend a few days. Native vegetation dominates the landscape, with a number of well-placed lakes. The course is generally flat, with some mounding created to provide texture.

Comments: There are some aspects of a typical Nicklaus course, and playing the tips would likely result in a dramatic test of golf. However, this layout is "resort driven" and more playable than Jack's usual designs. No doubt the freezing conditions made for a less desirable round. In addition to a sweater and rain jacket, I needed to wear my rain pants for some modicum of warmth. My brother and I were first off, which is always a formula for a quick round. We easily finished inside of three hours and were able to move up our tee time at The Conservatory, another of the Hammock Beach courses. This Tom Watson design is characterized by sand, sand and more sand…as well as plenty of water. The course plays somewhat more difficult than the Ocean Course. Although not as pristine, I enjoyed this layout more. If you end up in the Jacksonville area and find your way to Hammock Beach, be sure and play The Conservatory as well.

Round 52 TPC Sawgrass Stadium Course

Course Rank: 9

Date Played: February 13, 2012

Starting Time: 9:00 a.m. (scheduled). Frost delay until 10:40 a.m. We were the second group off.

Weather: Cold, although not as bad as the day earlier. When we arrived, the course looked like it was covered with snow. At the start the temperature was 51 degrees and rose to 65 degrees by the end of the day. The wind was variable at 5 to 15 mph.

My Score: 82

Number of Lost Balls: 1

Highlights: 1 birdie and 9 pars

Lowlights: 1 double bogey and 1 triple bogey

Excuse for Not Breaking 80: No. 14. After overcoming a bogey, double bogey start, I had righted the ship and was one over through No. 13. On 14, I came over the top on the drive and pulled the ball into the lake. The only drop area was in a trap, where it buried. From there I put another in the water.

Greens Fee: $196 as part of the stay-and-play package.

Playing Partners: Brother Andy and caddie Marco.

Practice Facilities: Very expansive and very nice except for my one pet peeve...they had an artificial strip of carpet from which to hit. These old carpets had plenty of lumps and "bubbles," and did not simulate typical lies.

My Rating: 9, a definite top 10 experience. The Island Hole is only part of the fun. The course has numerous great golf holes.

Absolutely Must Play: Yes! Do not miss this one.

Favorite Hole: I guess I will wimp out and say No. 17. After all, this is the signature hole and one of the most famous shots in golf. According to our caddie, there are 40,000 rounds played each year, and 120,000 balls pulled out of the lake. It is not a tough shot...just a wedge, with no wind, but it apparently works on the psyche. Both my brother and I were inside of 15 feet on the tee shots (no birdies). Personally, I think the Island Hole at Coeur d'Alene is tougher. Nevertheless, there is great anticipation as you get closer, and you have a great view from No. 16. The last three holes are all exceptional. I thought Nos. 1, 4 and 13 were also great.

Location Characteristics: Located in Ponte Vedra south of Jacksonville, the course is several miles from the ocean. However, there is water on every hole that reminds you that you are never too far from trouble. Nearly all of the fairways are lined by pines, with plenty of water, and the usual undulations found on a Pete Dye course. The setting is pristine and serves as home to the PGA.

Best Story: Although we had the first scheduled tee time, we were bumped to allow for a tour pro to play first. It turned out to be Tom Kite and two of his boys. Our caddie told us not to worry; they would be gone in a "New York second," and we would never see them again. They were riding, and probably finished in less than 3.5 hours; however, my brother moves very quickly, and I do not waste a lot of time. Thus, even though we were walking, Mr. Kite graciously allowed us to play through at the turn, as we had been waiting on several holes. We had previously met Tom Kite at the First Tee Open, and while the seniors are generally very genial, Tom certainly is one of the more gentlemanly. We would be honored to play behind him anytime, but really appreciated his letting us by.

Comments: TPC Sawgrass is a level course. It is typically cart paths only, so you will walk a lot regardless. I strongly suggest using one of the professional caddies and walking. Marco was excellent at telling stories, while providing above-average reads on the greens. This is particularly important as grain factors in heavily. Even though I missed numerous short putts, it was not his fault. Overall, this was one of the more enjoyable rounds, and well worth the frost delay. The layout reminded me a great deal of Harbour Town, another of Pete Dye's great designs. The terrific condition, great holes and setting really brought out my game. TPC Sawgrass definitely deserves its place in the top 10.

Round 53 — Bay Hill

Course Rank: 51

Date Played: February 14, 2012

Starting Time: 7:30 a.m.

Weather: 48 degrees to start, warming to 70 degrees, calm and sunny.

My Score: 86

Number of Lost Balls: 1, as I tried to cut it too close across the water on 6. (I repeated this mistake the next day.)

Highlights: 8 pars

Lowlights: 4 double bogeys

Excuse for Not Breaking 80: Bay Hill was in the process of preparing for the PGA tour event. As such, the rough was up. With the cool air, morning wetness and length, the course played extremely tough. Apparently my short game was also in hibernation.

Greens Fee: $185, as part of a stay-and-play package.

Playing Partners: Brother Andy and Brad from Colorado, along with Rick the forecaddie.

Practice Facilities: Very nice and in very good condition

My Rating: 8+, for terrific condition, great facilities, excellent staff and some very nice golf holes.

Absolutely Must Play: Yes, there is enough history and unique golf holes to make for an enjoyable round.

Favorite Hole: I liked Nos. 2, 3, 6 and 17, but No. 18 is the real gem. The approach shot is very difficult and demands precision from distance. Overall, the 16, 17, 18 finish is especially memorable.

Location Characteristics: Not too far from Disney World, Bay Hill is located in a throwback community not unlike that patrolled by Beaver Cleaver. Arnold Palmer's stamp is all over the resort and golf operation. There is a gentility that overcomes the somewhat dated nature of the surrounding improvements. The course is characterized by level, rolling fairways, guarded by lakes that demand accurate tee shots and often come into play on the second shot. Trees seldom come into play, with most being of the smaller variety.

Comments: Bay Hill is as much an experience and glorification of the life of Arnold Palmer as it is a golf course. The history associated with the PGA event lends an additional benefit. Playing the course several weeks before the tour arrives ensures pristine fairways and greens, although the narrowing of the fairways and increased rough will impact the score. The greens are difficult to read so you should listen to your caddie. On our second day we chose to walk the course. This is a great way to take in the ambiance and is not much more expensive than the mandatory forecaddie. Stop by the grill room...but remember to take off your cap.

Round 54 — Innisbrook Copperhead

Course Rank: 79

Date Played: February 16, 2012

Starting Time: 7:30 a.m.

Weather: 66 degrees to start, 82 degrees at finish, muggy, minimal wind

My Score: 80

Number of Lost Balls: 0

Highlights: 10 pars

Lowlights: 1 double bogey

Excuse for Not Breaking 80: A bad cart path bounce on 10 cost me a double bogey.

Greens Fee: $180

Playing Partners: Brother Andy. We completed the round in 2 hours and 45 minutes.

Practice Facilities: Really nice and in pristine condition.

My Rating: 8+, based upon the great condition of the course, tranquil setting and history associated with a PGA tour event.

Absolutely Must Play: Yes. Copperhead is a regular tour stop. The facilities are nice and the condition three weeks prior to the tournament was exceptional, albeit more difficult.

Favorite Hole: The course starts very strong with a couple of nice holes. The par 5s are especially good. I liked Nos. 3, 13, 14 and 16, but my favorite was No. 5, a monstrous par 5 up a hill with the second shot being blind, and the third shot back down with a dogleg left. This one takes all good shots and measures 570 yards from the green tees.

Location Characteristics: The Innisbrook Resort is located north of Tampa, in a gate-guarded community. There are four golf courses, of which Copperhead is the most renown, although some like the Island Course better (not me). The course has more elevation than your typical Florida layout, and more mature trees as well. Pines line most of the fairways, with ample lakes and ponds that necessitate strategic golf. The squirrels are friendly, but will steal your food. Several large nests (possibly osprey) are located in the mature trees, which are also adorned with ample Spanish moss. Travel around the Tampa area is a mess, but there is plenty to do within close proximity to the resort, and lots of golf. Copperhead occupies an idyllic setting.

Comments: My biggest complaint is the large number of blind tee shots confronting the golfer. Without GPS on the carts, it is sometimes difficult to know what dangers lurk ahead. Only a wayward tree branch kept me out of the hidden pond, which impacts the second shot on No. 14. Otherwise, the condition was immaculate, the fairways lush, the greens excellent and the surroundings terrific. The course plays tough from the green tees, with a huge premium on driving distance and accuracy. The staff is very friendly and the experience top notch. The resort itself is expansive, although the improvements are older...and a bit drab on the outside. Inside, they have been upgraded, consistent with a high-end resort.

Round 55 — World Woods Pine Barrens

Course Rank: 18

Date Played: February 17, 2012

Starting Time: 8:34 a.m.

Weather: 70 degrees and threatening, with some drizzle and minimal wind.

My Score: 84

Number of Lost Balls: 0

Highlights: 6 pars

Lowlights: 1 double bogey

Excuse for Not Breaking 80: The flatstick was not working. I left myself in terrible positions on the putts, and could not chip close.

Greens Fee: $85.00

Playing Partners: Brother Andy, and Florida citrus industry workers Joe and Mike. Despite decent games, they elected to play from the up tees. We probably looked liked idiots from so far back.

Practice Facilities: Pretty decent, once you make your way from the clubhouse…about a ten-minute drive. Because of travel time, we had less opportunity to hit balls. Practice greens are also available.

My Rating: 7, but maybe I was tired and we had played a number of courses in great condition. There were interesting holes, but I was getting frustrated with the putting. This is a typical Fazio course that provides a good challenge, without being "in your face." Despite the *Golf Magazine* ranking, Pine Barrens would not be in the top 50 on my list.

Absolutely Must Play: No, as it is a bit out of the way. However, if you find yourself in the Tampa area it may be worth the hour drive to the middle of nowhere to test it out, as well as the sister course.

Favorite Hole: There were plenty of interesting holes, with 12 and 18 being notable, however, Nos. 4 and 14, a couple of challenging par 5s, would top my list. The architect has made each of these holes unreachable in two to most, and requiring three precision shots in order to make par, with No. 4 having a heavily elevated, blind green that adds to the enjoyment/pain.

Location Characteristics: I did not know there were pine woods along the coast in central Florida. World Woods is situated at the end of the toll road, in the opposite direction as indicated by my GPS system. There did not appear to be any civilization in the general area. As such, the setting is serene, with large trees and bountiful sand ready to impede any wayward shot. Overall, the lack of civilization makes for a back-to-nature experience that probably accounts for the high rating.

Comments: World Woods Pine Barrens has the feel of a municipal facility. The people were great, but there was no sense of exclusivity, with a mediocre pro shop and grill, along with a pricing policy on food, accessories and rounds that attracts the "thrifty" crowd. Now, I'm not one to complain about low prices, but sometimes you get what you pay for (see Rustic Canyon). After playing TPC Sawgrass, Bay Hill and Copperhead in tournament-ready condition, it was a bit of a downer to finish with this one. There is a second course at the facility (Rolling Oaks), so a long day of affordable golf is a possibility. I am told the second course is nice as well. If I lived in the area I might like this option, but am not sure it deserves the prominent rating assigned by *Golf Magazine*.

Trip Summary:

One of the best golf vacations is the swing through northern Florida. Jacksonville is reasonably accessible via air from most points in the United States, and the drives to Orlando and Tampa are not overly taxing. During the trip you have opportunities to play at four stops on the PGA tour including the "Fifth Major" at TPC Sawgrass, as well as Bay Hill, the Magnolia course at Disney World and Copperhead, north of Tampa. We scheduled the trip before the tour hit, meaning the courses were generally getting ready for the Pros, and the conditions were excellent. The temperatures, however, were unseasonably cold.

Florida is generally not my cup of tea, but each of the top 100 courses occupied an attractive location, and the topography and condition of each surpassed my expectations.

No doubt, TPC Sawgrass is a top 10 course, even if the island hole (No. 17) is less daunting than I expected. Personally, I found No. 18 more challenging. Despite its lower rating, my second favorite was Copperhead at Innisbrook. Perhaps this was due to the pristine, pre-tournament condition, but I thought the holes were great. No. 3 would be Bay Hill. This is a more traditional Florida design: fairly open, with lots of water. The best holes may have been at World Woods Pine Barrens; however, despite the interesting setting, the project felt over-utilized. Financial issues may have also impacted Ocean Beach at Hammock Bay. This course was less distinguished, with few memorable holes, but occupies a great location along the ocean. I enjoyed the sister course (Conservatory) more, as the holes displayed more character. I should note that the development recently changed hands (same owner as Innisbrook) and may be on the rebound.

It is likely that most addicted golfers will eventually make their way to this hotbed of great golf. I found the more northerly courses to be more fun than those closer to Miami. It should not be hard to get the family to Disney World on vacation, so if you cannot get your regular foursome to make the trek, take the family and drop them at Epcot Center while you head for the local golfing venues.

Chapter 30

Sin City Reprise

The top-of-the-line golf facilities in Las Vegas are targeted to those who drop big bucks in the casino, rather than the golf fanatic. For this reason, they set exorbitantly high greens fees so the "whales" feel like they are getting special treatment for dropping $50,000 at the blackjack tables. The casinos do not care if anyone besides the high-stakes gambler plays their course. Golf operations are not designed to make money, but rather to serve as an amenity. Shadow Creek is the epitome of this. The Wynn course had been equally exclusive, although in recent years they have begun to allow some outside play. However, with a green fee rivaling Pebble Beach, very few non-serious golfers will "ante" up.

I had played Wynn several years earlier, as well as the Desert Inn (prior name of the course before Steve Wynn began imploding the Vegas skyline). My recollection was a facility in impeccable condition, but not necessarily worth the money. However, Wynn is on the list and I like Las Vegas. I knew as I hopped in my car for the 4.5-hour run to the Paris Hotel that I would enjoy the golf, in spite of the dent in my wallet.

Round 56 — Wynn Golf Club

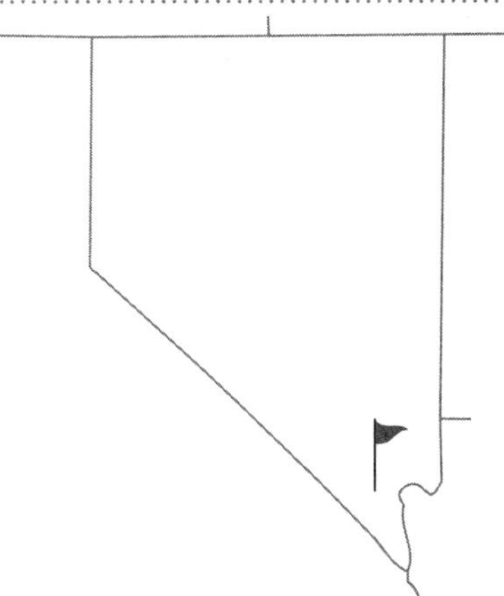

Course Rank: 66

Date Played: March 20, 2012

Starting Time: 10:45 a.m.

Weather: 51 degrees, sunny with mild wind. It never really warmed up.

My Score: *77*, although I would have been DQed for signing an incorrect scorecard...if I had signed the scorecard.

Number of Lost Balls: 0, as I managed to pull one shot out of the water.

Highlights: 2 birdies and 8 pars

Lowlights: 1 double bogey

Excuse for Not Breaking 80: Fortunately, a 35 on the back nine overcame my 42 on the front (par 34), so I easily snuck in under 80, despite the flag stick incident on No. 6 (more to follow)

Greens Fee: $500 (same rate on weekends, twilight, etc.)

Playing Partners: Brad (who was also my forecaddie and driver). The course allows the mandatory forecaddie to play with you if you are playing as a single, so long as you agree, which I was glad to do. Brad, being a teaching pro, as well as a scratch (or better) golfer, was handicapped with the rental clubs used at Wynn (which really are not so bad, unless you are exceptionally good) and provided great competition, especially on the backside when I shot one under and probably edged him by a stroke...but who's counting? As with many professional caddies, he had lots of great stories. This is probably truer of Vegas courses, where so many rounds are "comped" to guys who have lost tons of money but are not necessarily golfers. The free round is not much of a consolation prize but allows them to attempt to recover lost funds via huge bets on the course.

Practice Facilities: A bit cramped for a $500-per-round facility attached to a luxury resort. The range is limited to private nets, so that is a point against, although the quality of range balls was well above average. The practice putting green was O.K., and I did not make it to the short game area.

My Rating: 8, for fabulous condition. This is the former Desert Inn course, and has been redesigned and renovated in recent years. Wynn is very similar to Shadow Creek, which should be no surprise since Steve Wynn was involved in each. I like Shadow Creek better, but this one was still nice.

Absolutely Must Play: At $500 per round, it is hard to justify. No way; Pebble Beach is not a better value at a similar price. If money is no object and you are in Las Vegas there are worse options, but I would try Shadow Creek first and make a run to Wolf Creek before taking on Wynn's course. Of course, if you want the gold bag tag, you will have to give it a shot.

Favorite Hole: All of the holes are good, but the finishing two are exceptional. Many of the locals prefer No. 17, which is a ridiculously tough par 4, with a killer second shot over water to a tough green. Make your caddie take you to the championship tees for a stellar elevated drive. Despite loving No. 17, I am going to choose No. 18 as my favorite. This is a tough driving hole with a creek running along the left side, which becomes a huge factor on the second shot to the comparatively long par 4. What seals the deal, however, is the giant waterfall behind the green. I tried to get the caddie to tell me whether Wynn or Trump was the first to go with this superfluous, albeit fun, attraction, but he was not sure. Anyway, it fit well in Las Vegas.

Location Characteristics: Wynn Golf Course is located on the strip in Las Vegas, just behind the Wynn hotel. Driving by on the surrounding streets, you will not see the facility, due to the fencing and hedges. For a flat desert location, there is an amazing amount of undulation. There is also plenty of water that comes into play. The fairways are generous, and, if you avoid the water, the course can be tamed. Most of the views involve other casinos, including the Wynn, Encore, Stratosphere, etc. Because of the landscaping, if you can ignore the high rises, the atmosphere is relaxing...at least by Vegas standards.

Comments: Wynn and Shadow Creek both view themselves as bastions of exclusivity, existing primarily to compensate gamblers who have already given their fair share to ensure the viability of the gaming industry. Neither course has allowed the USGA to rate the facility, holding themselves above the rest. I feel Shadow Creek does the superior job of creating this aura, but Wynn is not far behind. For the inclusive, politically correct crowd, these are not your courses. For those of us who wish to play a first-class facility in terrific condition, then it is not a day wasted. I am probably too cheap to play this course often, but enjoyed the experience with one exception. No. 6 is a comparatively short par 3, which requires a precise shot over water. On the day I played, the pin was tucked to the far left, with a bunker right behind the hole. Brad suggested playing for the middle of the green given the "sucker pin," but I told him I did not come there to lay up, and would hit a high fade with a nine iron. The shot was perfectly executed. While Brad was shouting for it to get down, I was confident a short birdie putt would await. All of a sudden the sound of ball striking metal could be heard, indicating that I had squarely hit the pin. The next thing I saw was my ball bounding to the left and back toward the tee box. I turned, frustrated that my birdie would be lost, but knowing I would have an easy chip. At this point, my caddie started yelling "sit, sit!" I turned around just in time to see my ball catch a slope and nosedive into the lake. It was little consolation that I was able to retrieve the ball and also little consolation when I chipped close and made the putt. Investigating the ball mark indicated that my shot had probably hit no more than six inches up the flag stick. Thus, I had almost "canned" the shot for a first ever hole-in-one. I was so exasperated that I wrote a 3 on the scorecard, and told Brad throughout the round that "at least I saved par." He must have thought I was an idiot. The next day, driving back home, I was replaying the round in my mind and realized I had, in fact, bogeyed the hole, and that my 76 was really a 77. Being the good caddie, and hoping for a larger tip, Brad had never corrected me. So Brad, if you ever read this, please know that I understand the scoring, but if that stupid pin had not been in the way, my mind might have been better able to deal with simple arithmetic.

Trip Summary:

My trip to Las Vegas was a quick one, designed to get my daughter, who had recently turned 21, and some of her East Coast friends out to the desert for spring break. Wynn was better than I had remembered, and my game was firing on all cylinders, especially on the back side. No doubt, this led to a greater appreciation of the course. Access to the Wynn is directly through the casino, which is somewhat unnerving but affords the opportunity to view early morning gamblers, a different breed unto themselves. You may feel cheated as you hit practice balls into a net, but most of the high rollers are probably too intoxicated/hungover to notice. The forecaddies help with pace of play, and Brad was great as a partner, even if he did not correct my scoring (or maybe because of it). Overall, "Viva Las Vegas," but unless you are a compulsive, addicted golfer who must play the top 100, give a few of the other venues a chance. There are plenty of excellent, more affordable golf options in the Vegas area.

Anything long is coming back to the green. Boulders South.

Is a cactus 90 percent air? Brother Chris is trying to figure out a line of flight in Arizona.

John Laubach with one of his better lies at Pacific Dunes.

The largest sand trap I found during the trek, fourth hole at Pebble Beach.

Now that wasn't so tough. Andy and I both reach the 17th at TPC Sawgrass on our tee shots. Neither made a birdie.

Best not to miss left on the 12th at the Challenge at Manele.

A decent finish to my swing as well as to Harbour Town. The classic 18th "lighthouse" hole.

The only course in America that actively tries to discourage players . . . Bethpage Black. I decided to play it anyway . . . once I got a reservation.

With son Charlie at Wolf Creek.

My favorite golf architect at the Pete Dye French Lick Resort. I would go to Everest . . . if it was on the list.

Are alligators a loose impediment? John Laubach at Caledonia Golf and Fish Club.

Ah, those traditional New Englanders. The clubhouse sign at Taconic Golf Club.

Joe Strong finds himself with another challenging lie at Spyglass Hill. I think he saved par.

The famous par 3, 7th. That is not my ball next to the hole. I sailed mine over the green and into the water.

This was not the only time during my adventures I was plugged into the face of a trap. I saved a triple bogey on this short par 3 at Caledonia Golf and Fish Club.

How does Joe Strong seem to draw all the crazy lies? Pinehurst No. 8. (No animals were hurt during the round.)

Typically snow and golf do not go together, but this is a great view of son Charlie teeing off at Crosswater at Sunriver.

Crosswater at Sunriver is the only course I know where you have to clear the canoers to reach a green.

A scene that could only come from the mind, and wallet, of Donald Trump. Trump National in Los Angeles.

Henry Wilde (Charlie's son) is about to be swallowed up at Arcadia Bluffs.

Crazy lie at Wild Horse in Nebraska. Another triple bogey on a short par 3.

I do not believe they were referring to the cart girls. Atlantic City Country Club.

Getting some good extension at Old White at Greenbrier.

Charlie Wilde doing his best Scottish impression at Arcadia Bluffs.

Yes, that is an observatory at Primland.

Scott Rand from the hay at Whistling Straits "Irish." The sheep had missed a spot.

Whistling Straits "Straits" with Scott Rand. There are a few bunkers/waste areas.

These bunkers are easy. Brother Andy advances ball 18 inches.

Scott Rand at Whistling Straits "Irish." It was wetter than it looks.

Chapter 31

Let It Snow, Let It Snow, Let It Snow

I have never been to the Blue Ridge Mountains (or the Allegheny Mountains), and was eagerly awaiting the opportunity to play at The Greenbrier and The Homestead resorts. Per usual, I decided a "discounted" trip during the swing season made sense, and was less likely to be influenced by mosquitoes and/or humidity. Given that Linville (which should have been part of this trip) did not even open for a month should have been a clue that my frugal leanings might result in less-than-perfect golfing conditions. However, being a glass-is-half-full guy, I booked a mid-April excursion.

One major character flaw I possess (and my wife will tell you there are many) is that I am a chronic weather watcher. I usually start 10 days in advance and check the forecast every few hours. In San Diego, such weather watching is unnecessary, as any idiot can do a 200-day forecast in advance and seldom be wrong. Unfortunately, weather changes so quickly in other areas of the country that my compulsion leads to an emotional roller coaster ride. The initial prognosis for our trip was great weather, which changed to a wet forecast, and back to sun…and that was still 8 days out. As recent as two days before the trip, we were looking good. Thus, it proved depressing upon disembarking to learn that a "freak" snowstorm was headed into North Carolina.

After touching down on another successful Southwest flight, we made our way through Enterprise Rent-A-Car without incident and headed for the Blue Ridge Mountains, destination the Primland Resort in Meadows of Dan, Virginia. I maintained a sense of denial, knowing that snow in April was not possible. Alas, as we made our way along the five-mile drive from the gate off the main highway to the resort, it became readily apparent that, once again, weather would play a factor. At least the resort was nice.

Round 57 Highland Course at Primland Resort

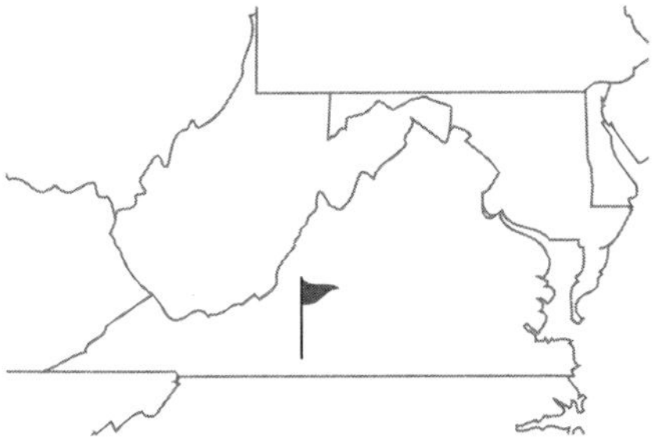

Course Rank: 49

Date Played: April 22, 2012

Starting Time: 10:00 a.m.

Weather: 49 degrees, drizzle, 10-15 mph wind

My Score: 83

Number of Lost Balls: 0

Highlights: 9 pars

Lowlights: 1 triple bogey

Excuse for Not Breaking 80: Cold, wet weather led to a triple bogey six on No. 2, a simple par 3.

Greens Fee: $125 as part of a stay-and-play package.

Playing Partners: I flew solo, as no one else was stupid enough to challenge the weather. As a result, I was able to complete the round, as well as a discounted replay round, in a combined 5 hours.

Practice Facilities: The driving range allows one to launch balls down the mountain. Given the weather, my efforts were limited, but it appears to be a nice facility. There is also a putting green, which is highly recommended in order to check out the uphill and downhill speed.

My Rating: 8, based largely upon the dramatic terrain and tree-lined fairways.

Absolutely Must Play: I am somewhat ambivalent on this point. The resort is out of the way, and it takes a big commitment to make the trek. On the other hand, the natural surroundings are exceptional, and the resort is terrific. My opinion may be slightly biased due to the inclement weather, ultimately detracting from the experience.

Favorite Hole: Although Nos. 16, 17 and 18, represent a great finish, my favorite hole was No. 1. This is a downhill par 5 that requires navigating between a rock outcropping. The promise of this great starting hole, however, is not matched by the ensuing 17.

Location Characteristics: The Highland Course at Primland Resort is situated in the Blue Ridge Mountains of western Virginia. The course was constructed to complement the fantastic natural terrain, framed by thickets of dense trees. Be prepared for plenty of walking, even with a cart, as the topography is very sloping, and you cannot drive the carts close to many requisite locations. I was exhausted after the two rounds.

Overall: It was unfortunate that Mother Nature did not cooperate on my visit. A planned second round the following day was canceled due to snow flurries and 25-plus mph winds. Nevertheless, it is impossible not to appreciate the serenity and beauty of the course. Nearly every hole involves an uphill or downhill shot, often both. My recollection is that most holes involved hitting downhill to the fairway, and uphill to the greens. The condition was very good. Bottom line, the course is well above average, but there is something missing. Perhaps a babbling brook running across the front of a green, or along one side of a fairway, would have enhanced the experience. I suspect the designer did not want to alter the existing landscape. You will not be disappointed with the experience, and while clearly deserving of top 100 status, there are other courses I prefer. My primary recommendation for the club is that they reclassify the tees. I have never previously played red tees (traditionally women's), and almost played the impossibly difficult black tees just so I would not have to admit to playing red. The slope from the red tees is 140, which is deserving of a more masculine color.

Round 58 — The Greenbrier

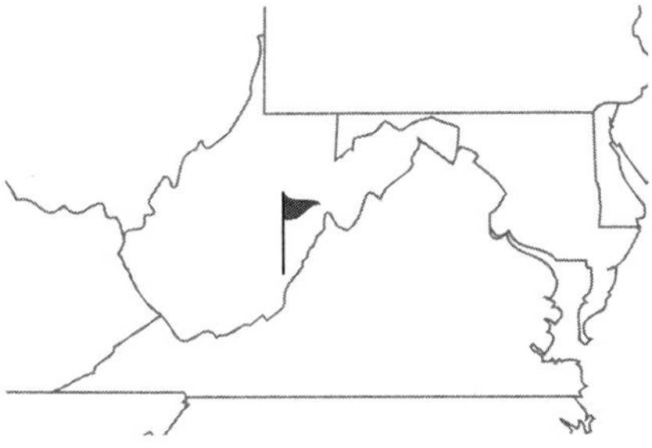

Course Rank: 58

Date Played: April 25, 2012

Starting Time: 9:03 a.m. (Ultimately 9:45 after a frost delay)

Weather: 50 degrees, calm and clear

My Score: 80

Number of Lost Balls: 0

Highlights: 2 birdies and 8 pars

Lowlights: 2 double bogeys

Excuse for Not Breaking 80: My hubris on No. 9. After a bogey/double bogey start, I had recovered to only two over after eight. I was already thinking of a sub-40 front side, when I failed to finish my swing on this easy par 3, leading to a double bogey.

Greens Fee: Part of the golf package, but listed at $225 in the pro shop.

Playing Partners: Given the weather conditions predicted for the following day, I decided to try to quickly finish the round and make my way to Hot Springs, Virginia, for an afternoon round at The Homestead's Cascade Course. Much to my dismay, not only was I third off, but there was a frost delay. I quickly identified the single who had secured the first tee time, and was able to convince him to let me tag along. Clearly an avid but climate-challenged golfer from Pittsburgh, Mike ultimately was joined on the fourth hole by a member of his company. At that point they graciously allowed me to play through, and the round was completed in two hours, placing me back on schedule for the second 18.

Practice Facilities: Very good, with an expansive driving range, putting greens and practice areas. These facilities service the three courses at Greenbrier. It was frustrating that, due to weather, I had to hit off mats as they could not accommodate a tee, thus foregoing use of the driver. This may account for errant tee shots on the first few holes.

My Rating: 8. Overall, the course is well designed with several fun, distinctive holes. The Jack Nicklaus influence is clear. My putting and chipping were surprisingly good for one of his courses. The layout is comparatively flat, and did not provide for much "wow" factor, but Nicklaus would rather create his courses with more subtlety than some of the other modern designers. Overall, the round is challenging, with plenty of good, if not, memorable holes. The redesign of the classic Macdonald TPC Old White Course is really nice and rates out at an 8+ in my book, even though it did not crack *Golf Magazine's* top 100.

Absolutely Must Play: Yes, especially since the trip allows for play on a second great course, as well as a chance to stay at The Greenbrier, which immediately became one of my favorite resorts.

Favorite Hole: I thought 15 and 16 were great par 4s, but preferred No. 2, as it creates an early challenge, forcing a very accurate drive (water on the right), with a long iron shot to a green bordered by the same lake. There is not much of a bailout area on the left, either off the tee, or on the approach.

Location Characteristics: The Greenbrier is situated in the Allegheny Mountains (not sure when we left the Blue Ridge Mountains) of West Virginia. Although not as mountainous, the course still offers plenty of character, and is influenced by the surrounding hills. Several lakes and numerous creeks and rivers that wind through the grounds also characterize the courses. The waterways are teeming with trout, and the location is a favorite of fly fisherman.

Overall: Greenbrier is an exceptional resort, with two first-class golf courses (maybe three, but I did not play the Meadow Course) located in a pristine setting. Although White Sulphur Springs, West Virginia, is comparatively dull, you never have to leave the facility. The tree-lined fairways, coupled with numerous waterways, put a premium on shot making, with the Greenbrier Course a bit narrower than Old White. The experience is memorable, and we will definitely be making the trek back to this facility again.

Round 59 — The Homestead (Cascades)

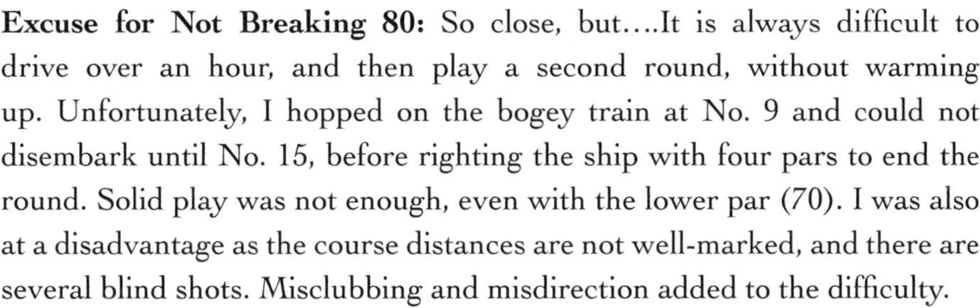

Course Rank: 24

Date Played: April 25, 2012

Starting Time: 2:10 p.m.

Weather: 65 degrees, partly cloudy, 10 mph wind

My Score: 80

Number of Lost Balls: 0

Highlights: 8 pars

Lowlights: None

Excuse for Not Breaking 80: So close, but….It is always difficult to drive over an hour, and then play a second round, without warming up. Unfortunately, I hopped on the bogey train at No. 9 and could not disembark until No. 15, before righting the ship with four pars to end the round. Solid play was not enough, even with the lower par (70). I was also at a disadvantage as the course distances are not well-marked, and there are several blind shots. Misclubbing and misdirection added to the difficulty.

Greens Fee: My kudos to the ownership of La Costa, who also owns The Homestead. As a member at La Costa, I was comped the round, paying only $25 for the cart. The green fee is typically $170.

Playing Partners: The course was largely deserted in the afternoon. As such, I took off on my own for another sub three-hour round. I could have played faster, but spent time enjoying the experience.

Practice Facilities: Like everything else, Cascades does things differently. The driving range is located on the opposite side of a hill that is accessible via a circuitous route that can only be traveled by licensed vehicles (i.e. no golf carts). I saw the facility the next day. It looked fine, with balls driven up a hillside. There was a putting green near the first tee.

My Rating: 9, with my initial reaction being an 8. However, the more I thought about the round, confirmed by a rain-drenched second effort the next day, the more impressed I became. I was able to recollect every hole, which was no easy feat given I had played a morning round at Greenbrier. Everything was so unique and so clever that the course easily deserves its ranking in the top 25. Is it a top ten? Almost, but not quite.

Absolutely Must Play: Yes. A side trip from Greenbrier, about 45 minutes away, and a night at The Homestead (with dinner at 1766 Grille) is the icing on the cake for a trip to western Virginia/eastern West Virginia. Try to play twice, as it takes some time to understand the layout.

Favorite Hole: There were a slew of great golf holes, including Nos. 4, 5, 9, 12, 15, 16 and 17, but my favorite was No. 13, a devilish par 4 that compels you to play right, given the creek running along the left side of the fairway. However, the right side is well trapped, with several trees, and given the dogleg makes a par very difficult if you are safe off the tee. A great many of the holes are designed in a similar manner, with clear risk/reward.

Location Characteristics: Like Greenbrier, The Cascades is situated in the Allegheny Mountains. The setting is exceptional, with the course carved into the hills, affording numerous uphill and downhill shots. It is a shot maker's course, and you will need to hit nearly every club in your bag. Thick forests line the fairways and play havoc with the errant shots. There is plenty of water on the back side, with lakes on the finishing holes, and creeks running throughout. The town of Hot Springs and The Homestead resort are very quaint. We were turned away for dinner at Sam Snead's Tavern, but did get to see the memorabilia inside. There are two additional courses affiliated with The Homestead, but weather did not permit playing them during my visit.

Overall: Cascades Golf Club is a truly unique and enjoyable experience. From your first view of the clubhouse (maybe the coolest old building I have visited), to the unusual par 70 format, in which there is only one par 5 in the first 15 holes, the experience is memorable. The setting is great, the holes challenging and the condition excellent. The greens were exceptionally soft, allowing for shots to hold on the small surfaces. At the same time, they were very quick and true. Of the four courses on this journey, Cascades stands above and continues to impress, even as I write this from 35,000 feet on my return to the much balmier San Diego climate.

Round 60 Golden Horseshoe (Gold)

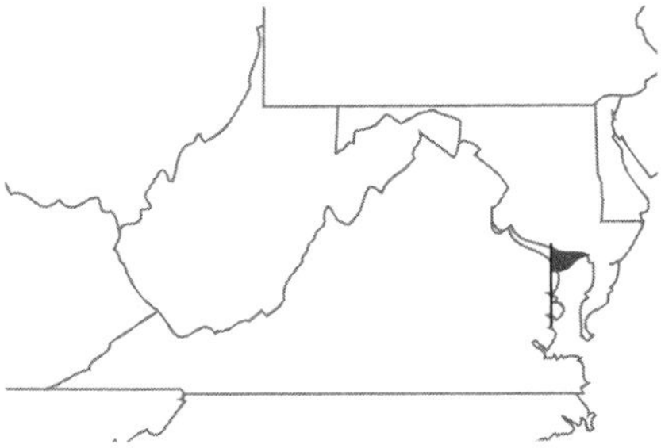

Course Rank: 63

Date Played: April 27, 2012

Starting Time: 1:30 p.m.

Weather: 69 degrees, clear, with 10 mph winds.

My Score: 83

Number of Lost Balls: 3

Highlights: 7 pars

Lowlights: 1 double bogey

Excuse for Not Breaking 80: Having driven four hours and racing to make my tee time, I was a bit distracted.

Greens Fee: $149

Playing Partners: Again, activity on the course was minimal, so I played alone.

Practice Facilities: Not extensive, but certainly adequate. There appeared to be large practice areas farther from the tee and clubhouse, so there may be more than meets the eye. The putting green adjacent to the first tee is a must, as you need to be prepared for the downhill speed putts.

My Rating: 8. There was a lot to like, and not much I would change. The par 3s are fun, albeit not in the category of Harbour Town, but certainly better than most. Given the small greens, proper club selection is vital. I may have enjoyed the course more from the blue tees, which offered more elevation and more distance.

Absolutely Must Play: Maybe...well, yes, as you must visit Williamsburg. Stay at one of the hotels in the historic Williamsburg area and you can walk to everything, including the golf course. This Robert Trent Jones, Sr. design has plenty of character and can challenge golfers of all levels.

Favorite Hole: I liked all of the holes, but until I reached No. 15, nothing was standing out. At 15, you are confronted with a 600+-yard par 5, with tree trouble if you get wayward. I always like a par 5 with a 6 in front of the yardage, although I seldom play them well. At No. 16, there is a monument indicating the next two holes are ranked in the top 500 in the world. No. 16 is a terrific par 3. It is not long and may be the forerunner for many of the "Island Holes" now regularly found on newer courses. No. 17 is a brutal, long par 4, uphill to a small, well-protected green. This is truly a great hole. No. 18 is another long par 4, with a dogleg left, downhill to a small, well protected, attractive green. All of the holes rated at the top of my list. Suffice it to say, this is one of the better finishing stretches.

Location Characteristics: Situated in the heart of historic Williamsburg, the course offers a coastal Virginia backdrop, augmented with several ravines and plenty of water. Like most of the south, the fairways are lined with thick trees. The course does not offer the terrain of Highland at Primland or Cascades, but they have created plenty of topography with many greens being elevated and sloped downward from back to front. (Do not miss long on these holes.) The region has great historical significance. This is a terrific trip for the family, and should give the golfers in the group an excellent diversion. There are additional well-regarded courses in the area; however, our tight schedule made play on these tracks impossible.

Overall: I am not a history buff, but I really liked Williamsburg. The accommodations in the heart of historic Williamsburg are terrific, and the concierge service can help design the perfect day, capped off with great meals. I appreciated the thought that went into the Gold Course at Golden Horseshoe. Being able to walk to the course was an added benefit, as was the affordable greens fee. Great golf, great location and great history makes this an attractive stop for any golfer, especially one with non-linksters in tow.

Trip Summary:

The Greenbrier Resort and Cascades Golf Course were nearly enough to make me forget being stuck in ski weather. The Blue Ridge and Allegheny Mountains offer some of the most scenic roads in America. In addition, there are plenty of Civil War locales, including the burial site of Traveller, Robert E. Lee's horse, not to mention the General himself. The back roads around Hot Springs, Virginia (Homestead), were amazing, even if it meant we were lost. Our GPS system had a few problems in the area. Primland is a very cool resort, and we topped off the trip by staying in historic Williamsburg. This is one of those trips where golf almost takes a back seat to the experience...almost. Ultimately, Cascades is borderline top 10 in my book. The Greenbrier courses were nice, and Old White, despite not being on the list, should definitely be included in the itinerary. Primland offers a spectacular setting that would have benefited from better weather. Golden Horseshoe is a more typical sea-level course, with interesting Trent Jones features. The biggest drawback to this trip was the amount of travel required between destinations. Ultimately, there are better places to take your regular foursome. This one is best suited for the family and will definitely score some wife maintenance points that may be necessary when you schedule your next Bandon Dunes vacation.

Chapter 32

Marathon Golf

I had not planned to return to Raleigh-Durham so soon, but golf historian and sometime golfing partner, Charlie Wilde, decided we needed a Pinehurst blitz. With less than four weeks' notice, I would have to work around the Senior Club Championship at La Costa, as well as a gala for the Flying Leatherneck Aviation Museum in San Diego (my wife sits on the board). Since I would be in the area, I felt a trek to Linville, North Carolina, could be added. Lastly, in a moment of insanity, I decided to add the three courses in Myrtle Beach. The odds of putting this one together were pretty slim, but I decided to give it a shot, especially as my American Airlines free round trip tickets were set to expire shortly.

Armed with free airfare and the promise of covering the rental car with my AMEX points, I called Joe Strong, the most reliable and available of my regular golfing partners. Surprisingly, he was enthusiastic, but we had to work around his anniversary. Despite the logistical nightmare, I was able to book a round trip to North Carolina that would include playing at least eight courses, later pushed to 10, in six days, while allowing enough time to traverse both North and South Carolina. Ultimately, I made it work for Joe, but we had to stop and visit his sister in Winston-Salem.

We landed late on Saturday night in Raleigh-Durham, and got into our hotel in Winston-Salem early Sunday morning. This began a string of consecutive nights with less than five hours' sleep and ultimately proved to be my undoing in the La Costa Senior Club Championship that began the next Saturday when I returned. My biggest concern was that the trip would be a blur, but I could not resist the challenge of checking so many courses off the list in less than a week. First stop: the Linville Resort.

Round 61 — Linville Golf Club

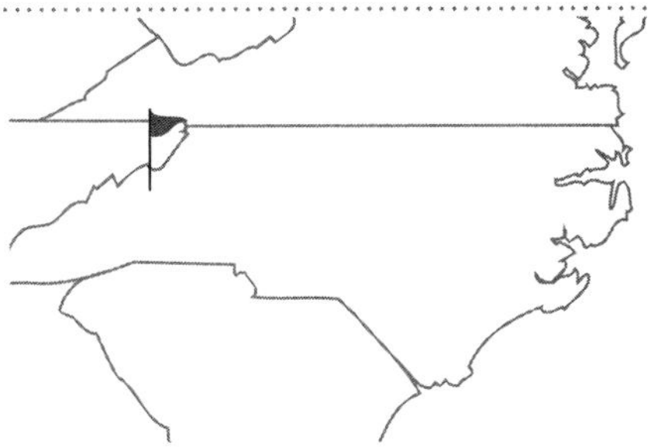

Course Rank: 61

Date Played: June 3, 2012

Starting Time: 2:08 p.m.

Weather: 68 degrees, 15 mph wind, cloudy

My Score: 86

Number of Lost Balls: None

Highlights: 1 birdie and 7 pars

Lowlights: 3 double bogeys and 1 triple bogey

Excuse for Not Breaking 80: The sadistic Donald Ross greens.

Greens Fee: $120; however, you cannot play the course unless you stay at the lodge.

Playing Partners: Joe Strong.

Practice Facilities: Nice driving range and practice facility, as well as putting green next to the attractive clubhouse.

My Rating: 8+, for the overall experience, including the classic Donald Ross layout. There are terrific golf holes set in amazing surroundings.

Absolutely Must Play: Yes. Despite the outlying location and limited golf season, you will not regret making the trek. Even if the golf is tough, the lodge will make it all good.

Favorite Hole: Nearly all of the holes were memorable; especially Nos. 7 and 10 with the ridiculously sloped greens, where being above the hole will guarantee a three- putt…minimum. However, my favorite hole was No. 3, a brutal par 4 that requires an excellent drive (but not too far, or you are in the creek), with an approach shot to an elevated green.

Location Characteristics: Situated at 3,800 feet above sea level in the Blue Ridge Mountains, Linville occupies a pristine forest setting amongst a backdrop of hillsides. There are great mountain views from the elevated tees on the back nine. There are numerous creeks running throughout the course, some of which are hidden. It is worth driving up the blind fairways to take a look…I should have done so.

Overall: Both Joe and I were very pleasantly surprised with the entire experience. The Eseeola Lodge is a very cool, 24-room facility constructed in 1892. The dining experience is exceptional, with a terrific menu. The staff is top-notch, as are the bar and common areas. And the golf? It is the icing on the cake. This Ross course is potentially top 25, in my opinion. Linville is one of the more underrated on the list, perhaps because it is only open from mid-May to mid-October. I strongly recommend finding time for this one.

Round 62 — Barefoot Resort (Love)

Course Rank: 86

Date Played: June 4, 2012

Starting Time: 2:04 p.m.

Weather: 70 degrees, cloudy skies with 10 mph wind.

My Score: 81

Number of Lost Balls: 1

Highlights: 4 birdies and 5 pars

Lowlights: 4 double bogeys

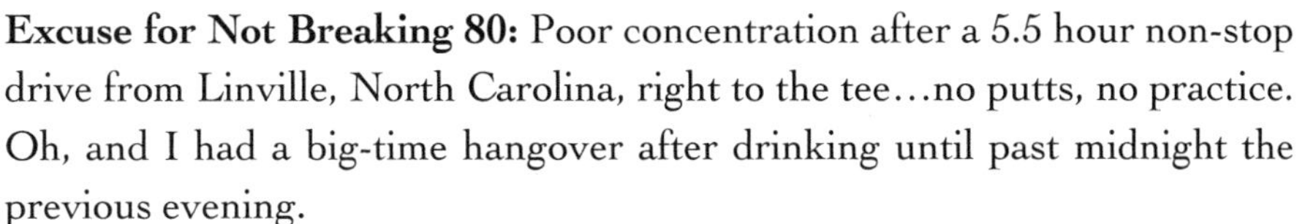

Excuse for Not Breaking 80: Poor concentration after a 5.5 hour non-stop drive from Linville, North Carolina, right to the tee...no putts, no practice. Oh, and I had a big-time hangover after drinking until past midnight the previous evening.

Greens Fee: $104, as part of the stay-and-play package.

Playing Partners: Joe Strong.

Practice Facilities: There was a putting green on the way to the first tee. The driving range required a shuttle. Given the time constraint after the drive, we decided to "wing it."

My Rating: 7, with an above average design, offset by average condition and service.

Absolutely Must Play: No. The layout is fine, but there are a number of more desirable courses in the Myrtle Beach area...maybe even the Fazio, Dye and Norman layouts at the Barefoot Resort.

Favorite Hole: No. 18 is a challenging par 5, with water on the left of the green influencing the second and/or third shots. I chose to lay up to a smallish landing area, which proved to be a good strategy. Most of the other holes would be described as good but not great.

Location Characteristics: Barefoot Resort is situated inland, in the North Myrtle Beach area. There is plenty of water, but no ocean influence. The course is set up in a generally links design, with few large trees. The highlight is the remaining structures left over from the original plantation house that can be found on the front nine. Although part of a master planned community, the houses do not come into play. Barefoot Resort is generally level, with the challenges coming from the large number of lakes eager to swallow up the errant shot.

Overall: I was satisfied with the Davis Love design. There were plenty of challenging holes, and the GPS in the cart was very useful. Our afternoon round was leisurely, with the course largely to ourselves. However, the greens were in average to poor condition. To be fair, these bent grass greens were scheduled to be replaced with Bermuda several months after our visit; however, it did not stop me from being annoyed when my birdie putt on No. 18 went airborne after hitting a dead spot. Despite this, the greens putted true, as evidenced by my four birdies on the front nine (or maybe that indicates poor greens that overcame my putting inadequacies). In addition to the condition, I was disappointed in the staff, aside from the bag boy who greeted us when we finished. All three courses stage from the same area, creating a mess that, I suspect, occurs more often than not. The golf was fine, but I found other local courses more appealing.

Round 63 — Dunes Golf and Beach Club

Course Rank: 48

Date Played: June 5, 2012

Starting Time: 8:00 a.m.

Weather: 73 degrees and rainy

My Score: 88

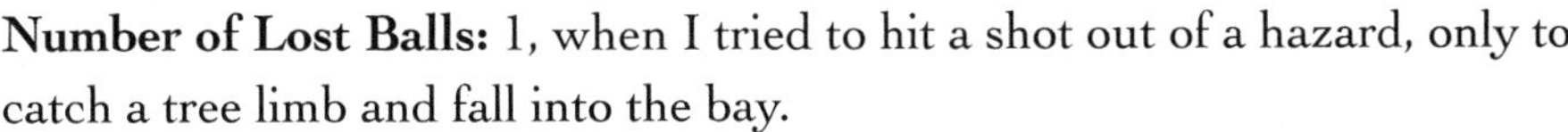

Number of Lost Balls: 1, when I tried to hit a shot out of a hazard, only to catch a tree limb and fall into the bay.

Highlights: 7 pars

Lowlights: 1 double bogey, 1 triple bogey and 1 quadruple bogey (ouch)

Excuse for Not Breaking 80: See weather. I could not get a good grip on the clubs.

Greens Fee: $109, as part of the stay-and-play package. The greens fees in Myrtle Beach in July are very reasonable.

Playing Partners: Joe Strong. We were later joined by Dan from Illinois, who had tied one on the night before, and was thinking too much about his 20-ounce lobster tail, on tap for his dinner that evening.

Practice Facilities: It was too early and too wet to hit many balls. I think I might have banged out ten before recognizing it would not be my day. The facilities were ample and nicely designed.

My Rating: 8. The Robert Trent Jones, Sr. design is a classic layout. The course was in good condition, but lacked the pizzazz of more preferred venues, despite having been a regular Seniors tour stop, as well as hosting numerous other tournaments.

Absolutely Must Play: Yes, if you are making a Myrtle Beach excursion, and you will, if just to play Caledonia Golf and Fish Club. The region is a golfing mecca, stuck in the center of tourist hell. I recommend taking your regular golfing group for a few days and making this one of the stops.

Favorite Hole: No. 13 is the signature hole, and for good reason. This horseshoe-shaped par 5 requires precise shot making, combined with real risk/reward. Although it is the number 1 handicap, a par is certainly possible...as is a snowman.

Location Characteristics: The Dunes course is situated along the coast, at the north end of Myrtle Beach, in a high demographic neighborhood. There are numerous mature trees as well as plenty of water. Trent Jones has utilized the bays from the Atlantic Ocean in a first-rate manner. Alligators are the theme of the course, so I presume they are in abundance...they are the logo on the hats, and there is a tribute to them on the course. This is a flat layout that could easily be walked.

Overall: I liked the classic Robert Trent Jones, Sr. design, and appreciated the history of the club. The staff was great, even if they could not turn off the rain. Despite my best efforts, I could not overcome the weather, but embraced the layout and enjoyed the surroundings. The Dunes Golf and Beach Club course was in very good condition and provides an excellent challenge for golfers of all ages. Make sure and check out the memorabilia in the clubhouse.

Round 64 — Caledonia Golf and Fish Club

Course Rank: 28

Date Played: June 5, 2012

Starting Time: 2:36 p.m.

Weather: 75 degrees and raining to start, with dry conditions after the first three holes

My Score: 87

Number of Lost Balls: 1

Highlights: 1 birdie and 5 pars

Lowlights: 2 double bogeys and 2 triple bogeys

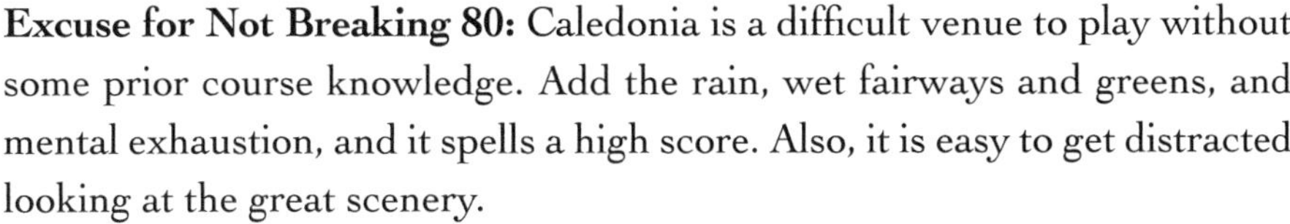

Excuse for Not Breaking 80: Caledonia is a difficult venue to play without some prior course knowledge. Add the rain, wet fairways and greens, and mental exhaustion, and it spells a high score. Also, it is easy to get distracted looking at the great scenery.

Greens Fee: $104 as part of the package.

Playing Partners: Joe Strong.

Practice Facilities: The driving range is located off site at the True Blue sister course. Given the weather and prior 18 holes, we saw no reason to abuse our middle-aged bodies. There is a putting green and practice area on the grounds.

My Rating: 9, for great setting, terrific holes and general "coolness."

Absolutely Must Play: Yes. Go to Myrtle Beach and play this course. You can try out some others, but this one definitely has the "wow" factor. I had never heard of Mike Strantz before this trip, but, along with Tobacco Road, have come to love his designs. I would describe his layout as Pete Dye meets Walt Disney. Tillinghast, Ross and MacKenzie might roll over in their graves, but for those crazy, addicted, Type "A" personalities like myself, this is nirvana.

Favorite Hole: This is a tough one, as the back nine rated four 9s and four 8+ scores on my card. Having previously seen No. 18 from the clubhouse, however, I have to go with that short but challenging par 4 that requires a very precise tee shot and knee-knocking approach over a large water feature to a narrow, very wide green. I am sure the natives sit on the porch of the clubhouse watching the golfers launch their Titleists into the water.

Location Characteristics: Caledonia Golf and Fish Club has it all. It begins with an impressive entryway, highlighted by stately trees filled with Spanish moss. The property is located on a former plantation, and is now an eco-project with all forms of flora and fauna. When the sun came out on the back side, we had to sidestep the gators sunning on the seventh tee box. The course had also planted flowers behind many of the holes, adding a nice touch of color. Although the project is not situated on the ocean, there are marshes and other water features throughout. The clubhouse is an attractive, tasteful building, with rocking chairs on the deck to watch the golfers hack it up on No.18. Caledonia is situated south of Myrtle Beach on Pawleys Island in a terrific location.

Overall: Caledonia is one of the true hidden treasures. While Myrtle Beach is not exactly my type of town, the golf is excellent, capped by this jewel. Sure, the course is a bit tricked up and very difficult the first time through, but the visual presentation is exceptional. Unfortunately, the course was very wet, which made scoring tough. Nevertheless, it was obvious the facilities are well-maintained. I am not sure this one will make my top 10 after I finish the process, but it will be darn close. Like Wolf Creek, Lake of Isles and Paa-Ko Ridge, this one was a terrific surprise.

Round 65 Pinehurst No. 2

Course Rank: 7

Date Played: June 7, 2012

Starting Time: 7:40 a.m.

Weather: 75 degrees, rising to 80 degrees, partly cloudy and calm.

My Score: 96

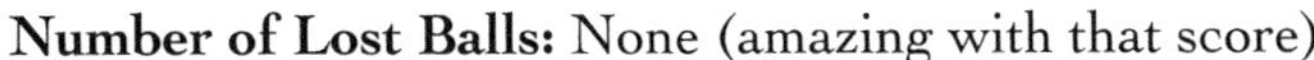

Number of Lost Balls: None (amazing with that score)

Highlights: 2 measly pars

Lowlights: 3 double bogeys, 1 triple bogey and 1 quadruple bogey

Excuse for Not Breaking 80: Let me count the ways: First, I should not have been talked into playing from the blue tees, as the distance is too much for an old man. Second, after 36 holes each of the prior two days, an average of five hours of sleep per night and too much alcohol, my game had fallen apart. My usually strong short game could not cope with the crowned greens, leading to nearly one extra stroke per hole. Ultimately, the quadruple bogey on the very easy third hole put me in a bad mental state, from which I could not recover.

Greens Fee: $349, plus $80 for the caddie's tip.

Playing Partners: Joe Strong, Greg Strong (no relation, but the same index) and Charlie Wilde. Charlie arranged the Pinehurst portion of the excursion. Greg is Charlie's friend from Utah, and was an excellent addition to the group.

Practice Facilities: Massive, as expected. It was too early, and I was too tired, to partake of the driving range, but rolled a few putts to try to gauge the speed.

My Rating: 8. Perhaps it was the lack of sleep, but I felt the course lacked excitement, other than watching your balls roll up and off the green. The links design was fun, but few of the holes were memorable. I felt like I kept playing the same 420-yard par 4, with crowned greens and waste areas on either side of the fairway. The Donald Ross layout (subsequently redesigned) provides plenty of challenge, especially around the greens. Given the history, as well as being a U.S. Open venue, adds to the interest, but this one did not rock my world.

Absolutely Must Play: Yes. Any opportunity to play a U.S. Open course should be at the top of a golf addict's list. Nevertheless, I preferred most of the other top 10 offerings.

Favorite Hole: All of the holes rated well, but few were standouts. I liked the par 5s at No. 4 and No. 16. However, No. 5 garnered my highest rating. This long par 4 plays into a tough green. I should have parred the hole, but could not get up and down from an easy front location.

Location Characteristics: Pinehurst is situated in the Sandhills area of North Carolina, just over an hour southwest of Raleigh-Durham. The region is inundated with golf courses, including many that are not part of the Pinehurst complex. The redesign for the 2014 U.S. Open is more links style than before, with minimal fairway rough, but plenty of native area. These areas, which border nearly all the fairways, are somewhat sparse, so finding balls is relatively easy; however, you are at the mercy of the golf gods as to the lies. Beyond these waste areas, where you can ground your club, are rows of pine trees that will take distance off the wayward drive. There is limited topographical change, so I recommend walking the course with a caddie. Water does not come into play on the course, and there are no exceptional views…just challenging golf.

Overall: I had played No. 2 in the mid 1980s, before the renovation. That round was also played in a sleep-deprived state. The rough, which vexed me at that time, is now gone, but the waste areas are no picnic. I took nearly 25 photos of unusual lies confronted by the members of our foursome, and would have had another 25 if I had six hours to finish the round. For a U.S. Open course, and one ranked No. 7 on the list, I was somewhat disappointed. It was still great golf, but it lacked the uniqueness of other top courses on the list. Perhaps it is sacrilege not to bow down to Pinehurst No. 2, but, like some of the Bandon Dunes courses, I felt the venue was overrated.

Round 66 Pinehurst No. 8

Course Rank: 100

Date Played: June 7, 2012

Starting Time: 2:09 p.m.

Weather: Partly Cloudy, 80 degrees, calm

My Score: 84

Number of Lost Balls: 1

Highlights: 2 birdies and 8 pars

Lowlights: 1 double bogey, 1 triple bogey and 1 quadruple bogey

Excuse for Not Breaking 80: Three over on 15 holes, and nine over on the other three. The quadruple bogey on No. 3 was the killer, with a bad break in a fairway bunker, leading to another trap, a sculled shot over the green and into a hazard. It was my second "snowman" on No. 3 (see Pinehurst No. 2) that day.

Greens Fee: $189

Playing Partners: The brothers Strong (Joe and Greg, who are not related) and Charlie Wilde.

Practice Facilities: Attractive facilities, with driving range, short game area and putting green. Once again, I was sleep deprived and mentally exhausted from the hectic schedule, and decided to forego the warm-up (bad idea), which led to a double-par-quadruple start.

My Rating: 8 for an enjoyable Fazio design, but like many of his courses, it does not have many memorable holes. This course is certainly top 100 worthy, and is underrated at 100 on the list.

Absolutely Must Play: Yes, as long as you are partaking of the Pinehurst experience. This is probably the second best course, and one that is highly regarded.

Favorite Hole: No. 18 is a great finishing hole, requiring a forced carry over water, and is uphill 417 yards back to the clubhouse. This one takes a couple of really good pokes.

Location Characteristics: Pinehurst No. 8 is situated several miles away from the main Pinehurst complex (which houses Nos. 1 to 5). There is moderate topography, and water comes into play on several of the finishing holes. No surprise, pine trees line the fairways, and there are a variety of birds circling the grounds, searching for rodents and other delectables. The highlight was the tortoise that decided to traverse the middle of the No. 10 fairway. At the rate he/she was going, it probably would have taken another hour, if Charlie and Greg had not provided an assist.

Overall: While I enjoyed the golf course, I was somewhat turned off by the operation. Charging for a cart seems excessive, when no one is going to walk and the green fees are already at a premium. In addition, the course was not well-marshalled. The group in front of us not only played at a tortoise pace, but were exceedingly loud, frequently making excessive noise which could be heard several holes away, and regrettably occurring during several of my backswings. In addition, I observed them failing to rake the bunker on 16, right before I launched my drive into the same sand. The swearing, tossing of clubs and lack of course etiquette should have been brought under control. Otherwise, the round was enjoyable, with the course being fairly typical for a Fazio design.

Round 67 Pine Needles

Course Rank: 52

Date Played: June 8, 2012

Starting Time: 7:10 a.m.

Weather: 60 degrees to start, rising to 78 degrees, sunny and calm.

My Score: 90

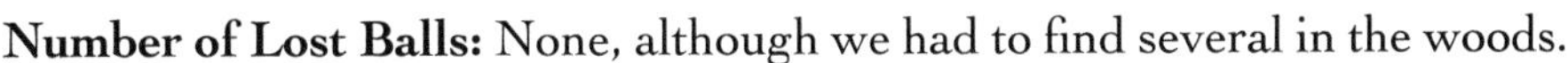

Number of Lost Balls: None, although we had to find several in the woods.

Highlights: 1 birdie and 3 pars

Lowlights: 3 double bogeys and 2 triple bogeys

Excuse for Not Breaking 80: O.K., now I was *really* sleep deprived. A late dinner at the Pine Crest Inn (highly recommended), followed by the early wake up call (5:45 a.m.) turned me into a basket case. A bad start was followed by an even worse finish, with a double and triple on Nos. 17 and 18. Without a warm-up, the round was doomed from the start, but I had to make it to Tobacco Road for a 12:50 starting time, and then to the airport. For this golf marathon, I had hit the wall.

Greens Fee: $145

Playing Partners: Joe and Greg Strong and Charlie Wilde. Greg rallied tremendously after an 11 on the opening hole.

Practice Facilities: Once again, they looked good, but no way were we going to get there in time to hit a few balls.

My Rating: 8, as there was nothing to complain about on this Donald Ross design, although I was less attentive, as I sleepwalked through the round. Further, I did not see much of the actual course, as I chose this round to begin spraying my drives.

Absolutely Must Play: Absolutely? No, but the course is only a few miles from Pinehurst, and is probably more interesting than some of the resort venues. Any chance to play a Donald Ross course should be taken.

Favorite Hole: I liked No. 10, a big dogleg par 5 that offers a true risk/reward tee shot. A bunker hugs the left side of the fairway, which, if successfully navigated, can lead to a comparatively short approach, and likely birdie. I decided to play right, ended up hitting next to a tree, followed by a left-handed punch across the fairway into the aforementioned trap, leading to a double bogey. Most of the holes rated 8 in my book, but did not necessarily get the juices flowing.

Location Characteristics: Not surprisingly, Pine Needles is situated amongst numerous pine trees, with beds of needles lying just off the fairway. I finally mastered the art of hitting off pine needles, a skill that is totally irrelevant on my usual venues. Bug spray is highly recommended here. The course has an adequate amount of water and elevation changes to make for an interesting round. Accurate driving will take most of the flora out of play. Nevertheless, there was a feeling of being in the woods.

Overall: It is hard to find anything to dislike about this course, other than my poor effort. The design is fair, and unlike Linville, this Ross course lets you see everything. The greens are typically crowned, and tough to read the first time through. There are few sand traps, but all are well placed, and I found many. The condition was above average and the staff friendly. This is a course I could play everyday, and be content, however, it does not scream: "I am special." While playing Pine Needles, you can run across the street to Mid Pines, which is less expensive but still a nice track, albeit in average condition during my visit.

Round 68 — Tobacco Road

Course Rank: 97

Date Played: June 8, 2012

Starting Time: 12:20 p.m.

Weather: 85 degrees, sunny, calm

My Score: 84

Number of Lost Balls: 1

Highlights: 10 pars

Lowlights: 2 double bogeys and 1 quadruple bogey

Excuse for Not Breaking 80: Exhaustion, both from the heat and lack of sleep. The game fell apart once we ran into the group in front of us (No. 9), when the speed slowed to a crawl, and there was some danger we would miss our flight.

Greens Fee: $89, easily one of the best deals going.

Playing Partners: Joe Strong.

Practice Facilities: We were too rushed to check it out, but the range looked O.K.

My Rating: 9. O.K., it was really "tricked up," but was a fun finish to the hectic vacation. (We are still talking about this round.)

Absolutely Must Play: Yes, if for no other reason then to see what you missed, and be able to grouse about it to your other golf addicts.

Favorite Hole: Other than a few par 3s, which seemed too short, nearly every other hole had something to offer. I thought No. 1 was a great starting hole and prelude to the adventure that was just beginning. This par 5 has two blind shots (get used to it).

Location Characteristics: Tobacco Road is located about 30 minutes north of Pinehurst, but may as well be located in a different country. Situated amongst tobacco farms, the course appears to have been developed in the middle of a quarry. There are no sand traps per se, but waste areas abound. On several holes, a drive into the waste area can cut off significant distance to the green, making par 5s reachable in two. I purposely drove into the waste areas on Nos. 5 and 11, setting up great birdie opportunities, both of which I missed. You can drive your carts into many waste areas and ground your club. Tobacco Road has plenty of pine trees, although few come into play. The topography creates a visually stimulating and intimidating layout, with numerous blind shots. Fortunately, there is not much water. Bells are located along the course to ring when you clear blind fairways and greens. For the first-time player, confusion can result from the layout, with a premium placed on ball control.

Overall: Tobacco Road can be summed up as a Pete Dye course on steroids. Designed by Mike Strantz, who also was the architect at Caledonia Golf and Fish Club, the course will not be everyone's cup of tea, but is perfect for someone who appreciates a unique design. Sure, the blind shots will drive you crazy, but if you can stay in control, it is not impossible to score well. Distance is irrelevant, as the course is short, but requires target golf, and the use of most clubs in the bag. No. 16 is a bit crazy, but if you follow the directions is an easy par. The clubhouse is small, but works for this rural facility. As a golf sadist/masochist, I found Tobacco Road to be a satisfying afternoon. The biggest negative is that the blind shots create relatively slow play. As we had to catch a flight 2.5 hours after our estimated finish time in Raleigh-Durham, it was frustrating when it took five hours to complete, despite a comparatively quick front nine. Golf purists may cringe, but I am a huge Mike Strantz fan, with Tobacco Road and Caledonia being highlights of this trip.

Trip Summary:

The whirlwind tour of North and South Carolina yielded a number of pleasant surprises and some disappointment. My three favorite courses were Caledonia, Linville and Tobacco Road, all rating higher with me than

Pinehurst No. 2. Not that the U.S. Open venue was not appealing, but the layout lacked the thrill of the other three. The Linville experience, including staying at The Eseeola Lodge, was well worth the travel. I would rate the course a cut below Cascades, but still a lot of fun. Caledonia and Tobacco Road are both Mike Strantz designs that are great if you love blind shots and interesting views. The back nine of Caledonia is definitely top 10 worthy, and the front is no slouch. I cannot begin to explain Tobacco Road, but trust me; it is worth the 30-minute drive from Pinehurst.

Pinehurst No. 2, like many top links designs, is more subtle in its approach. With a great history, it is worth grabbing one of the knowledgeable local caddies and walking the sand hills. Once again, I believe this course suffered from inflated expectations. The other Pinehurst courses are nice and offer good options if you are there; however, I would play Pine Needles before venturing on these other layouts.

Both Pinehurst and Myrtle Beach are vacations that should be restricted to serious golfers only. Pinehurst, because there is not much else to do, and Myrtle Beach as it is too "cheesy" for my tastes. On the other hand, Myrtle Beach is a mecca for many families on vacation, so if you are into that sort of touristy stuff, by all means drag the young ones along. An intense golf vacation could include both venues, although I would have preferred to spread them out. You might save Linville for the Primland/Greenbrier/Homestead trip, and allow for an extra day or two. For what it is worth, the golfing value in Myrtle Beach is much better than at Pinehurst, although Tobacco Road is quite affordable.

Chapter 33

Planes, Trains and Automobiles…… and a Cruise Ship

Nothing screams "golf vacation" like an invitation to do an Alaskan cruise—especially when your parents are offering to pick up the tab. Thus, when my overly generous, octogenarian parents proposed a family cruise to Alaska "on them," my first instinct was to look up golf courses in the 49th state.

My lifeline to the top golf courses is the *Golf Magazine* website devoted to this issue. A quick check of the site's interactive map yielded no courses in Sarah Palin's backyard that would make bringing the sticks along worthwhile. What a shock! Not a single golf course in that massive state had made the top 100. Shoot, now what was I going to do on a cruise ship for seven days? Not a problem; I would just find one of the best courses in each port for my excursions. As part of their review, *Golf Magazine* lists the top 10 courses in each state. Unfortunately, someone forgot to tell the Eskimos (that is who live in Alaska, right?) about America's Favorite Pastime. The top 10 list included only five courses, and the one closest to a port we were visiting was a nine-hole track in Anchorage. *Nine frigging holes!* Are you kidding me? A week without golf. I was already getting the shakes thinking about it. My last hope was the vague recollection that you can drive golf balls off the back of cruise ships, although having been on a number of voyages, I have never known this to be the case. I will admit the thought of trying to take down a bald eagle did give me a perverse charge, but, alas, a review of the Princess Cruise ship we were to take did not reference an on-board driving range.

To be fair, I had always wanted to experience the Alaska cruise, but who knew there would be no golf? Since a prolonged absence from the links would be difficult, I decided to overdose immediately before the trip (just like carbo-loading before a marathon). The cruise ship was leaving from Vancouver, Canada, so I figured a side trip to the Pacific Northwest was in order. There are three top 100 courses in the region (I don't count Bandon Dunes since it is too far out of the way), so I worked out a tour that would take us to Pumpkin Ridge, Crosswater and Chambers Bay. I had previously been to Bend, Oregon, to play Crosswater as well as other local venues, but only remembered one long hangover.

Logistically, the biggest problem was what to do with the clubs. On past cruises I had carried them along, but if you have ever been in one of those cabins you know that space is at a premium, and my wife did not want to sleep with my TaylorMades again.

During another late night watching some throwaway instructional show on the Golf Channel, the answer came to me. I had always enjoyed the ads, but it had not actually occurred to me that I could ship the clubs back home via Federal Express. Hey, if it is good enough for Ponce de Leon's map, why not my clubs? Why not, you ask? Well, check out the pricing sometime. For a cheapskate, it is hard to justify buying an airline ticket for an inanimate object. This led to another brainstorm: I could use some of my excess mileage points to purchase tickets for my son, who could fly them back (no charge on Southwest) when I left the States for Canada. Ultimately, the plan took shape to have Charlie join me for several days of golf, after which I could drop him off at the airport in Seattle, along with my clubs and the rental car, and take Amtrak Cascades to Vancouver.

Yes, it ultimately cost more for his meals and greens fees than the FedEx shipping, but it was great to have Charlie around. Further, the one thing you will not get from my son is inane conversation. The kid has an IQ off the chart and reads everything (well, most everything, think *The Economist* not *People* magazine). He could also serve as navigator for the trip as he is a whiz on the GPS system. This is good since professionally he works in satellite technology.

Despite all the great planning, it was still with a bit of trepidation that I set off on a trip that would conclude with eight consecutive days of no golf. I would have to go cold turkey. Before this golf drought, I was determined to get it out of my system with some top-flight rounds. First stop: Portland, Oregon.

Round 69 **Pumpkin Ridge Ghost Creek**

Course Rank: 47

Date Played: July 13, 2012

Starting Time: 10:30 a.m.

Weather: 72 degrees, sunny and calm.

My Score: 86

Number of Lost Balls: 2

Highlights: 6 pars

Lowlights: 3 double bogeys

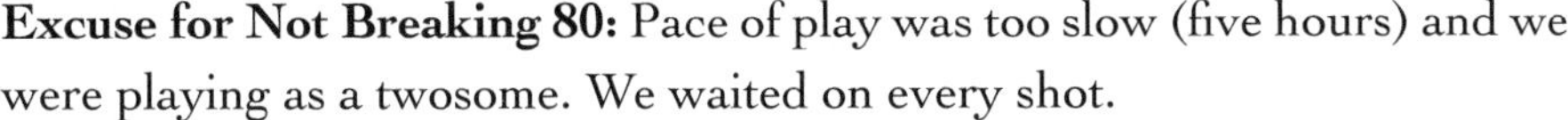

Excuse for Not Breaking 80: Pace of play was too slow (five hours) and we were playing as a twosome. We waited on every shot.

Greens Fee: $150, plus $16 for a cart. I noticed a lot of walkers, but there was some topography, so it would not be for everyone. It was cart paths only, so pace of play was further impacted.

Playing Partners: Son Charlie, who was distracted/agonizing over whether to accept admittance to the Wharton Business School or continue a few more years with his engineering position. He only had 72 hours left to decide.

Practice Facilities: The requisite facilities were available, including an ample driving range, large putting green and short game area.

My Rating: 8, with the front nine surpassing the back nine in terms of overall ambience.

Absolutely Must Play: No; however, it is not a course to be missed if you are in the Portland area. Had the back nine lived up to the promise of the front, my opinion would have been different.

Favorite Hole: None of the holes were completely memorable, except No. 14, where my son almost got a hole in one. I liked No. 4 the best. This is a par 5 through the woods that slopes right to left, with trouble on both sides of the fairway, especially as you near the green.

Location Characteristics: Pumpkin Ridge is situated in the farmland outside of Portland, Oregon. The course is unique in that the front nine works its way into heavily wooded forest, with an ever-present creek winding along the holes. Holes 2 through 8 are especially serene, and offer great views. For those remaining holes situated back in the farmland there is not too much exciting, other than the occasional presence of the creek and a looming lake on No. 18. The course is very playable, with some modest topography adding to the pleasure.

Overall: The course was in excellent condition the day we played, as the LPGA tour event was just around the corner. I would have preferred if they had reversed the nines, as I enjoyed the front nine much more than the back side. The greens putted well and the course offered a good challenge. The biggest negative was the pace of play. For the most part the course was not marshalled, allowing for a foursome several groups in front to take nearly three hours on the first nine holes. (Ultimately, the pace picked up on the final six holes after someone came out to tell them to keep moving.) As the course is very open, such a slow pace seemed ridiculous. This was exacerbated by our playing as a twosome. Despite the speed, it was a great day for golf and a nice environment for knocking the ball around.

Round 70 — Crosswater at Sunriver Resort

Course Rank: 39

Date Played: July 15, 2012

Starting Time: 10:39 a.m.

Weather: 70 degrees, sunny, 15 mph winds

My Score: 81

Number of Lost Balls: 1

Highlights: 1 birdie and 10 pars

Lowlights: 3 double bogeys

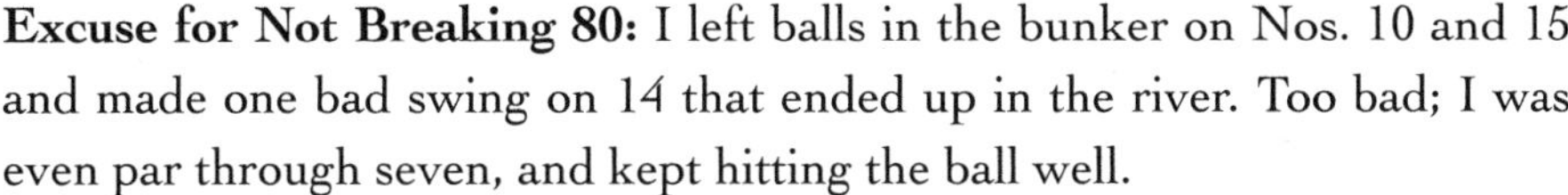

Excuse for Not Breaking 80: I left balls in the bunker on Nos. 10 and 15 and made one bad swing on 14 that ended up in the river. Too bad; I was even par through seven, and kept hitting the ball well.

Greens Fee: Part of the package. You must stay at the resort to gain access. Reported greens fee is $175.

Playing Partners: Son Charlie, and George and Tammy from Boston, by way of Southern California. They were playing many of the top 100 courses, although without the formal structure. We were able to compare notes on a number of venues.

Practice Facilities: Very good. The practice range is sufficient, with a designated area for members. The practice putting green was in great shape, and there was a large short game area, with a couple of bunkers.

My Rating: 8+, for a couple of very interesting holes, combined with several less memorable ones.

Absolutely Must Play: Yes. The venue is terrific, although the access is challenging. I recommend a family vacation in Bend, and, if in the area,

Crosswater is a definite must. In addition, Bend has several other excellent courses including Tetherow and Pronghorn, both of which appear in the *Golf Digest* top 100.

Favorite Hole: The signature hole is No. 12, a great par 5 with a wide river running the entire length of the hole on the left side and forest/vegetation on the right, with narrow landing areas. At 572 yards, the hole requires three excellent "knee knocker" shots. Both Charlie and I parred the hole, and George had a birdie. The par 5s were the most interesting.

Location Characteristics: Crosswater is situated in central Oregon. The location is isolated, but the drive is terrific through heavily forested national parks. The course itself is characterized by rivers, which often come into play. These are wide waterways that attract local rafters and canoers. It is especially interesting on No. 18 as you hit your second shot over the river traffic. The course is pseudo-links style, with a limited number of trees; however, there is some vegetation off the fairways that can lead to unplayable lies, or lateral hazards. Much of the layout is dominated by wet marshland that swallows up the errant golf shot. Be careful with the tee shots as several of the fairways end abruptly at the marshes. Overall, the setting is attractive, especially with snow-capped Mount Bachelor in the background. This is a comparatively level venue.

Overall: You cannot go wrong with a day at Crosswater (assuming the weather is good). Bring a few extra golf balls, as there are plenty of hazards—both seen and unseen. Once the ball gets into the thick rough lining the course, it can be difficult to find. Bend is a terrific resort area that offers snow sports during the winter months. There are plenty of great golf courses in the area including two others at Sunriver, in addition to the other aforementioned top 100 venues. In my opinion, a golf vacation in Bend should be somewhere on the list. By itself, Crosswater may not be worth the travel, but the additional local amenities make a visit worthwhile, and makes for a terrific family vacation.

Round 71 — Chambers Bay

Course Rank: 13

Date Played: July 16, 2011

Starting Time: 9:26 a.m.

Weather: 72 degrees, 10-15 mph winds, sunny

My Score: 84

Number of Lost Balls: None

Highlights: 7 pars

Lowlights: 1 double bogey

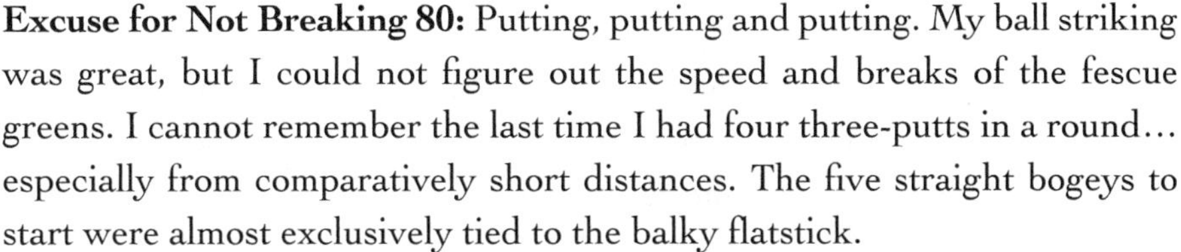

Excuse for Not Breaking 80: Putting, putting and putting. My ball striking was great, but I could not figure out the speed and breaks of the fescue greens. I cannot remember the last time I had four three-putts in a round... especially from comparatively short distances. The five straight bogeys to start were almost exclusively tied to the balky flatstick.

Greens Fee: $141.90 for out of state residents.

Playing Partners: Son Charlie, and Rich and Barry (two doctors related by marriage) and our caddies Beau (us) and Brian (them).

Practice Facilities: There is a large driving range, practice putting green and short game area located away from the first tee. A van provides access, but only runs every ten minutes. This van also drives you from the parking area/pro shop up top, down to the golf. As such, you should arrive at the course early if you want to warm up.

My Rating: 9. This was very close to a top 10 course in my book. For a county-owned facility, Chambers Bay was a pleasant surprise. I liked every hole.

Absolutely Must Play: Yes. This site of the 2015 U.S. Open is very similar to Whistling Straits, albeit not quite as spectacular.

Favorite Hole: This one is tough, as I rated every hole an 8 or higher. The par 3s were especially memorable, generally offering elevated tee boxes. I rated No. 3 the highest, which may have related to the respective tee and pin positions. Only 145 yards, this heavily bunkered hole offers an excellent risk reward, when the pin is tucked left. Despite this, there are numerous other great holes, including challenging par 5s, most of which are uphill, and a drivable par 4 (No. 12).

Location Characteristics: Chambers Bay is a links-style design situated along the shores of Puget Sound, south of Seattle, in the city of University Place. There is plenty of rolling topography that lends itself to elevated greens and elevated tee shots. The water is visible throughout the course, with some excellent photo ops. On the course there is no water in play, but plenty of waste areas and knee-high fescue.

Overall: You must walk Chambers Bay. I strongly recommend hiring one of the experienced caddies. I am not sure of their green-reading talent, but line of flight is vital on the blind shots. You can count on a five-hour round, despite not having to look for a lot of golf balls due to the open links design.. However, should you find yourself in knee-deep "hay," take your medicine and get back to the fairway. The alternative is spending your day threshing the grounds for the city of Tacoma. Chambers Bay is a terrific golf course that should not be missed. I understand they hope to have the course even longer than the currently insane 7,547 yards for the U.S. Open. I am not sure this is a top 10 course, but definitely warrants an honorable mention.

Trip Summary:

It is always great to end a trip on a truly exceptional course. Tobacco Road on my previous boondoggle and Chambers Bay both filled this bill. It was especially important on this trip given that I would not be playing again for over a week. This, I believe, would be my longest layoff from golf since beginning my quest to play the top 100. You really need to be a golf fanatic to take on the Pacific Northwest tour. I think another day or two in Bend and a couple of extra days in the Seattle area would have been a good idea.

Ultimately, the trip came off well, as our flights, reservations and even the train were as scheduled. As for the cruise, it was pretty good. Alaska is an amazing venue. Despite having seen most of the continental United States, there is nothing to match the beauty of the place. I gained some understanding as to why there are no golf courses in Alaska. The entire region is comprised of glaciers. While this would greatly assist the roll on your drives, it would probably be hard to putt (maybe a 25 on the stimpmeter). My biggest complaint was the lack of a sports bar on board the ship. I had selected Ernie Els in my golf fantasy league for the 2012 British Open, and you know what happened there.

The Pacific Northwest is beautiful country and the golf courses are worth the effort, assuming it is not raining, which is probably a 50/50 proposition… during prime season. Take the family to Bend for a vacation. There is plenty for them to do while you feed your golf addiction. Chambers Bay is a terrific facility, occupying a great location that makes you forget the drive through some seedier areas of Tacoma to get there.

Chapter 34

Senior Moment

Some of the biggest worries confronting golfers are the effects of aging as related to the golfer's motor skills. We buy ultra thick grips for our putters to avoid the yips, or alternatively putters we can anchor to our ever-expanding midriffs. Graphite shafts are a concession to age, although the most macho will continue to flail away with steel shafts. We buy exercise programs to improve the core, and read everything we can find on increasing distance. This includes contradictory articles that appear regularly in the most popular golf magazines. And, of course, we need to own a wide variety of tools and instructional videos that grace the airwaves via that wonderful device known as the infomercial. Alas, we continue to lose distance faster than the golf club and golf ball manufacturers can keep up.

I have long ago accepted my fate. At least golf is a sport in which you can participate well into your 80s. At some point we no longer seek that elusive round of breaking par, but rather desire to "shoot our age."

What concerns me more is not the deteriorating physical capability, but rather coping with the mental loss. This became very apparent during my trip to the lower peninsula of Michigan.

It had never occurred to me that Michigan was a hotbed of golf. With a three-month season (give or take), there seems little point in developing great courses. Thus, when originally planning my golf excursions, I was mildly surprised to find four courses in the top 100 located in the state. (As a side note, *Golf Digest* had nine Michigan courses on its recent list). As such, a Michigan excursion was in the offing. This also afforded the opportunity to join up with Scott Rand for a third consecutive year at Whistling Straits. Given the itinerary of golf courses, I labored for days scheduling the vacation such that I could play the entire Wisconsin and Michigan courses in one week. This was no small feat, but, despite my increasing age, I retain excellent organizational skills.

We flew into Milwaukee using more Southwest Airline miles. With the free luggage, the only cost was $10 for the TSA. The next day we were on the road to Sheboygan, after numerous delays trying to get out of Milwaukee, which had the world's worst road improvement project underway. An afternoon round at The Straits course went well, with great weather and a somewhat better score than on past attempts. The next morning I took on the River Course at Blackwolf Run that had humiliated me the prior year. If not for the triple bogey on the ridiculously stupid, par 3 No. 13, (you try playing this hole with a fade swing), I would have broken 80 on what I consider to be one of the most difficult courses I have ever played. An afternoon round at The Bull at Pinehurst Farms was completed before dark, and I was able to get another bowl of my favorite corn and sausage chowder at Blackwolf Run.

The next day it was a morning jaunt around the Irish course, and a mad dash to catch a ferry across Lake Michigan. This got us to Arcadia Bluffs just before the restaurant closed, and in time for a good night's rest before tackling the Links course at this resort. Despite the weather turning cold and wet, we continued to make progress on the itinerary without a hiccup. After Arcadia Bluffs it was up to Boyne Mountain Resort, from whence I was able to drive about 90 minutes to Forest Dunes, and back in time for a great Italian meal. The next morning it was off to Bay Harbor for another highly successful, enjoyable round. That night we trekked down to the Grand Traverse Resort, where I had a 7:00 a.m. time on the Bear Course (not top 100 in *Golf Magazine*, but on the *Golf Digest* list). It was dark when I teed off, and there was no one behind me when I made the turn. This two-hour and twenty minute round was critical, as we needed to make the two-hour trip to Tullymore for the afternoon round. This is where disaster struck.

I had been doing so well on my itinerary that I chose not to consult my notes on the way to the final course. Even with detours I arrived in time to tee off and finish before dark. It was disconcerting, however, when I arrived at Tullymore-St. Ives only to be informed that I did not have a tee time.

I almost went ballistic, but they said it would not be a problem to get me out. In checking their computer, they noted that I had inadvertently made a starting time at the "other" Tullymore course. After previously correcting an error made by Bay Harbor, I was willing to overlook "their" mistake, so long as I could get out and play. St. Ives was a nice course, with some interesting holes, but struck me as a marginal top 100 layout. I shot an 84, with a couple of blow-up holes, but was satisfied that, despite the obstacles, I had pulled off the trip with no issues.

Flash forward to 2:00 a.m. I awake from a fitful sleep with a feeling of dread. With limited light, I traipse over to my computer bag and pull out my itinerary. A review of the final day notes suggests that, in fact, I should have played the Tullymore Course and *not* St. Ives at Tullymore. Unfortunately, because this was the last of the courses on the trip, and I needed to leave that morning for San Diego, I did not have a backup plan. My heart sank as I realized I had experienced a senior moment. As a result, this fabulous trip could not be considered a true success. An expensive return to Michigan was now necessary.

Round 72 — Arcadia Bluffs

Course Rank: 30

Date Played: September 17, 2012

Starting Time: 10:00 a.m.

Weather: 65 degrees, cloudy, some drizzle and 25-30 mph winds.

My Score: 89

Number of Lost Balls: 0

Highlights: 8 pars

Lowlights: 5 double bogeys and 1 triple bogey

Excuse for Not Breaking 80: I have never been a good wind player, but this was ridiculous. At its most blustery it was impossible to keep my high-ball flight on line.

Greens Fee: $160, plus minimum $50 caddie fee (you can take a cart if you like).

Playing Partners: Tom, a golf professional at Grand Geneva Resort and Billy, my caddie.

Practice Facilities: Decent range, including a short game area. The putting green was adequate.

My Rating: 9-. This is a really nice links-style course, with great views of Lake Michigan. I think it is just a cut below Whistling Straits.

Absolutely Must Play: Yes, especially in combination with the other two great courses in the area (Forest Dunes and Bay Harbor). If you like a links design, with some topography and views of the lake, you should love this one

Favorite Hole: There were plenty of good holes. I thought No. 10 was great, but preferred No. 11. The latter is a long downhill par 5 (594 yards), with a narrow landing area and a tight green. I think my enjoyment related to achieving a par despite an enormous head wind. I hit driver, 3 metal, 3 metal and pitching wedge…with the last shot rolling to within two feet of the hole for a tap-in par.

Location Characteristics: Arcadia Bluffs is situated along the Lake Michigan shoreline, in the middle of nowhere. After departing the ferry from Wisconsin, we drove more than an hour to the resort, with few (if any) businesses being open. We arrived just after the "season" and the Lower Peninsula was beginning to shut down. Even in season, there appeared little to do in the immediate area other than golf. This is great for me, but my wife had trouble keeping occupied. Like many links courses, there is long fescue grass lining the fairways. As they had a drought this year, the grass was thinner, and most balls could be found and played. The course offers rolling topography with panoramic views of Lake Michigan from nearly every hole.

Comments: I absolutely enjoyed my round at Arcadia Bluffs, the gusty conditions notwithstanding. Most people choose to take a cart, many with a forecaddie. The topography was mildly challenging to an old guy like me, but we finished the round in about 3.5 hours. I recommend the caddie if you have a day to recover, or are part mountain goat. It was a bit easier to walk than Bethpage Black. The black tees were longer than I might have preferred, but the white tees seemed a bit short. If you can, stay at the resort for a relaxing experience and good meals. By the way, the 19th hole at Arcadia Bluffs is rated in the top 10. As the first leg of the big three, Arcadia Bluffs is a must.

Round 73 — Forest Dunes

Course Rank: 45

Date Played: September 18, 2012

Starting Time: 10:40 a.m.

Weather: 50 degrees, 10-15 mph wind, schizophrenic, with sun, then clouds, then sun, then clouds, literally changing every hole. Craziest weather I have seen…and cold.

My Score: 82

Number of Lost Balls: 0, although I had to dig one out of the water hazard on No. 8.

Highlights: 2 birdies and 7 pars

Lowlights: 3 double bogeys

Excuse for Not Breaking 80: Mental lapses on Nos. 4 through 9, where I was seven over, with a couple of truly uninspired shots. My 38 on the backside was one of my best nines in a long time.

Greens Fee: $100 special booked through Boyne Mountain Resort. The usual cost is still a bargain at $115.

Playing Partners: John, from Cincinnati. A really fun guy, who ingratiated himself by treating me to a single malt after the round. Despite a recent stroke, he had done a great job of adapting his game.

Practice Facilities: Very good, with plenty of open areas to work on all parts of the game. The most important is undoubtedly the putting green. I think they were rolling at 12 on the stimpmeter when I played. The greens were very true as evidenced by my lack of three-putts. Arrive early and get the game tuned up.

My Rating: 8+, with a series of terrific golf holes in great condition. The course is a bit out of the way, and had light play when I was there…again, after the "season." Nearly every hole offered something to appreciate.

Absolutely Must Play: Yes, again in concert with Arcadia Bluffs and Bay Harbor; you will have an exceptional golf vacation. Combine it with a trip to Whistling Straits (just across the lake) and it becomes an amazing golf experience.

Favorite Hole: The course begins strongly, with a picturesque front nine, meandering through the forest. No. 2, a long par 4, was my favorite, as it places a premium on an accurate tee shot and precise approach with a low iron. The hole provides a good preview of coming attractions.

Location Characteristics: Forest Dunes occupies an isolated location away from most of the Lower Peninsula resort areas. I booked the round through Boyne Resorts, even though my room was over an hour away from the facility. Once in the neighborhood (you may need to ignore your GPS), it is a scenic drive through the forest. The course includes numerous water hazards. I am not sure if the location led to the crazy weather, but I alternated between two and four layers of clothing during the round. The great condition in concert with the rural scenic environment makes Forest Dunes a must. Many of those I spoke with during the trip indicated this layout to be their favorite of the public courses in Michigan.

Comments: I had a great time at Forest Dunes. It helped that I was generally playing well, and hitting a lot of great shots. The fast but true greens helped my putting. Although it was cold, the wind was down somewhat from the rest of my trip, so I did not experience the frustration of watching a ball get tossed into the rough…or worse. This course was a pleasant surprise, a borderline top 25 venue on my list. This is one that should not be missed, even if you have to spend some time in Michigan.

Round 74 — Bay Harbor (Links/Quarry)

Course Rank: 38

Date Played: September 19, 2012

Starting Time: 10:00 a.m. schedule, pushed back to 10:40 a.m. as the resort screwed up the booking, and had me originally playing the Links/Preserve combination.

Weather: 50 degrees, cloudy, with 10 mph winds. It never got much warmer.

My Score: 81

Number of Lost Balls: 1, a stupid fade into the water on No. 13.

Highlights: 11 pars

Lowlights: 2 double bogeys

Excuse for Not Breaking 80: Too cold. After a brilliant front side of 38, frostbite set in (O.K. maybe that is a bit of an exaggeration from a SoCal native) and I went six over on Nos. 11 through 14.

Greens Fee: Quoted rate is $159; however, I booked it as part of a very affordable golf package at Boyne Mountain.

Playing Partners: Shawn and Chuck from Detroit. They struggled a bit on the challenging layout, but both had good swings and kept the pace moving.

Practice Facilities: Good, although it was a bit confusing finding the driving range across the street. You are supposed to follow some colored lines.

My Rating: 8+, with a slight nod to the Links nine over the Quarry. Despite freezing, the views were excellent, especially along the water.

Absolutely Must Play: Yes, see Arcadia Bluffs and Forest Dunes. Bay Harbor is a very cool layout, and like the other Michigan courses, offers a unique and enjoyable experience. It is definitely a top 50 course, and maybe top 25.

Favorite Hole: Ironically, although I liked the Links nine better, my favorite holes were No. 12 and 14 on the Quarry. Hole 12 begins the adventure into the quarry, and is a challenging par 5. My favorite, however, is No. 14, a long par 4 with a forced carry over water, and an approach, again over water, to a green backed by a steep quarry wall (reportedly with a waterfall, although I missed that part). Every hole on the Links nine rated highly in my book.

Location Characteristics: Playing Bay Harbor is slightly reminiscent of Pebble Beach or the Ocean Course at Kiawah, in that you must enter an exclusive gated residential community. The place oozes exclusivity on a level matched by few (although not quite like Shadow Creek). The course is situated on the bluffs above Lake Michigan, with views down to an enclave of spectacular waterfront homes. There are dramatic panoramas during the early holes of the Links nine. The Links course is of a links design (duh!) with few trees but plenty of trouble, especially down the embankments. The Quarry nine heads into the woods, before emerging into a quarry with 40-foot sheer walls and plenty of water, and ends with two holes along the lake. It is a fascinating location, characterized by numerous unique golf holes, and, to some extent, defies any specific definition.

Overall: Bay Harbor was the third of the "big three" Lower Peninsula golf courses that were included in this journey. Because of the huge differences between the nines, there was great variation, which I personally enjoyed. I suspect The Preserve nine would also be interesting, and would like to play that layout as well. In combination with Arcadia Bluffs and Forest Dunes, Bay Harbor made for a terrific three days of golf. The setting of Bay Harbor, once I reconciled with my GPS, was terrific. Other than the unseasonably cold weather, I thought the golf was exceptional.

Trip Summary:

Despite the mental lapse at Tullymore, the Wisconsin/Michigan boondoggle was one of my favorite trips of all time. I was again reminded of why I recommend Whistling Straits to anyone who will listen. Further, all three of the Michigan courses were clearly top 100 worthy. In fact, all three are definitely in my top 50. The entire flight back from Milwaukee was spent trying to figure out which of three courses I liked best. No obvious selection jumped to mind. I then asked myself if I could only play one of them again, which it would be. Each offered such unique and compelling characteristics that it was impossible to make a final determination. My recommendation is go out of your way to play the Lower Peninsula (side trip to Wisconsin if you have the time) and play each of them. Your preference is likely to be highly personal. The best recommendation I can make is to create a perfect itinerary, and stick to it. The logistics are complex, and, if you are like me, the aging brain can only process and remember so much.

Chapter 35

The Home Stretch

It has now been five months since the embarrassment of my Tullymore golf bungle. In that time, I have made no inroads on my quest to complete the top 100, due primarily to a lack of warm weather sites remaining. *Golf Magazine* released the new list (2012). Fortunately, there were only five new courses, and only one, Pronghorn in Bend, Oregon, in the top 50. I have made the executive decision, after consulting with myself, and my bankbook, that I will stick to the 2010 list.

During my self-imposed exile, I was working to solve logistical issues related to finalizing my journey. It is my hope to complete the top 100 by February 2014, when we are planning a trip to Kauai to celebrate Greta Strong's 50th birthday, and will knock out Princeville at that time. This assumes they do not decide to redo the greens again (see Chapter 21). To be successful, I will need to play the remaining 26 courses in 12 months. With "The Donald" closing Doral for renovation in April, and the WGC event in March, an expedited trip to Florida is a must. I may be pushing it, but a trip to Reynolds Plantation will be added to this trip. I have two Mississippi courses scheduled for the first week in April, as it is on the way to Boston (sort of) to see my daughter perform again. Her graduation in May provides another opportunity to finish off the East Coast, with Atlantic City and Bulle Rock on the schedule. I will need to bring a chauffeur to New Jersey, as I may have an outstanding bench warrant (more on that later). After, completing the East Coast swing, things get a bit dicey. I was conned (quite willingly) into agreeing to join Charlie Wilde on a crazy Scotland golf extravaganza. As best I can tell, there are no top 100 USA courses across the pond. We will, however, play a number of top 100 in the world, which Charlie assures me should be the subject of my next book.

By the time I return from Scotland the first week in June, I will still have 17 courses remaining. I can check off five with a scenic Des Moines, Galena (IL), Peoria, French Lick and Columbus trek. O.K., not so scenic, but it will be cheap. In September I am considering a quick trip to Tulsa and back to Austin for another three, and October is a good time for CordeValle in Northern California, as well as the big three on the Monterey Peninsula. With the finish scheduled in Hawaii, that only leaves the dreaded final four.

To date I have spent numerous hours trying to plan trips to Branson, Missouri; Bismarck, North Dakota; and North Platte, Nebraska, not to mention a return to Grand Rapids, Michigan for Tullymore…again. The problem is that none of these trips are particularly compatible with one another. Even putting two together is proving a challenge. Due to weather concerns I will probably have to complete these courses between June and September, and that may be pushing it for Bismarck.

Aside from golf planning, the last five months have been largely uneventful, with the exception of learning that my boy Rory took the big bucks and switched to Nike. He has now played horribly in back-to-back events, and I cannot help but feel the clubs are part of the problem. His talent, however, like Tiger's, will likely win out in the end. But, alas, I am still not buying any products with a swoosh.

Chapter 36

Dad, Are You Sure You Want to Do This?

I always like golfing with my son. He is unfailingly practical, and usually willing to tag along on my crazy golf excursions if I will pay the bill. It was not surprising that he rolled his eyes when I offered a proposed itinerary for late February. By necessity, I needed to get to Doral before Donald Trump closed the course after the WGC golf event. His planned renovation will undoubtedly add some "Disneyesque" flavor to the course, but I cannot wait a year to check this off the list if I want to finish by February 2014. I had hoped to combine the Doral round with a cruise over the Christmas holidays, but that idea never gained traction. A single trek to Miami and back for one course seemed wasteful, so I studied the map and determined that the Atlanta area would be open for business during my proposed trip.

"You know, the weather might not be very good that time of year," my son casually remarked. However, I figured I was due for some good luck, so I added the two Reynolds Plantation courses and Cuscowilla to the itinerary. A quick flight from Fort Lauderdale to Atlanta was all that was needed for three additional check marks.

Later, as I was planning my Mississippi excursion, I realized that the Alabama course was much closer to Atlanta then to Biloxi. As such, I added the Grand National "Bobby Jones Trail" course to the Florida/Georgia itinerary.

By the time I was done, I had a seven-day trip that included a flight to Fort Lauderdale from San Diego (one lost day) and two days in Miami, before flying out the second night to Atlanta. A 90-minute drive from Atlanta to Cuscowilla for one night, and then a short jog to Reynolds Plantation for two nights and two rounds, followed by a three-plus hour drive to Opelika, Alabama, for two nights and one round each on the Grand National courses, before a mad dash to Atlanta to catch a flight back to San Diego. Logistically, this was a well-conceived way to knock off five courses, albeit not a very relaxing vacation. My son, being the good sport that he is, agreed to take a week off work and put up with my addiction. I was not too worried about the weather in Florida. As for the *rest* of the trip...

Round 75 — Doral Blue Monster

Course Rank: 98

Date Played: February 26, 2013 (unilaterally changed by the pro shop from February 25)

Starting Time: 8:00 a.m.

Weather: 82 degrees, rising to 86, with partly cloudy skies and 20 mph wind gusts…not to mention high humidity.

My Score: 86

Number of Lost Balls: 3, including two on No. 10 where I pulled my Tin Cup impression…again.

Highlights: 1 birdie and 6 pars

Lowlights: 1 double bogey and 1 quadruple bogey

Excuse for Not Breaking 80: Mostly it was the 10th hole. A duck hook into the lake on this horseshoe shaped par 5, followed by an ill-advised attempt to cut too much of the corner on the third shot, led to a quadruple bogey. Four, three-putts on the last 10 holes did not help.

Greens Fee: We partook of the stay-and-play package, which is probably the only realistic way to go, as they charge $315 otherwise. The golf package has an upcharge for playing this course, as opposed to the other four offerings on-site.

Playing Partners: Son Charlie and Elmer, a retired corrections worker from outside of Buffalo. Elmer is one of those lucky government workers who can quit after 25 years with a huge pension and then screws it up by staying in upstate New York. We were also joined by Jonathon, our walking caddie, who had four years of experience on the Blue Monster, but was being displaced by Trump during the renovation. As such, he had decided to embark on a new career.

Practice Facilities: I did not spend much time at the practice facilities, which seemed like they would get a bit crowded trying to serve four courses. There was a large putting green, and, I suspect a short game area near the Jim McLean Golf Academy. Special note: they have free 30-minute golf schools for guests at the hotel. I elected not to partake, as I figure they are just used to promote more lessons.

My Rating: 8. I was pleasantly surprised because, as noted earlier, I generally do not care for South Florida golf, but the Dick Wilson (same architect as my home course at La Costa) design was fun. But, like La Costa, there are too many sand traps. There was also plenty of water. I suspect the condition was a bit better than usual, as the WGC Cadillac Championship was scheduled to commence a week after we played. The rough was up and the greens were very true and very fast.

Absolutely Must Play: No. The course was better than the 98 rating; however, the experience of getting to Miami and dealing with the people (more on this later) mitigated the pleasure. Nevertheless, if you find yourself in Miami, or are taking a cruise out of Fort Lauderdale, you should try and find your way to Doral. Take a second day to play the Great White Course. The last six holes of this second venue are great.

Favorite Hole: The Blue Monster (No. 18) actually lives up to its billing, although I brought it to its knees with a great drive into the wind and a four iron to the green. (We won't talk about the three putts because of the ridiculous pin position.)

Location Characteristics: Located in the teeming and trying metropolis of Miami, Doral is situated under the flight path to Miami International Airport. Those great big birds landing on the tarmac just a mile away are the highlights of the wildlife. Actually, the flat landscape is highly improved with palm trees, lakes and mounded greens, as well as a plethora of sand traps waiting for the stray shot. Prevailing winds add to the difficulty of the course.

Overall: I enjoyed my round at Doral, more so than I expected. It was hot and humid, but after a comparatively cold winter in San Diego, I was ready for some warmth. Further, it takes no time to warm up. I strongly recommend the walking caddie. They will assign you a forecaddie anyway, and once they put up the ropes, you will walk farther from the cart. It is less windy in the mornings, so you might think about an early tee time. The golf shop is well stocked, and, despite trying to operate four courses from one central staging area, things went smoothly…until the valets forgot to send down my clubs and I had to wait 20 minutes, killing any chance to warm up. I liked the golf more than the resort, but Trump is planning to renovate everything, so things may change. Regardless, the exact course I played will not be available in the future.

Round 76 Cuscowilla

Course Rank: 33

Date Played: February 27, 2013

Starting Time: 11:00 a.m. Due to limited play and our caddie's golf match later in the day, we moved this time up to 10:15.

Weather: 55 degrees, partly cloudy with 10-15 mph winds.

My Score: 85

Number of Lost Balls: 1

Highlights: 1 birdie and 5 pars

Lowlights: 4 double bogeys

Excuse for Not Breaking 80: Aside from the punched greens, which are brutal even when perfect, the course was saturated with water. Depending upon whom you believe, they had experienced seven inches of rain in the prior five days, or 14 inches in the last two weeks. Either way, I probably hit at least eight "splats" that caused my approach shots to come up short.

Greens Fee: We booked a stay-and-play package with the resort, with the quoted rate being $120. This includes the forecaddie.

Playing Partners: Son Charlie, and our caddie, Jay.

Practice Facilities: Cuscowilla is situated in a gate-guarded community with no shortage of land. The driving range occupies a very wide area, although only a few stations were set up. It is not the most exciting view (barn in the background), but serves the purpose. The practice area is very good and the putting green ample, although this was also aerated.

My Rating: 8+. The Coore & Crenshaw design is loaded with excellent golf holes. We were playing during the swing season with dormant fairways, leafless trees, punched greens and waterlogged fairways, yet the attractive nature of the golf course could easily be discerned. I liked the mix of holes, which required all kinds of shot making.

Absolutely Must Play: Yes; as part of the greater Reynolds Plantation excursion, this one is not to be missed. There are too many excellent golf holes, and the environment is very pleasing.

Favorite Hole: I loved the intimidation factor on No. 10, but this was equally present on No. 14. This latter hole is a 590-yard par 5 with a forced carry over a large lake. After 300 yards generally downhill, the hole rises dramatically to an elevated green. I hit the ball very well on the hole, including a driver, 3 wood and a 4 iron. It did not help that the wind was in our face. The green is also well-bunkered.

Location Characteristics: Cuscowilla is situated outside Eatonton, Georgia, on Lake Oconee. This massive lake is also home to Reynolds Plantation, which houses two top 100 courses. The area is defined by rolling hills, pine trees and numerous lakes, ponds and creeks. The project is situated about 45 minutes south of Augusta, and becomes a "hopping" place during the Masters. The natural features of the terrain and landscape make an excellent canvas upon which to create a fabulous golf course. Weather is definitely a factor, with wet and cold winters, and hot and humid summers making golf less attractive to the non-addict.

Overall: We enjoyed the round at Cuscowilla. Jay was well-versed in the course, got the distances right and coped well on the reads, despite the aeration. He had plenty of good stories, including the variation on the novice golfer trying to teach the more novice golfer how to play the game while firing a 66 on the front side. It should be noted that public play on Cuscowilla is only available Tuesday to Thursday, although you might check with the resort to see if packages are available on weekends. You will definitely enjoy the par 70 Coore & Crenshaw design, which offers several short holes, but more than compensates with some very difficult ones. It is a testimony to the attractiveness of the golf course that I was so impressed despite the weather, soggy fairways, dormant grass and punched greens. This one is definitely worth the 90-minute trip from Atlanta.

Round 77 Reynolds Plantation (Oconee)

Course Rank: 57

Date Played: February 28, 2013

Starting Time: 10:30 a.m. (shotgun start, we were sent off No. 10)

Weather: Cold (48 degrees to start), breezy (15-20 mph) and partly cloudy.

My Score: 81

Number of Lost Balls: 1

Highlights: 10 pars

Lowlights: 1 double bogey

Excuse for Not Breaking 80: As with Cuscowilla, the saturated fairways led to several sloshy shots that tacked several strokes on to the final tally.

Greens Fee: $250, although you probably will get a package deal, as you need to stay in one of the participating resorts.

Playing Partners: Son Charlie, who was starting to wear down. He enjoys golf, but does not have the addiction.

Practice Facilities: Adequate, with short game practice area and putting green. Because of the shotgun start, the practice areas were crowded.

My Rating: 8+. A really classy layout that does a great job of incorporating the natural surroundings, especially the lake.

Absolutely Must Play: Yes. A true addict needs to play the Reynolds Plantation courses, with a side trip to Cuscowilla. The finishing holes are exceptional, with very good par 3s, and plenty of differentiation in the layout and design. Oconee requires precise shot making.

Favorite Hole: No. 16 was a terrific hole, but they had a similar one at Great Waters that was my favorite at that venue. Each of the final four is exceptional in its own right, but I liked No. 9 best. This very challenging par 4 has trouble all along the right side, consisting of Lake Oconee, with the second shot into this green being quite daunting as the green is tucked into the lake.

Location Characteristics: Like Cuscowilla and Great Waters, the course is situated in the Lake Oconee area 90 minutes outside of Atlanta, on the way to Augusta. The holes are either lined with thick pines, or bordered by the lake. We were too early for the blooms, but dogwood and azalea are common throughout these courses. The rolling topography and a few well-utilized creeks add to the ambience. Given the proximity, this facility is likely to mirror the visual appeal of Augusta in season.

Overall: My penny-pinching decision to attack this course during swing season resulted in less than ideal conditions. The water-logged fairways severely limited the roll and caused several fat shots. The dormant fairways are not as attractive as during the peak season. Nevertheless, this type of golf is some of my favorite, and the Rees Jones design offered interesting views, and required great shot making. Atlanta offers good access, so there is no excuse not to take advantage of the great courses northeast of the city.

Round 78 Reynolds Plantation (Great Waters)

Course Rank: 37

Date Played: March 1, 2013

Starting Time: 10:30 a.m. (shotgun start, we began on No. 16)

Weather: A chilly 45 degrees, rising to 52 degrees, with 5-10 mph winds and partly cloudy skies.

My Score: 84

Number of Lost Balls: 1

Highlights: 8 pars

Lowlights: 2 double bogeys

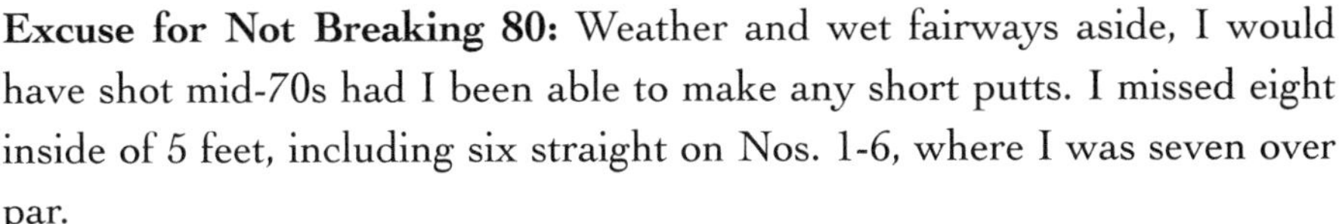

Excuse for Not Breaking 80: Weather and wet fairways aside, I would have shot mid-70s had I been able to make any short putts. I missed eight inside of 5 feet, including six straight on Nos. 1-6, where I was seven over par.

Greens Fee: $250 if you are staying at the resort and are not on a package.

Playing Partners: Son Charlie, who thinks Jack Nicklaus is a sadist.

Practice Facilities: Pretty similar to Oconee, with the requisite driving range, short game area and large putting green. They had a second putting green near the first tee box. I especially liked the new TaylorMade range balls at both Reynolds Plantation courses.

My Rating: 8+, although in combination with Oconee and Cuscowilla represents a 9 overall experience. Again, the rating might have been higher in season, with dry fairways and warmer temperatures.

Absolutely Must Play: Yes. I suspect these courses provide the closest experience to Augusta of any in the top 100, plus the added benefit of the lake influence.

Favorite Hole: Great Waters offers plenty of great holes, with Nos. 9, 16, 17 and 18 getting honorable mentions. My favorite was No. 5, which, like No. 16 at Oconee, offers a meandering stream running along the left side of the fairway, before turning across in front of the green, making the approach shot challenging. On both of these holes I dropped a ball in the greenside creek. Nevertheless, these are exciting golf holes, with each shot being terrific, and both greens offer additional challenges.

Location Characteristics: Generally, very similar to Oconee, with a bit more lake influence, and a few more level shots. The housing along this course, which is situated outside of the primary Reynolds Plantation area, is attractive to those of us that enjoy some non-natural surroundings.

Overall: I usually have trouble with Nicklaus courses; however, despite the weather I was striking the ball very well. The putting was my fault…just one of those things. I liked this course as much as Oconee, although it was good to get some variation.

Round 79 — Grand National (Lake)

Course Rank: 88

Date Played: March 2, 3, 2013 (Due to weather, the round was completed over two days.)

Starting Time: 1:30 p.m. and 8:30 a.m.

Weather: Snow flurries, sleet, 34 degrees, 10-15 mph wind (25 windchill factor)

My Score: 86

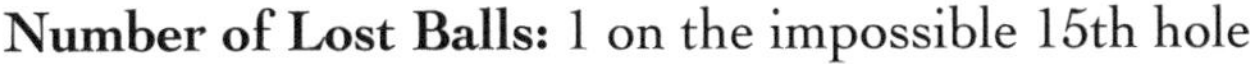

Number of Lost Balls: 1 on the impossible 15th hole

Highlights: 9 pars

Lowlights: 5 double bogeys

Excuse for Not Breaking 80: See weather. This is the coldest I have ever been in my life, especially on the second day. Four layers of clothes were about three too few. I had no feeling in my hands and the ball felt like a rock. Despite the weather, the course was packed.

Greens Fee: $82, plus $17 for the cart.

Playing Partners: Solo for the back nine, son Charlie and a couple of ringers for the front nine, until they gave up due to the cold.

Practice Facilities: Seemed O.K., but with a distinct "municipal" feel. The range was a long, cold drive from the pro shop. There was ice in the bucket to wash your clubs.

My Rating: *7*, heavily influenced by the weather. There were some interesting holes, but the condition was inferior. The course gets a lot of play (where else would they be fully booked in arctic conditions?) and does not have the exclusive feel of some of the more resort venues.

Absolutely Must Play: No, although the course is part of the Bobby Jones trail, which is probably a must for the avid golfer. Grand National also offers the Links Course, which is almost on par with the Lakes. Thus, you have two good layouts together. For the budget conscious, this facility offers excellent value.

Favorite Hole: The sadistic No. 15, a 182-yard par 3 into the wind playing 200+ yards with the back right pin placement, and water in play the whole way. This was also my least favorite hole. Over two rounds I put three straight in the lake, as the wind pushed every shot right of the green, and short. Maybe with a little warmer weather it would have been possible, but no lay up area made it a nightmare.

Location Characteristics: The Lake Course at Grand National is situated along a lake in the woods of eastern Alabama. It was too cold to notice much of the surroundings, but know the pine-lined fairways are ready to snag the errant shot. The water has been nicely incorporated into the design, and comes into play on about half the holes. As for Opelika, Alabama, there is little reason to visit. A couple of nice restaurants in the redeveloped downtown district offer good food, but the neighborhood is generally depressing. This is SEC country, with Auburn University located nearby and dominating local development. The best hotel in town, the Marriott, was substandard by this chain's normal operations. After Doral and Reynolds Plantation, everything was a step down.

Overall: I am sure the Bobby Jones Trail is a great experience when the temperature creeps above 40 degrees. Granted, it was "swing season," but it should have been more comfortable. The unusual cold definitely detracted from the experience. The dormant Bermuda grass made it less attractive, but you could still discern an overall beauty to the course. Special kudos to the staff, who worked diligently to get me on the back nine on Saturday, knowing that between an expected frost delay and flight from Atlanta Sunday afternoon, I was not going to be able to complete the entire round on Sunday morning.

Trip Summary:

I used to think Dave Barry was a great and inventive comedic writer. Having spent two days in the Miami area, however, I now know the real secret. If I lived in Miami, I could easily write great comedy merely by observing the local populace. I have never seen a more dysfunctional group of people. Without a doubt these are the worst drivers in the cosmos. I had people pass me at over 100 miles per hour on the freeway, in the slow lane, while having to slam on my brakes when running up the rear end of a doddering octogenarian going 35 mph in the fast lane. What's worse, this occurred during my first three miles on the freeway. It was so bad that we had to detour to the airport on our way back from the car rental lot, when a black Mustang that had just been the subject of an upgrade by the counter clerk had a major accident leaving the parking lot. I found much of the local populace to be quirky, arrogant, ignorant, slow, fast and generally eclectic. I cannot think of a better match than Donald Trump and the Miami citizenry. Doral is worth the effort if you find yourself in south Florida.

Reynolds Plantation, outside of Atlanta, is something special for golfers. All three of the top 100 courses in the area were exceptional despite the weather, wetness and dormant fairways. There are a couple of good local eateries, but not much else. After Miami, that was fine. I will definitely make a return trip.

Likewise, I will probably make the sojourn again to play the Bobby Jones Trail in Alabama, although it will be a trip unto itself. Hopefully, some of the other venues will offer more than Opelika. With the affordability of the trail comes some concession with respect to condition, overplay and general course ambience.

Only a crazy person would plan a golf trip around the Miami, Reynolds Plantation, Alabama troika, but being the Type "A" person that I am, I welcomed the challenge. I was able to complete Trump's course before it was closed, while knocking off four other out- of-the-way venues. Overall, the trip was hectic, but ultimately proved successful (despite the frostbite). I really should rethink the swing-season trips.

Chapter 37

Mississippi Has Golf Courses?

Since I began my adventure I have been joking about having to travel to Choctaw, Mississippi. I figure coastal Mississippi is bad enough, but three-and-a-half hours north of the Gulf cannot be something anyone would enjoy. My only consolation is the belief that a course must be pretty exceptional to get a decent ranking, especially when located in the middle of nowhere.

I had the Rolodex working overtime trying to recruit a partner (or partners) for this little adventure. The good news about Mississippi is that it is not too expensive. The bad news is that it is Mississippi. The silence was deafening as I put out feelers. My son was still recovering from his recent frostbite adventure. The more daring Charlie Wilde was too busy trying to figure out how to break it to his wife that he was going to Scotland...again. My brothers were excited about a golf trip, but wanted to go someplace where English was spoken. Joe Strong was only committing to the high-end locations, and was headed to the Yankees' spring training camp. The members back at La Costa were too busy planning their Bandon Dunes trip, which I would be missing for my daughter's graduation (and a couple of other top 100 venues). Scott Rand wanted to thaw out after a delightful Wisconsin winter, but was out of vacation time. Ultimately, my expectations were met...no one wanted in on this one. I finally convinced my wife to go (though not a golfer), but she wanted to stop in New Orleans on the way to check out another military museum. She would take care of the culture, and I would spend my time on Bourbon Street, the exact opposite of culture. We could then meet up to enjoy the local cuisine.

With expectations low, I packed up the sticks and a few days' worth of clothes and headed for the Big Easy. The real highlight of the trip was going to be the added days in Boston to see our recently blonde daughter perform the role of Elle Woods in *Legally Blonde*. Initial weather reports were O.K., with some rain possible, but temperatures above 50 degrees were predicted at both golfing locales. This would feel like a sauna after the Alabama fiasco.

Round 80 Fallen Oak Golf Club (at Beau Rivage)

Course Rank: 27

Date Played: April 1, 2013

Starting Time: 9:00 a.m.

Weather: 60 degrees, with 5-10 mph winds and cloudy skies. As the skies cleared, the temperature rose into the 70s.

My Score: 82

Number of Lost Balls: None, although I had to pull a ball out of the lake on No. 3.

Highlights: 1 birdie and 8 pars

Lowlights: 2 double bogeys

Excuse for Not Breaking 80: My notoriously slow start, which left me six over par after five holes.

Greens Fee: $200, and you must stay at Beau Rivage Resort and Casino. The round is "comped" if you bet enough money at the tables. Unfortunately, that would probably increase the cost of the round by at least tenfold.

Playing Partners: I played this one on my own. Of course, they only had seven players scheduled the entire day. As a result, the round took less than 2.5 hours…so I played a second round, nicely comped by the head pro.

Practice Facilities: Significantly above average, despite the minimal level of play. There is an attractive range, an exceptional short game area and several putting greens. It is worth getting there early.

My Rating: 9, for the terrific condition, great staff, exceptional facilities and highly attractive Fazio design. Fallen Oak is the poster child for how a golf facility should be run. Of course, it is largely subsidized by the gamblers. Thanks, losers.

Absolutely Must Play: Yes. They model themselves after Shadow Creek in Las Vegas, and while they are not quite on that level, it is nevertheless an exceptional experience, beginning with the gated entry, to the attractive drive back to the clubhouse, to the well-maintained and very comfortable golf carts. The generally low level of play results in a round that keeps moving. I have no suggestions for improvement...unless they could locate somewhere closer to Southern California.

Favorite Hole: Fazio courses do not always offer the most dramatic holes, but there were plenty of very good ones at Fallen Oak, especially those that utilized the local water features. No. 18 stood above the rest, with the hole slightly reminiscent of other great finishing holes I have played. The hole offers water on the left side, and plays extremely long if you are conservative off the tee. This downhill, 429-yard par 4, has nasty bunkering along the left, which is only marginally better than the lake just beyond. To the right is an enormous oak tree that blocks all shots into the green (I was stymied behind this tree each time I played the hole). I also had to deal with grandstands that were being removed after completion of a Senior PGA Tour event played there the prior week. The long approach shot is difficult, with the lake on the left collecting errant shots.

Location Characteristics: Fallen Oak is situated about 20 minutes north of Beau Rivage, where you will be staying. This hotel is located on the Gulf of Mexico, and is regularly frequented by hurricanes. The golf course itself is tucked away from the water, although the elevation is not that high. Fallen Oak is a relatively level layout, with generous fairways (typical of a Fazio course) lined with thickets of unforgiving pines, or water elements, including several large lakes. There are a number of oaks from which the course gets its moniker, but few come into play, with the exception of the signature tree on No. 18. The course brags about the presence of an alligator, Hogan, who makes his home in the pond adjoining hole No. 1. I do not recall any parallel fairways that are not fully protected by pines. As such, if there are other golfers, you may not see them until the 19th hole, which, by the way, is one of the best around.

Overall: Over the course of my travels I have run into several extremely well-run courses. While some may be the equal of Fallen Oak, few provide a more relaxed golfing atmosphere, while offering a great eighteen holes of golf. If you like Shadow Creek, you will enjoy this experience as well, and at 40 percent of the cost. Sure, you miss the limo ride, but the exclusivity is readily apparent. Do not plan to take a shuttle from the resort, as one does not exist. You will need a car. From start to finish Fallen Oak is terrific, while being amazingly under-promoted by the hotel/casino. The $200 greens fee is about the same cost as 45 minutes at the $10 minimum blackjack tables. For those who stay at the hotel and do not partake of the golf, you are missing a treat.

Round 81 — Dancing Rabbit

Course Rank: 32

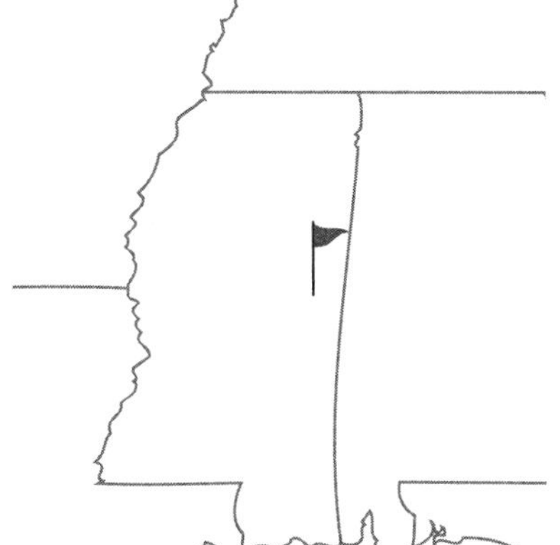

Date Played: April 3, 2013

Starting Time: 8:20 a.m.

Weather: 45 degrees, cloudy and drizzly with light winds. Bad enough that I had to don the rain gear.

My Score: 87

Number of Lost Balls: 2, despite some good finds in the forest and pulling one out of a creek.

Highlights: 3 birdies and 3 pars

Lowlights: 6 double bogeys

Excuse for Not Breaking 80: The very wet conditions that made the course play close to 7,000 yards. I had at least three drives back up in the fairway.

Greens Fee: $75, making it one of the better deals.

Playing Partners: With the weather conditions, everyone else was canceling, so I had the course to myself. I had played a practice round the day earlier with Joe, Jonathon and Brian, a regular group who make the sojourn to Dancing Rabbit from Austin twice a year. The solo round was a 2.5-hour tour of the course, despite spending plenty of time searching for missing balls.

Practice Facilities: Adequate, but not as inviting as Fallen Oak. The range was pretty beaten up and the balls were older. I did not see a short game area, but was hard pressed for time.

My Rating: 7+. A higher rating may have been in the offing had the greens not just been punched, the azaleas been blooming and the fairways less wet. The individual holes were, at times, brilliant. This Coore & Crenshaw course did not disappoint in terms of design and interesting holes. The condition, however, was not commensurate with the design quality. I suspect that the low greens fees encourage too much play for this course to absorb, especially in the swing season.

Absolutely Must Play: No. Although if you are looking for great value, there are few top 100 courses to match Dancing Rabbit. The golf package is very low priced, and there is a casino for evening activity. On the other hand, Choctaw is in the middle of nowhere, being a bit more than an hour from Jackson, Mississippi, a city that has never been on my bucket list.

Favorite Hole: There were several nice golf holes that incorporated the pine-lined fairways, elevation changes and small ponds and creeks running through the property. My favorite hole was the par 4 No. 9, a 403-yard dogleg right that requires a precise drive down the left side (which I failed to execute) in order to have an open line to a narrow, sloping green that is bounded on the left by a creek, and on the right by thick pines. Honorable mention goes to Nos. 5, 8 and 18, the latter of which is a sadist's treasure.

Location Characteristics: Situated in the central portion of Mississippi, Dancing Rabbit occupies a location that most will never experience. It is surprisingly beautiful country, with plenty of pines, birds, water features, etc. The crowds and weather discouraged many of the native species; however, several box turtles were sunning themselves along the pond at No. 18 the day earlier. The rolling terrain, amongst thick forests and water features, provides a pleasant atmosphere. Despite the outlying location, the roads were surprisingly good, consisting of two-lane highways in each direction, separated by a grass median. The tax dollars required to build and maintain these lightly traveled routes must be huge. Access is available via Jackson International Airport (a lightly utilized, expansive facility that also must also be highly subsidized).

Overall: The excellent Coore & Crenshaw design, no doubt, contributed to the very high *Golf Magazine* ranking, despite the isolated locale. The affordable greens fees, lodging, etc., are also attractive. I appreciated the fact that the local Native American tribe had committed to finding jobs for its members (this is not always the case at similar projects), however, by doing so, they appeared to have eschewed some outside assistance from experts. As a result, the effort was there, but delivery lacking. By comparison to Fallen Oak, the experience comes up short. The golf carts were old and dirty. Golf tees were not included in the carts. The GPS was state-of-the-art, but may have had some calibration issues, as distances did not match my rangefinder, and I was constantly warned I was too close to the green, despite being more than 100 yards away and often on a cart path. Ultimately, Dancing Rabbit is good, not great, and you get what you pay for. If you have not been pampered at some of the nation's exclusive resorts, this may be O.K.

Trip Summary:

I was pleasantly surprised with the Mississippi trip (low expectations). I found the state to be cleaner and more modern than I expected. Biloxi had some good restaurants, and Fallen Oak is an exceptionally well-run facility, offering first-class golf. Dancing Rabbit is a nice layout with some attractive golf holes that does not place a huge damper on the budget. However, it lacks some of the amenities offered at the majority of the top facilities. Having never been to New Orleans, I was glad I took the extra day to spend time in the French Quarter and try out the renowned Creole cuisine of the city. It was well worth the effort, and just a short drive to Biloxi. This may be a once-in-a-lifetime excursion for me, but I really think a golf junkie should find his way to Fallen Oak.

Chapter 38

Too Close For Comfort

My daughter completed her undergraduate education in the requisite four years, meaning that upon her graduation I will free up nearly $60,000 annually to pursue more practical endeavors (i.e. my golf game). It may even allow for some international travel. The prospects of said additional cash were cause for celebration, so my wife and I elected to go back and watch the graduation ceremony...just to make sure. Traveling to the opposite side of the country also provided an opportunity to knock off the last of the East Coast courses, namely Atlantic City Country Club and Bulle Rock, a Pete Dye layout dangerously close to Washington, D.C., outside of Baltimore.

I am always hesitant to go anywhere near the nation's capital. Being entrenched on the West Coast, it is easier to ignore professional politicians. However, this becomes more difficult as one nears the D.C. area. I was particularly perturbed by the breaking information that the IRS has been targeting conservative groups and donors for extra scrutiny. This only served to enhance my paranoia regarding my least favorite government entity.

The intrusion of Big Brother has long been a concern, but, to date, they have largely left the golf world alone. Nevertheless, I am always worried about new federal legislation and can envision such idiocy as the following:

Par would be increased by one stroke on each hole, thereby making the standard course a par 90. This would allow golfers to feel better about themselves.

Courses would be required to allocate 15 percent of rounds played to low and moderate income individuals at green fees equal to their ability to pay.

All courses would immediately be required to become ADA (Americans with Disabilities Act) compliant. Shuttles would be provided between holes, moving walkways would be installed to allow access to elevated tees, etc.

Caddies would immediately be recognized as part of a union, with all of the attendant benefits. Should caddies become tired while looping, they could request the golfer to carry their own clubs for up to three holes.

Golf tee times would be allocated in direct relation to the demographic makeup of the respective community.

The hole would be increased in size to allow for lower scoring.

Anchored putters would be legalized again.

Am I a cynic? It is amazing that the bastions of exclusivity (America's oldest country clubs) are still allowed to exist. I plan to steer clear of Washington during my travels.

First up, however, is a detour to Atlantic City, America's second "Sin City." It was fortuitous that my wife was along on this trip, as I may or may not have a bench warrant out for me in the state of New Jersey. It seems several years ago, upon arriving on a red-eye flight, I parked in a handicapped space at the Sheraton Newark Airport Hotel. There were numerous parking spaces available, but apparently the one I picked was designated handicapped. Even after receiving the citation the next morning, I could not see any evidence of the space being restricted, other than being adjacent to one with a blue sign. Although I will maintain my innocence forever, I still attempted to pay the fine by mail. The check was returned to me, indicating that I needed to make a court appearance in New Jersey. Needless to say, that has not happened. I have not heard anything since, but being locked up would make it difficult to arrive by my tee time at the Atlantic City Country Club.

Round 82 — Atlantic City Country Club

Course Rank: 91

Date Played: May 13, 2013

Starting Time: 11:10 a.m.

Weather: 60 degrees, with 10-15 mph winds and partly cloudy skies.

My Score: 81

Number of Lost Balls: None

Highlights: 1 birdie and 6 pars

Lowlights: 1 double bogey

Excuse for Not Breaking 80: Seven bogeys on the front side doomed my chances.

Greens Fee: $145

Playing Partners: Joe Strong, who had returned to his old stomping grounds for a family reunion.

Practice Facilities: Adequate; however, our driving range practice was interrupted by the landing of a private helicopter. Apparently, some of the rich locals like to arrive in style.

My Rating: 8, based upon the history of the club (constructed in 1897) and the bayside links design. The front nine is nothing exceptional, but the finish is worth the visit.

Absolutely Must Play: No, unless you find yourself in the area. I am not a big gambler, and Atlantic City is a bit of a dive. That said, I liked the golf. For a golf historian a detour might be warranted, as the ancient clubhouse has significant memorabilia and plenty of history.

Favorite Hole: No. 11 is a very sophisticated design that challenges any golfer, and No. 13 is a terrific and difficult par 5, but the most interesting hole is the short par 4, No. 14, which includes a blind carry over the bay, and a severe dogleg right to a small green, tucked against a lateral hazard. The approach shot is influenced by strong winds. The hole is not long and will yield some birdies, but double bogey or worse is always in the cards.

Location Characteristics: Atlantic City Country Club is a classic design, situated on the bay on the opposite side of downtown Atlantic City in a residential area of eastern New Jersey. Many of the holes offer views across the water to the casino towers. The course itself is relatively flat, and probably should be walked. The facility is home to a number of foxes, one of which spent much of the day following us around in the futile hope that we would offer some crumbs. This was the first time I had encountered domesticated foxes. They burrow into the bunkers, which can make for an interesting shot, especially when you have not previously noticed them and they make an appearance in your backswing (which actually did happen to us). There are few trees and not a lot of trouble, except where the bay encroaches, and everything slopes in that direction.

Overall: The facility is deserving of a top 100 ranking, but is properly located toward the bottom of the list. There are a few good holes, lots of great history and domesticated foxes. The opening tee shot off the practice putting green is also unique to this course. This par 70 layout is there for the taking, but subtle breaks and tough chip shots keep the scores up. The greens had been aerated just before we arrived and were difficult to navigate. In the final analysis, I think you will enjoy the course if you get there, but I would not plan a vacation around this one, unless taking the family to the Jersey Shore.

Round 83 — Bulle Rock

Course Rank: 36

Date Played: May 15, 2013

Starting Time: 9:00 a.m.

Weather: 60 degrees, cloudy with 5 to 10-mph winds.

My Score: 83

Number of Lost Balls: None

Highlights: 1 birdie and 7 pars

Lowlights: 2 double bogeys

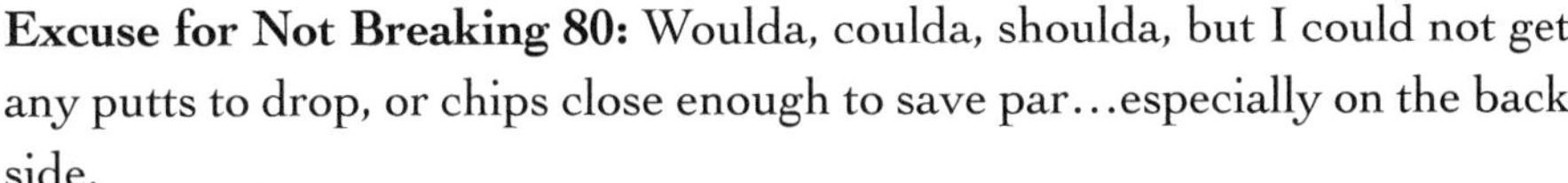

Excuse for Not Breaking 80: Woulda, coulda, shoulda, but I could not get any putts to drop, or chips close enough to save par…especially on the back side.

Greens Fee: $130.

Playing Partners: Joe Strong made his way down from New Jersey after running into Governor Christie and Prince Harry surveying Hurricane Sandy damage.

Practice Facilities: The range was a haul from the clubhouse. You might give yourself an extra fifteen minutes if you wish to warm up properly. Also, it is crucial to roll a few on the practice greens, as the stimpmeter reading was supposedly 13. Given the typical Pete Dye course, a three-putt is always lurking.

My Rating: 8+, given the great setting, number of terrific golf holes, value and one of the better-run operations.

Absolutely Must Play: Yes, although you need to flirt with the bad vibes surrounding Washington, D.C. I love Pete Dye designed tracks, and this one does not disappoint. Unfortunately, the course is not located within close proximity to other top-rated venues, so is more likely to be part of a non-golf holiday. Plan on playing a couple of rounds, as it will take several tours to appreciate all of the Dyeabolical design. Bulle Rock would be an excellent cornerstone of a dedicated golfing vacation if there were other, similar courses available.

Favorite Hole: Ironically, I am usually enamored of Pete (and Alice) Dye's par 3s; however, aside from No. 12, they were only good, not stunning. Instead, the par 5s were especially good, with No. 2 and No. 15 being special. However, my favorite hole was probably No. 13, a long par 4 that reminded me a bit of No. 8 at Pebble Beach. An aggressive drive would put you in trouble, with the proper tee shot leaving a long second to a very difficult elevated green (at Pebble Beach you hit down to the green). Par on this hole will be rare for the mid-to-high handicapper, with double bogey not being a bad score.

Location Characteristics: Situated on an old horse farm north of Baltimore, the location is bucolic, with gently sloping fairways and greens, as well as several creeks and lakes. There are forested areas, as well as open, links-style holes. The entrance features a long drive off the main road, and includes a stop sign for one-way traffic under a railroad bridge. New homes have been constructed above the course, but do not intrude upon the experience. Nearly everything about this course is first class, and the location only contributes to the enjoyment.

Overall: According to one of the employees on site, Bulle Rock was developed at about the same time as Whistling Straits. Apparently, both owners were seeking to create a facility that could host a major championship. Since Pete Dye was developing both, he was essentially given carte blanche to develop world-class golf courses on each site. As the story goes, the competition between the two developers was quite keen, with each attempting to outdo the other. Ultimately, what resulted were two great golf courses, but the Kohler people were hell-bent on outspending anyone in their way and therefore, Whistling Straits was able to play host to the PGA Championship. Despite finishing second in the "competition," Bulle Rock stands on its own as a great golf course. The proximity to Washington notwithstanding, the environment, the staff, the condition and the design all make this a worthwhile stop on your golfing journey.

Trip Summary:

I had expected to devote much of this chapter to my dislike and distrust of the federal government, but I steered clear of Washington, never venturing south of Baltimore. (My wife did make a run down to a museum in Quantico, and experienced the crazy traffic that characterizes the D.C. area.) Instead of Washington bashing, which I can save for another day, the trip was more influenced by my perception of Atlantic City. Having been to Las Vegas on many occasions, I was expecting a mini version on the East Coast. Instead what I found was a somewhat seedy community that had none of the buzz associated with Vegas. Granted, the newer hotels such as Harrah's, where we stayed, are standalone facilities that cater to every compulsive gambler's needs and were fine as far as accommodations. The Boardwalk was interesting for the first 500 feet, but then became redundant. The parking situation is ludicrous. Atlantic City has the only casinos I know of where they charge for parking. Similarly, you need to pay to park near the Boardwalk. The local area is characterized by public housing, and does not seem particularly safe.

As for the golf, both courses were fun, with Bulle Rock getting my vote as the better experience, but the history of Atlantic City Country Club should not be ignored. Both are good stops along the way, if you are vacationing in the region. Ultimately, I was, once again, reminded of how much I enjoy a Pete Dye course.

Chapter 39

Getting Sidetracked...Again

I like to think I have a reasonable level of self-control over my life decisions. I am generally good at saying no, but somehow my reasoning abilities get lost at the mention of golf, ergo the addiction. I had absolutely no business agreeing to a Scottish golf vacation, especially given my push to finish America's top 100. Yet, when frequent golf partner and certified golf geek Charlie Wilde approached me about joining a foursome set to conquer the great links courses of Scotland, I only hesitated for a moment before agreeing.

Ironically, Scotland was never at the top of my golf wish list. Sure, it is ground zero for golf history, and home to numerous recognizable tracts, but links golf has never had the same allure as a walk in the park with babbling brooks on a warm, sunny day. Links is bland. No trees, no lakes, thin lies and putting from 30 yards off the green is not my idea of golf. Add some wind, cold and rain and the appeal is lost on me. Crazy? Maybe, but I am one of the few who thinks the Bandon Dunes courses are overrated. Sure, I liked Arcadia Bluffs, Chambers Bay, Whistling Straits and Erin Hills, but I am not sure I would travel to a foreign land just for the pleasure of hacking around in a bunch of gorse.

And yet, I found myself boarding a red-eye flight from San Diego, through London Heathrow and on to Edinburgh to attack a new golf adventure that I thought could wait another decade. I always knew I would make the trek to play the great courses of Scotland; however, I never figured it would happen so soon. What makes someone throw his entire life into turmoil, spend the big bucks and mess with well-laid plans in order to whack a little white sphere all over a foreign land in hopes of losing it in small hole, only to start all over again? This is my cross to bear. On the plus side, I intend to chronicle the effort at some future date and seek additional tax write-offs. Further, I can now supplement my boring golf small talk with additional "international" insights, possibly assuring I will never get invited to another social gathering.

Chapter 40

If It's Wednesday, This Must Be Peoria

I had prolonged the inevitable as long as possible, but ultimately it became necessary to book a trip to America's heartland. I have nothing against the wonderful people living in Middle America, but let's be honest; few people choose to move to French Lick, Indiana. Originally, I had tried to arrange the trip to coincide with one of my true bucket list events, either the Kentucky Derby or Indianapolis 500. (Ironically, both events are held at venues within approximately two hours of French Lick.) Having failed on two occasions to pull it off, I resigned myself to a 36 hole-a-day marathon across the cornfields of the three Is (Indiana, Illinois and Iowa), with a quick stop in Ohio.

My initial analysis suggested one could fly to Columbus, Ohio, and work west to Des Moines. However, the drive from Columbus to French Lick was daunting, so we chose the alternative, which included flying to Ohio for a day, then taking a second flight back to Des Moines, from where we would make our way across the Mississippi River at Dubuque, duck down to Peoria, take a quick stop in Champaign, Illinois, for some business deductions...I mean meetings, and head on down to French Lick, before flying home from Louisville. At this point, you might want to skip this chapter, since no one, except the true junkie, would expose himself to such an excursion.

Aside from the travel nightmares, the choice of timing was also problematic, since there is no prime golf season in these areas. Winter is out, as the courses are likely to be closed. No one ever knows when spring will actually occur, creating huge risks with early planning. A second problem with early planning is that most courses do not allow reservations to be made more than 30 days in advance, unless you are on a stay-and-play package, which are not available at some of the venues. In summer, the likelihood of heat and humidity is very high, and in fall (which many deem to be the best season), you are likely to play with mosquitoes. I elected to take my chances during July, hoping the heat and humidity would only be bad for a day or two (I miscalculated on this one).

The most amazing thing about booking this trip is that I was able to convince my brother to join in the excursion. It turns out one of his childhood friends lives in Peoria. Even better, Scott Rand, my Wisconsin golf partner, disappointed that we would not be reprising Whistling Straits again, agreed to drive down and chauffeur us from Des Moines to Louisville. Always the joker, he arrived at the airport with his official chauffeur's hat and sign bearing the Laubach name. As such, what I envisioned as a solo expedition turned into a threesome. I suppose this made the incredible heat more bearable. Scott, apparently immune to both heat and humidity, seemed to relish the long hours in the sun. In fact, while Andy and I were meeting with business partners in Champaign, he went out and walked 18 holes at one of the local courses.

Did I mention the corn? We drove about 800 miles through the Midwest. Amazingly, nearly 30 miles of that total were *not* planted on either side of the roads or highways with corn. At least you will not waste many photos on the scenery. However, if you happen to be headed to Longaberger Golf Club, make sure and have the camera ready to take a picture of the Longaberger corporate headquarters building, which is designed to look like a basket. Alternatively, look it up online, and save the time.

We could not prevail upon Scott to make the trip to Columbus, but that is where we started our crazy Midwestern journey.

Round 84 — Longaberger Golf Club

Course Rank: 56

Date Played: July 14, 2013

Starting Time: 1:00 p.m.

Weather: 85 degrees to start, with 75 percent humidity, sunny skies and 5-10 mph winds.

My Score: 78

Number of Lost Balls: 2

Highlights: 3 birdies and 7 pars

Lowlights: 1 double bogey

Excuse for Not Breaking 80: None

Greens Fee: $50, as this was a replay round. The morning round was $99, which is their premium rate.

Playing Partners: Brother Andy. We were joined on hole 5 by Kevin, a member who plays 72 holes every weekend. The foursomes in front were speed challenged, so it was nice to get a partner.

Practice Facilities: They have an elevated driving range, which is nice, although my station had a downward slope. This is good for working on downhill lies, but threw me off. The range was somewhat chewed up and the balls were older. There were a couple of putting greens.

My Rating: 7 with some good holes, but nothing great.

Absolutely Must Play: No, but you will get good value if you are in the area. Longaberger is situated nearly an hour east of Columbus, Ohio, making access problematic for most.

Favorite Hole: Most of the holes were decent, but not spectacular. I liked Nos. 4 and 18, but thought No. 8 was the most interesting. This 420-yard par 4 offers a split fairway and green surrounded on three sides by water.

Location Characteristics: Longaberger Golf Club occupies a typical Midwest location, in the rural area outside the city limits of Columbus. The area is characterized by numerous farms, most of which grow corn. There is a bit more topography to the course than one expects in the area. The first twelve holes are situated amongst wooded terrain, before exiting into a farmland area, with few trees. There are creeks and ponds that come into play throughout.

Overall: Longaberger Golf Club is borderline top 100, with difficult accessibility and minimal local synergy with other golf courses. I would be surprised if I made the trek back again, although I found the golf fine. Ultimately, there is nothing compelling enough about the facility that would warrant going out of your way.

Round 85 — The Harvester Golf Club

Course Rank: 53

Date Played: July 15, 2013

Starting Time: 7:30 a.m.

Weather: 70 degrees, rising to 85 degrees by the time we finished, with partly cloudy skies and minimal wind. We played in steam bath conditions due to the humidity, which began to impact the round on the back nine.

My Score: 77

Number of Lost Balls: None

Highlights: 3 birdies and 7 pars

Lowlights: None

Excuse for Not Breaking 80: None needed; my "A" game showed up.

Greens Fee: $129

Playing Partners: Brother Andy and Dr. Scott Rand.

Practice Facilities: They had a driving range and putting green, but we had an early starting time and chose not to warm up. It probably would have been good to test the speed of the greens, which were really slick.

My Rating: 8+, with a number of great and near great holes. The Harvester is a borderline top 25 course on my list.

Absolutely Must Play: Yes. I hate to tell anyone they must go to Des Moines, but this is really a great layout.

Favorite Hole: There were so many great and unique holes. No. 2 is a terrific par 4 with an elevated green that gets the juices flowing. Nos. 3, 6,

7, 9, 14, 15, 16 and 17 all got high ratings, with the 525-yard, finishing par 5 being my favorite. This horseshoe shape around a large lake is reminiscent of holes at Bay Hill and Blackwolf Run.

Location Characteristics: The Harvester is situated in the farm country of Iowa, just east of Des Moines. It is amazing how much topography exists, which is enhanced by a large lake in the middle of the property. The course is a links-style design with limited trees. Most of the surrounding development includes farmland. Although the surroundings are not particularly unique, you will probably not notice as you attempt to avoid the numerous pitfalls awaiting stray shots.

Overall: I liked The Harvester Golf Club despite an iffy start. To begin with, there was no one at the club at 7:00 a.m. when we arrived. Nor had they arrived by 7:30 when we teed off. Apparently, they had messed up our reservation and assumed no players would be arriving at the course until around 8:00 a.m. There was some work being done in the parking lot, which resulted in a temporary staging area. All of this was quite confusing. However, the well-conceived golf holes and slick but true greens made for a great golfing experience. It did not hurt that I played very well. In addition, this round offered some of the best weather on our trip, which is not saying much. It is too bad The Harvester is located in such an outlying area, as I would love to tackle this layout again.

Round 86 — Eagle Ridge Golf Club

Course Rank: 95

Date Played: July 16, 2013

Starting Time: 8:00 a.m.

Weather: 75 degrees rising to 92, sunny, minimal wind, lots of humidity. The National Weather Service issued a heat advisory.

My Score: 95

Number of Lost Balls: 8...*are you kidding me?* I had to buy a dozen new balls in the pro shop. A practice round the day before resulted in 11 lost balls.

Highlights: 2 birdies and 5 pars

Lowlights: 3 double bogeys, 2 triple bogeys, 1 quadruple bogey and 1 quintuple bogey.

Excuse for Not Breaking 80: I wish I could blame the heat, but this is the most punitive golf course I have ever played.

Greens Fee: $90, but you need to add a premium for lost balls.

Playing Partners: My Midwestern team of Andy and Scott. We combined to lose several dozen balls over two rounds.

Practice Facilities: The General at Eagle Ridge does not have a range on site. However, the North Course at Eagle Ridge, located several miles away, can be used, but at a cost. There is a putting green on site.

My Rating: 8, based upon a compilation of great golf holes, with huge elevation changes, offset by the frustration created as a result of losing golf balls on shots that appear to be well struck.

Absolutely Must Play: No; however, there may be some who love the layout. If you are hitting the ball directly down the middle, with excellent distance control, then you have a chance.

Favorite Hole: There were a ton of great holes. Unfortunately, in total, they were overwhelming. No. 15 was a long par three, requiring significant carry. Since I birdied the hole, I am going with this one, but rated Nos. 9, 11, 14, and 15 similarly. No. 14 is the signature hole, with a massive elevated teeing area to a very narrow landing area.

Location Characteristics: The General at Eagle Ridge is a woodland course with huge elevation changes. Elevated tee boxes are followed by elevated greens, which make distance estimates difficult. There are a number of forced carries and plenty of inaccessible woods. The resort itself is nice and the adjoining town of Galena is worth a visit. Galena is just across the Mississippi River from Dubuque, Iowa, in a hillside setting.

Overall: I have never played a course as punitive as The General. Any shot that did not land in the fairway or on the green had an excellent chance at being lost. The fairways are not very wide, so accuracy is at a premium. During an initial practice round I lost 11 balls, with no more than three really bad shots. Several times, approach shots were barely offline but were lost as they kicked off the sides of the greens. I rated the holes extremely high on an individual basis. However, this largely reflects the level of difficulty that creates numerous interesting shots, but taken as a whole can wear you down. It will also mess with your swing, as you begin to "steer" the ball. This resulted in a few shanks. Indicative of the difficulty is that during this Midwest swing I shot between 77 and 84 for the other 8 rounds I played, but did not finish the practice round (ran out of balls) and shot 95 when it counted. The views are great and it is never boring, but the course completely destroyed me, and that had nothing to do with the oppressive heat and humidity.

Round 87 — WeaverRidge Golf Club

Course Rank: 89

Date Played: July 17, 2013

Starting Time: 7:00 a.m.

Weather: 75 degrees to start, rising to 90 degrees with high humidity, partly cloudy and calm. A heat advisory was in effect.

My Score: 82

Number of Lost Balls: 1

Highlights: 2 birdies and 7 pars

Lowlights: 3 double bogeys

Excuse for Not Breaking 80: A bad finish, as the oppressive heat and humidity took their toll.

Greens Fee: $49, with the early morning discount.

Playing Partners: Andy and Scott. During the previous day's practice round, we were joined by Bill (Tweets) Streeter, our old neighbor from California who had relocated to the Peoria area. That made two members of the foursome who had gone astray.

Practice Facilities: A decent driving range and putting green were available, although we passed due to extreme heat.

My Rating: 7, for a course that provided a nice challenge, but lacked the pizzazz of many in the top 100. The condition was good, although some of the fairways appeared to be suffering from the heat.

Absolutely Must Play: No. There are more exciting venues in terms of location, design and challenge; however, the value was very good.

Favorite Hole: Most of the holes were fine, but nothing exciting. The finishing 18th hole was the most interesting, a par 5 from an elevated tee box, with too much trouble for my "iffy" game.

Location Characteristics: WeaverRidge has to overcome the Peoria stigma. This woodland course makes the most of the terrain, with enough undulation to keep the round interesting. The fairways are ample, with lost balls possible in the heather that lines some of the fairways. Ultimately, however, being stuck in the middle of Illinois limits the "wow" factor.

Overall: No course will shine when a heat advisory is in effect, but WeaverRidge presents a clean, well-conditioned look, with a variety of attractive housing surrounding much of the front nine. The second nine is more picturesque, with attractive holes situated in lush surroundings. The greens were not particularly fast, but putted true. The fairways were in average to good condition and offered ample width and plenty of rough that made the course seem fairly open. Ultimately, there was nothing especially memorable about WeaverRidge, but there was nothing to criticize either. The cost for the round was very reasonable. If I lived in the area I would play the course on a regular basis, but otherwise would not go out of my way.

Round 88 French Lick Resort (Dye Course)

Course Rank: 80

Date Played: July 18, 2013

Starting Time: 11:00 a.m.

Weather: 90 degrees, 90 percent humidity, virtually no wind and few clouds. A heat advisory had been issued by the National Weather Service, so we decided to play 36.

My Score: 82 on both rounds

Number of Lost Balls: None

Highlights: 2 birdies and 6 pars

Lowlights: 2 double bogeys

Excuse for Not Breaking 80: Heat, heat and more heat, not to mention the unbearable humidity. I actually played pretty well, but kept hoping to get it finished. Also, I double bogeyed No. 18, where I eschewed my caddie's advice as to the correct line on the drive.

Greens Fee: $350 or so, I am told. We booked the round as part of a package. It was unlimited golf, but you had to stay at the French Lick Resort. The cost is a huge obstacle that apparently results in the course getting very little play.

Playing Partners: Scott and Andy braved the weather again. We were joined by our forecaddie (required), who played the final nine holes with us, teaming up with Andy in an epic match that ended in a tie.

Practice Facilities: Exceptionally good, given the limited play. This is Pete Dye's baby, and they have attempted to do everything right. We saw an excellent range, putting green and short game area, although it was really too hot to partake.

My Rating: 8, for the quality of the experience. As usual, the Dye design did not disappoint.

Absolutely Must Play: This is a tough one. Getting to French Lick is a real pain, and there is not much to do, unless you spend time in casinos. However, the experience is on par with some of the best I have played because of the fabulous service, an excellent links-style design, and the impeccable condition of the course. Therefore, I am going to have to say maybe. I may go back someday, if I get to the Kentucky Derby, which is held just over an hour's drive away.

Favorite Hole: I generally liked most of the holes, although few were exceptional. As usual, Dye had some interesting par 3s. I enjoyed No. 16, although this 183-yard par 3 is really tough, with a lake lining the right, and no bailout area left. I took a triple bogey in the afternoon, costing me a shot at breaking 80.

Location Characteristics: Although situated in a somewhat rolling, woodland area, the course has been cleared to emulate a links-style design. It would have been nice if there had been some shade trees. There are a few strategically placed lakes/ponds that will capture the wayward ball, being particularly nefarious on No. 16. French Lick is a quaint little town, dominated by the resort and casino, and not what one would have expected of its most famous resident (Larry Bird). There are more attractive settings, but this one was a positive surprise.

Overall: Pete Dye's French Lick Resort brings to mind several of the other exclusive, somewhat expensive, venues designed for high rollers, and which get limited play. Notably, Shadow Creek and Fallen Oak come to mind. All are in great condition, with superior amenities and first-class service. Further, each serves as a loss leader for the casino, which makes the lack of play less of a burden on operations, and more enjoyable for the player who does not like to wait between shots. On the day we played there were only three other groups stupid enough to brave the weather. Because of the unlimited play, it was only natural we would abuse ourselves with a second round. Special kudos are due to the golf staff. This is the only facility I have ever played where they welcomed you when you arrived and shook your hand. (It is almost as impressive as the caddie line-up at Whistling Straits.) The true golf addict needs to add this one to the list, but plan it around some other trip.

Trip Summary:

My visit to the Midwest will forever be remembered for the extreme heat and humidity. Also, indelibly inked on my brain are the rows upon rows of cornfields. With the exception of French Lick the golf was very affordable, once you got there, and the courses were fun. The Harvester and Pete Dye layouts were memorable, and well worth the trip. The golf masochist will love The General at Eagle Ridge, and Galena, Illinois, is a really cool old town, even if they have over-hyped Ulysses S. Grant's influence on the community. It also gives one the opportunity to see the Mississippi River and cross into Dubuque, just so you can tell your friends you have been to Iowa. WeaverRidge Golf Club is no more necessary than Peoria, but you have to love the green fees. Longaberger Golf Club is fine, but, other than the company headquarters building, largely forgettable.

Chapter 41

I'm Taking a Mulligan

Once again, I am winging my way to Michigan to make up for last year's blunder (see Chapter 34). It has been less than one year since I insisted the resort had screwed up, which resulted in my playing the St. Ives course rather than the Tullymore layout. I am still haunted by that sickening 2:00 a.m. feeling the night after completing my erroneous round that I had blundered my way into a very expensive return trip. This time I have been very careful, booking one time on Sunday morning and one time on Tuesday morning, after I detour back to Forest Dunes and Arcadia Bluffs to play a couple of rounds with Charlie Wilde. It would be just my luck to have bad weather close the course, so I have hedged my bets. The good news is that the weather report looks promising for both days, and, much to my relief, it does not look like I will be reprising the weather of last month's fiasco in the Midwest.

Here we go again…

Round 89 — Tullymore Golf Club

Course Rank: *76*

Date Played: August 11, 2013

Starting Time: 8:00 a.m.

Weather: Cold, only 50 degrees to start, but warming to 68 degrees by the finish. The skies were partly cloudy with mild winds.

My Score: 82

Number of Lost Balls: 1, totally unfair on the first hole. I watched my second shot on the par 5 land in the fairway, but never found the ball.

Highlights: 9 pars

Lowlights: 2 double bogeys

Excuse for Not Breaking 80: The aforementioned lost ball on one, as well as a ticket on the bogey train for much of the front side.

Greens Fee: $160, which is the prime rate. You can do much better. My Tuesday round was $125.

Playing Partners: Played this one by myself in 2.5 hours.

Practice Facilities: Solid, with an ample range and putting area. The turf was a bit dug up on the range, affording few pristine lies.

My Rating: 8, for the picturesque nature of the course and surrounding development.

Absolutely Must Play: No, although I did go there back-to-back years. The resort has the advantage of two good courses, including the infamous St. Ives, which ultimately necessitated this trip.

Favorite Hole: There were plenty of good golf holes, although most of the par 3s were relatively short. There are five par 5s, which is always good for a few fun shots. The best hole is No. 18, a comparatively short par 5, but one that dissuades you from trying to reach in two, with a large tree protecting the green, and a sizable lake running along the left side of the hole. No. 18 leads back to the very picturesque clubhouse.

Location Characteristics: Tullymore is advertised as a links course; however, there are numerous trees, water features, marshes and other tricks that work against a true links designation. The resort is located about an hour north of Grand Rapids, making it somewhat isolated, although it could be a natural stop on a circular route starting in Chicago and meandering through Wisconsin and part of Michigan. Personally, I love the look of all the Michigan courses, with the forests, water and sand dunes. As with many of these locations, weather and bugs are the most significant issues.

Overall: I enjoyed both of my rounds at Tullymore. There are some quirky par 4s, short but with a bite, plenty of interesting par 5s, and very playable par 3s. I like Jim Engh golf courses, and this one is no exception. This is a shot maker's venue that requires hitting to precise locations. The greens are heavily undulated, which makes scoring difficult for the uninitiated. Tullymore is not a long layout, but the slope is indicative of the many problems that confront the golfer. Given a choice, I would focus on the courses farther to the north, including Arcadia Bluffs, Bay Harbor and Forest Dunes, but if the opportunity presents itself, this one is not too bad. The sister course, St. Ives, is generally on par with Tullymore, although the design is woodsier. Ultimately, this is a legitimate top 100 layout, and the setting is terrific.

Trip Summary:

My 2012 faux pas proved quite expensive: nearly $1,200 for the adventure. This is a bit rich for my blood, but I deserved it for being such an idiot. The trip was not a total loss, as I enjoyed Tullymore, and was also able to meet up with Charlie for rounds at Arcadia Bluffs, Forest Dunes and Manistee National (not top 100, but a pretty interesting and tough layout). The side trip reminded me just how much I enjoy Michigan golf, and reinforced how terrific Forest Dunes and particularly Arcadia Bluffs are as golf courses. Charlie and I are already looking at another Michigan/Wisconsin golf fest, once I have completed the top 100. The trip was short but sweet. I now have several weeks to catch up on my real job…although the lines are becoming blurred.

Chapter 42

TSA, TSA, TSA, TSA, TSA

Bismarck, North Dakota, and Gothenburg, Nebraska, are two of the toughest destinations for top 100 golf courses. My masochistic streak therefore dictated that I schedule both for the same trip. There is no simple way to make the itinerary work, unless you have a desire to spend quality time in Denver International Airport.

For this leg, I again persuaded my son to take a day off work for a long weekend of bouncing around the "flyover" states. Charlie is a good sport, and seemed to have thawed out after our Alabama boondoggle. Travel began on Thursday evening, with a flight from San Diego to Denver. We lucked out, and found a gap between flights that allowed us to pass through the TSA line in only 10 minutes. After spending the night at an airport hotel, we caught a morning flight to North Platte, Nebraska. The TSA line was somewhat more crowded; however, they were using dogs, and did not require the usual disrobing to pass through the scanners. They only checked for metal, and the exercise was completed in less than 15 minutes. The flight to Nebraska was only an hour, but with travel to the airport, TSA and waiting for the flight, it took about as long to fly (3.5 hours) as it would have taken to drive (4 hours). We spent the night at Quality Suites in Gothenburg after playing 18 holes upon arrival. We slogged through another nine holes in the morning before heading back to Denver on the way to Bismarck. The Great Lakes Aviation return flight only had 19 seats, and fewer than 10 passengers. It was not unreasonable to assume TSA would be a piece of cake. In fact, there are only two flights out of North Platte on weekends. Despite this, they have four employees. I suppose they were bored, but it took them 15 minutes to get the ten passengers through security.

We flew west to Denver, before changing flights and heading back east to Bismarck. Total travel time was seven hours. (Again, about the same amount of time it would have taken to drive from Gothenburg to Bismarck.) We lucked out in completing a round that threatened severe thunderstorms and it was off to the airport for a four o'clock flight back to, you guessed it, Denver. The TSA was much more efficient in Bismarck, moving us through the system in three minutes. At least we were done with security, or so we thought. It turns out I booked a crazy return trip (cheap!) through Phoenix before we headed back to San Diego. This involved changing from United Airlines to US Airways, with a change of terminals necessitating a fifth run through the TSA line in four days. Fortunately, it was late at night with few flights, so that line was only a 10-minute delay. By the time we had passed through the system for the fifth time, Charlie and I had perfected the process of getting through without incident.

Round 90 — Wild Horse Golf Club

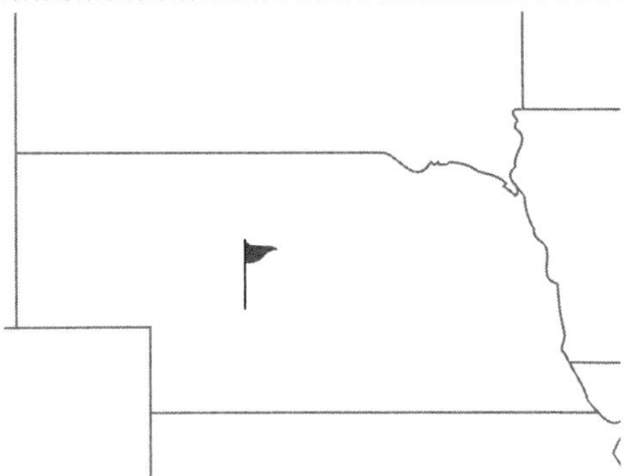

Course Rank: 67

Date Played: September 6, 2013

Starting Time: 2:00 p.m.

Weather: 100 degrees, sunny, 10-15 mph wind.

My Score: 82

Number of Lost Balls: 2, which is pretty lucky given the intrusive natural areas that consist of high grasses and thorny ground cover, which are regularly in play.

Highlights: 1 birdie and 10 pars

Lowlights: 4 double bogeys

Excuse for Not Breaking 80: Not ready for the intense heat, especially coming off the 19-seat turboprop flight into the North Platte airport immediately before the tee time. I double bogeyed the first two holes.

Greens Fee: $63 included a cart. Great deal for a round of golf, although the range balls were comparatively expensive at $3.50 for a small bag.

Playing Partners: Son Charlie. We had the course largely to ourselves.

Practice Facilities: Average. The range was a bit chewed up and the balls looked like they had been retrieved from the native areas, after sitting for a season. The putting green was pretty good, and necessary given the speed.

My Rating: 6, for uneven conditions (although the greens were uniformly good); however, there were dry and dead spots in the fairways and around the greens. The links-style design was less imaginative than most of the others on the list. Lastly, the access is problematic, with little else to do in the region, unless you can pull off an invitation to play Sand Hills.

Absolutely Must Play: No, there are too many better options with better accessibility and better local activities.

Favorite Hole: There were few holes that really got the blood pumping, but No. 11, a very short, 113-yard par 3, offers many pitfalls, including two gnarly traps in front of the green, and a huge downhill, back-to-front green that can easily lead to a four-putt if the tee shot does not find the right location.

Location Characteristics: Exactly what you would expect for the middle of Nebraska (i.e. comparatively flat, no trees, no water features…essentially a large farm). The course is constructed on the local sand hills, so there is some variation, and the designer created a few contours, especially on the greens, which help to make it more interesting. There were not a lot of great photo ops, although an old windmill is still drawing water. Unfortunately, it appeared to be spilling into a small pool that would be a great breeding ground for mosquitoes.

Overall: My son and I enjoyed the Great Lakes Airlines trek from Denver to North Platte. TSA is a lot simpler in the rural airports, and the small plane with one seat on each side of the row means you have both a window and an aisle seat. No screaming kids or dogs, like we had on Southwest going to Denver. The course itself was not exceptional, and it did not help that we experienced triple-digit temperatures. The people working the facility were great, but this is another golf course that has a "municipal" feel.

Round 91 — Hawktree Golf Club

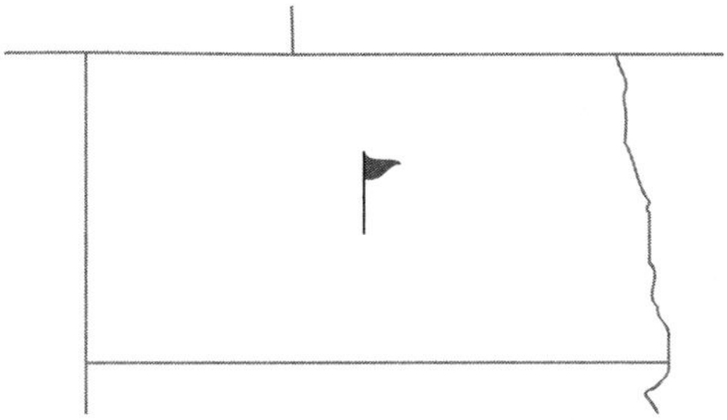

Course Rank: *74*

Date Played: September 8, 2013

Starting Time: 8:40 a.m.

Weather: Cloudy, showers, threat of thunderstorms, 65 degrees to start, and rising to 82 degrees, generally calm.

My Score: 80

Number of Lost Balls: 1 (first swing of the day I hit a cart path)

Highlights: 12 pars

Lowlights: 1 triple bogey

Excuse for Not Breaking 80: The cart path along No. 1.

Greens Fee: $69; the real cost is getting there.

Playing Partners: Son Charlie.

Practice Facilities: Basic, with a decent driving range and modest putting green. We passed on warming up due to the weather.

My Rating: 8, given plenty of topography, the interesting design and the unique nature of each hole. The condition was pretty good, especially given the greens fees.

Absolutely Must Play: There is really nothing necessary about Bismarck. The city is tough to get to, and does not have much else to offer. Nevertheless, Charlie rightly stated that if we were ever in the area, it would be great to play this one again. If Hawktree occupied a more accessible location, it would be a regular on my schedule.

Favorite Hole: There were a slew of interesting holes. Uniformly, the par 3s and par 5s were great, with most of the par 4s being fun as well. I preferred the short par 3, third hole, with an elevated tee to a narrow green. This is a classic design that creates a positive mood for the remainder of the day.

Location Characteristics: Hawktree is located outside the Bismarck city limits, winding through a new residential subdivision. There is a great deal of topographical change that lends itself well to picturesque vistas. There are several interesting blind shots, and a number of elevated greens. The topography requires careful club selection. For the most part, this is an open design with few trees or shrubs except on select holes. In addition, there are several interesting water features, including a great one on the drivable par 4 No. 16.

Overall: Hawktree Golf Club provides an enjoyable round of golf. The topography offers great character, with numerous fun and challenging holes. Keep your ball in play and you can go low. The green speed was a bit slow, and the heavy rough around the greens can be daunting, but the course is very playable. Despite threatening weather and some precipitation, the course was interesting enough to keep our attention. The people of Bismarck are great, even if there is not much else to the city. Even with several foursomes ahead of us, we completed our round in less than four hours. Ultimately, other than the access issues and iffy weather, I have nothing negative to say about Hawktree. Well, they could get a better selection of hats.

Trip Summary:

So, was it worth it to fly all over the country and deal with the TSA in order to play these two courses? No. The golf was fine, but even Pebble Beach would have been less enjoyable after the excessive travel. Further, the town of Gothenburg and the city of Bismarck have little to offer. Since we had some extra time on our hands, we drove through the town of Gothenburg. I would speculate that at least half of the local businesses had closed permanently. At best, Gothenburg appears to be a city going out of business. Bismarck, on the other hand, is riding the energy boom and appears to be growing rapidly. Overall this was a trying, long weekend, but at least these two courses could be checked off the list.

Chapter 43

Nirvana

No, "The Happiest Place on Earth" is not located in Anaheim, California, or Orlando, Florida. Anyone over the age of 12 who has ever swung a golf club knows that Heaven on Earth can be found within the confines of 17-Mile Drive, between Carmel and Monterey along the Pacific Coast in northern California. Driving through the gates to enter the Del Monte Forest and 17-Mile Drive is the most exciting event a golfer can experience. Within the gates can be found six golf courses (excluding Peter Hay), of which two are among the top 10 you can play and one of the private courses (Cypress Point) is among the top 10 golf courses in the world. Spanish Bay and Poppy Hills are great venues on their own, and the Monterey Country Club is reportedly an excellent track as well.

The location merges the rugged coastline of the Pacific, including several attractive coves that lure all kinds of sea life, with dense forests characterized by mature pines. Every time I enter the gates I can feel my heart begin to race in anticipation, as all the troubles of the world melt away. Even if you cannot afford the extravagant greens fees and hotel charges, it is worthwhile to pay the entry fee into 17-Mile Drive just to drink in the experience. Many complain about the expense, but there is no price you can put on golfing these wonderful courses.

This year I have added the additional experience of CordeValle to the itinerary, which has been hosting the annual Frys.com PGA event. The resort is reportedly quite special, so I am looking forward to this as a warm-up to the main event.

As in the past, we are joining Joe and Greta Strong, who seem to appreciate the environment almost as much as my wife and I. First stop: CordeValle.

Round 92 CordeValle

Course Rank: 64

Date Played: September 16, 2013

Starting Time: 10:48 a.m.

Weather: Sunny, 90 degrees, 5-10 mph wind

My Score: 89

Number of Lost Balls: 1

Highlights: 7 pars

Lowlights: 4 double bogeys and 1 triple bogey

Excuse for Not Breaking 80: Certainly not the weather. This was without question one of my worst days putting. In addition, I was blocking all of my irons.

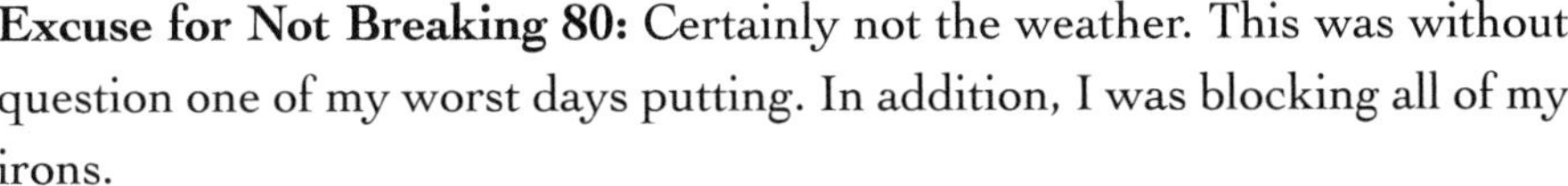

Greens Fee: $350, plus you need to have a caddie. In addition, you must stay at the resort. Plan on a big investment.

Playing Partners: I walked this one solo with my caddie, Carlos.

Practice Facilities: Very nice. The driving range was uphill and in very good condition. Good putting green and practice areas.

My Rating: 8, for terrific condition and nice setting.

Absolutely Must Play: No, but if cost is not an issue I recommend a stay at the resort. The rooms are great and the service terrific. But, hey, as long as you are there, you might as well play the course.

Favorite Hole: I liked the elevated tee on the par 4 No. 9, but preferred the drivable par 4 No. 8. The hole is 295 yards from the green tees, but plays shorter. A lake in front creates a great risk/reward opportunity, and the severe slope in the back of the green allows you to hit long, but with a great result.

Location Characteristics: CordeValle is situated in the vineyard-laden foothills of the Santa Cruz Mountains. Although worlds apart, the resort is only an hour from Pebble Beach. In general, the course has a links feel, with mature oaks and other native trees supplemented by several creeks and lakes. The resort is gated and caters to the more discerning crowd to which I aspire, but will never be a part. The attractiveness has induced a number of the rich and famous to acquire homes in the area. Many of the residents own small vineyards and produce their own wine.

Overall: CordeValle is a spectacular resort, with only 48 guest rooms. If you are not a member, you must stay at the resort in order to play the course. A stay-and-play package is semi-affordable, and can be upgraded to include a round at Pasatiempo. The rooms are single level, large and isolated with a large patio area. My wife plans on returning next year. I think she really enjoyed the outlet mall in Gilroy, but claims the spa was nice and enjoyed the walking trails. The Robert Trent Jones, Jr. design is reminiscent of others I have played. This includes large greens, rolling topography and subtle characteristics that make scoring difficult for the newbie. This is an excellent walking course, so I suggest a walking caddie versus a forecaddie. The condition is well above average due to somewhat limited play...although it may have benefitted from extra work completed prior to the U.S. Women's Amateur scheduled for the following week, and the Frys.com PGA event shortly thereafter. CordeValle is a challenging track that requires excellent shot making skills. Hopefully, I will putt better next time.

Round 93 Spyglass Hill

Course Rank: 8

Date Played: September 17, 2013

Starting Time: 2:30 p.m.

Weather: 65 degrees, 20-30 mph wind gusts, especially strong on the ocean holes.

My Score: 88

Number of Lost Balls: 2

Highlights: 8 pars

Lowlights: 4 double bogeys and 1 triple bogey

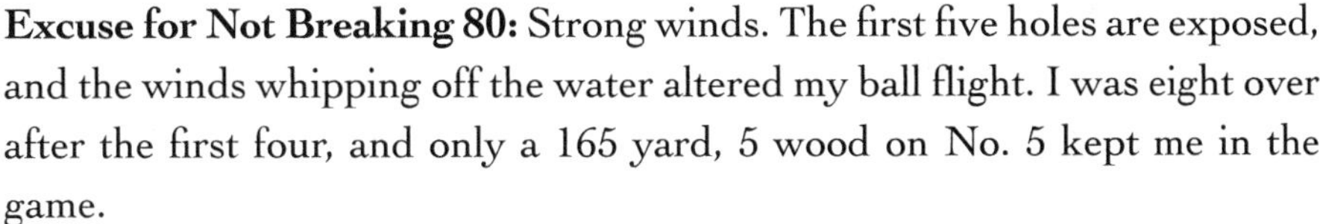

Excuse for Not Breaking 80: Strong winds. The first five holes are exposed, and the winds whipping off the water altered my ball flight. I was eight over after the first four, and only a 165 yard, 5 wood on No. 5 kept me in the game.

Greens Fee: $370

Playing Partners: Joe Strong.

Practice Facilities: Pretty good. As in past years, Bambi was roaming around the driving range, so there was a target (no, PETA, I did not try to hit the critter). The range was using mats, which always seems to be the case when I am there. The putting green is decent and there is a teaching area on site. Generally, however, you just mull around the small pro shop, and watch others getting ready to tee off.

My Rating: 9+, one of the great golf courses in the world.

Absolutely Must Play: Yes. Despite the steep green fees and heavy utilization, Spyglass Hill remains one of the great golf experiences. In combination with Pebble Beach, this twosome cannot be beat.

Favorite Hole: There are so many great holes it is hard to identify just one. I like the par 5 No. 14, which requires five good-to-great shots in order to get par, and No. 4 may have the most interesting green on the planet. However, I think No. 1 is one of the best starting holes in golf. This downhill, dogleg left, par 5 starts in the forest and requires a precise tee shot, with OB right and forest left. The second shot turns toward the water, with the prevailing wind in your face making this 529 yard hole (from the whites) play more like 629 yards. A well-bunkered, difficult green makes par a great score.

Location Characteristics: Spyglass Hill occupies a prime location within the best real estate in the world. A strong ocean influence, coupled with amazing, pine tree-lined forests, yields one of the most spectacular settings imaginable. Ultimately, it is impossible to fully describe the magnificence of the surroundings. The sand dunes of holes 2 through 4 are amazing. Despite the ocean proximity, there is plenty of topography. Most of the greens are elevated, making the course play significantly longer. The par 3s are on the short side, but winds and water hazards make each a difficult venture.

Overall: Many golfers believe that Spyglass Hill is better than Pebble Beach, and I can understand why; however, they are wrong. Nevertheless, this terrific golf course is a definite top 10, and one that cannot be missed if you love the game. From the great starting hole to the challenging par 4, No. 18, there is something to like about the entire layout. The course is so magnificent that you will quickly forget that you have used up a month of greens fees back home to play a municipal facility.

Round 94 Pebble Beach Golf Links

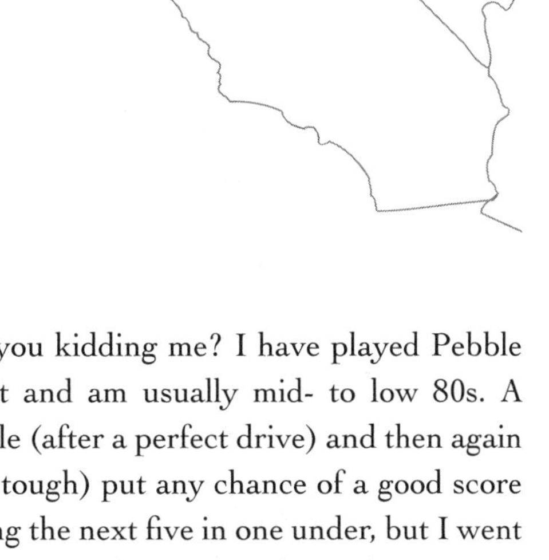

Course Rank: 2 (wrong)

Date Played: September 18, 2013

Starting Time: 7:00 a.m.

Weather: 60 degrees, 5-10 mph winds

My Score: 93

Number of Lost Balls: 4...*how??*

Highlights: 2 birdies and 3 pars

Lowlights: 4 double bogeys and 2 quadruple bogeys

Excuse for Not Breaking 80: Are you kidding me? I have played Pebble Beach at least 10 times in the past and am usually mid- to low 80s. A quadruple bogey on the easy first hole (after a perfect drive) and then again on No. 10 (tough hole, but not that tough) put any chance of a good score to rest. After the first, I rallied playing the next five in one under, but I went into the tank when I sculled my wedge over the green and into the ocean on the famous 7th hole. I will have nightmares about this round until I can get back out there.

Greens Fee: A bargain at $495.

Playing Partners: Joe Strong. We were matched up with Adam and Shane (from New York). Adam was getting in his last golf before getting married that weekend. They foolishly decided to play the gold tees, and paid the price.

Practice Facilities: The only downside to Pebble Beach is that the driving range is located off-site. As such, you cool down before the nerve-racking first tee shot. There is a large putting green between the hotel entrance and the Pebble Beach shops, just off the tee box. They are building a new practice facility and school across from the existing driving range. I assume it will be great, but still a bit of a trek from the pro shop and first tee.

My Rating: 10. Best course I have ever played. The setting, history and design are unique. I would play here every day if I could afford to absorb the cost.

Absolutely Must Play: Yes, unless the experience will ruin all other golf courses for you, or you get addicted to playing here and cannot afford the greens fee. In my opinion, this is the holy grail of golf available to the public.

Favorite Hole: There is something I love about every hole. Those located along the cliffs above Stillwater Cove (Nos. 4-10 and 18) are all spectacular, but the inward holes are no slouch. Most people would choose the famous 18th as their favorite, and it is spectacular, while others really like the short par 3, No. 7, which is also very cool. Being a contrarian, my favorite hole is the par 4, No. 8, which requires a well-placed tee shot (not too long depending upon the line) followed by the most difficult approach shot in golf. The green is small, with huge slope, adding to the challenge.

Location Characteristics: Pebble Beach is situated just above the quaint seaside community of Carmel. The area is characterized by sandy and rocky beaches, cliffs and pine forests. There is abundant sea life, including otters, sea lions (both regularly on display along the rocks below No. 7); there are all types of sea fowl as well, and the occasional migrating whale pops by. We also were entertained by a couple of dolphins on this trip. Deer are in abundance in the forest areas. The views of Stillwater Cove are magnificent and provide for spectacular photographs. There is no better setting in the world, although it can be subject to nasty weather. Wind and fog are regular features. I am told September and October are the best months to play. To date, I have had good luck, with the exception of a disaster at Spanish Bay several years ago.

Overall: There is plenty of topography, but this is a course that must be walked. Sure, you can take a cart, but it is cart paths only, so you are going to hoof it quite a distance. My recommendation is that the course be enjoyed with one of their professional caddies, most of whom have been there for multiple decades. They not only assist with the golf, but also serve as tour guides pointing out the homes of the rich and famous that border the course.

Opinions may vary as to the best golf courses in the world, but of those I have played, Pebble Beach is head and shoulders the best. Even on its worst day, the course is one that transcends the game of golf. I have not played Pine Valley or Augusta, but I will take Pebble Beach over any of the others on the list of the 100 you can play. I hate to build expectations too high, because they are seldom met; however, I cannot envision any real golfer not loving the experience. It is a joke to me that *Golf Magazine* could rate Pacific Dunes over Pebble Beach. There is nothing I do not love about the experience, aside from the inconvenient driving range. Pebble Beach is not about the golf, but rather about the experience. It is the only place I can think of where shooting a 93 could still leave me content and relaxed. Of course, I will have to go back and tame the course next year.

Round 95 — Links at Spanish Bay

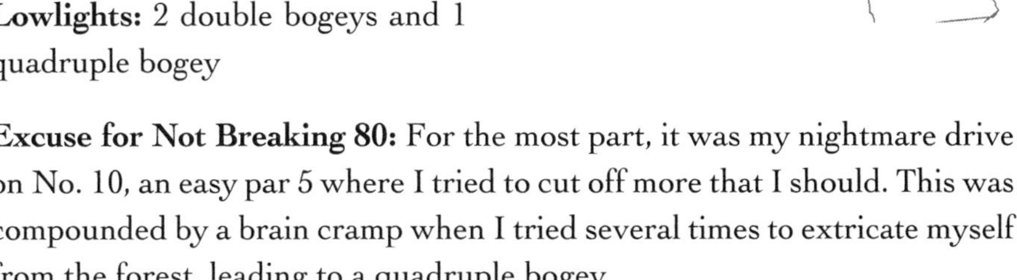

Course Rank: 42

Date Played: September 19, 2013

Starting Time: 8:10 a.m.

Weather: 62 degrees, sunny skies, 10-15 mph wind

My Score: 84

Number of Lost Balls: 3

Highlights: 1 birdie and 9 pars

Lowlights: 2 double bogeys and 1 quadruple bogey

Excuse for Not Breaking 80: For the most part, it was my nightmare drive on No. 10, an easy par 5 where I tried to cut off more that I should. This was compounded by a brain cramp when I tried several times to extricate myself from the forest, leading to a quadruple bogey.

Greens Fee: $265

Playing Partners: Joe Strong. We were joined by a Korean couple, Andrew and Ashley. He works for Morgan Stanley, but was on an extended vacation looking to play many of the top 100. I was able to preview for him the next 12 courses on his itinerary. He tried to play the back tees, but they won this battle.

Practice Facilities: Not great. There is no driving range nearby, so you are on your own. The putting green is expansive and steeply sloped, but not really like the greens on the course. You need to get your mind ready, since the swing will not be grooved. No doubt, this is the reason I always start slow.

My Rating: 8. It is always tough to play this one as the third in the rotation. By comparison, both Spyglass Hill and Pebble Beach are world class, with Spanish Bay being the less attractive younger sister. Much like the Irish Course at Whistling Straits, I am sure this one would be more enjoyable if played before the big two.

Absolutely Must Play: Yes, since you will be playing Pebble Beach and Spyglass Hill, and likely book into one of their packages, this should be on the itinerary. This links design has a slew of really good golf holes and should not be taken lightly. Often, the highest score of the three occurs at Spanish Bay.

Favorite Hole: There are numerous good holes. In fact, I rated each of them as at least an 8. Actually, I rated 17 of them 8 or 8+. The standout hole for me was No. 12, a brutal par 4 that requires a long, well-placed tee shot, and a long approach to an uphill green, over a large ravine. Par this one (I did with a magnificent 5 wood approach) and you have done something.

Location Characteristics: Like Pebble Beach, approximately one half of the holes are influenced by the Pacific Ocean, with the remainder moving into the forest, albeit not as thick as at Spyglass Hill. The setting is more exposed to the wind, with the finishing holes being particularly at risk. Some of the short par 4s, notably Nos. 15 and 17, typically play much longer. Be prepared to keep the ball low. This was underscored several years earlier when Joe and I played Spanish Bay during a monsoon. Forty- to fifty-mile wind gusts had the flags at 30-degree angles to the ground...when they stayed in the hole. The driving rain was actually painful. Being the troopers we are, we not only started the round, but were the only two, of the seven idiots who tried, to finish. Of course we had to play four holes twice, as they had closed several due to concern the local trees would blow down and injure a golfer. By comparison, my round at the Ocean Course at Kiawah was a walk in the park.

Overall: Spanish Bay is a nice course in a terrific location, but suffers from being located in the same area as two of the top 10 courses you can play. Fortunately for Spanish Bay, the resort offers the best value in accommodations within 17-Mile Drive, albeit still expensive. I recommend booking one of their two- or three-night packages that include rounds at all three venues. Request Spanish Bay first. However, if you do not book early, there is not much flexibility. If possible, pay for the whole thing up front and forget about it. Eat at some of the small bistros in Carmel, and take the wife's credit card away before she heads to the stores in the Village. Accept Spanish Bay for what it is: a really good test of golf in a great location that helps to supplement the greatest golf experience ever.

Trip Summary:

The northern California golf vacation is the best of the best. In fact, nothing can even come close. For my money (and it takes a lot), Pebble Beach and Spyglass Hill are my two favorite courses in the top 100. The greatest setting on the planet is 17-Mile Drive, which only serves to enhance the experience. The Links at Spanish Bay provides a fun golf challenge and the accommodations on this site provide a great staging ground. You can also partake of Poppy Hills, another fun, albeit not top 100 golf course. In addition to everything else, some of my favorite restaurants are situated in Carmel, just outside the gates of 17-Mile Drive. Despite the cost, this is one terrific place.

An added bonus is that the CordeValle Resort is situated about an hour away and provides excellent golfing within a terrific setting. This resort is also top-notch. But wait, there's more. A side trip to Pasatiempo may easily be included in this golf extravaganza, generally on the way between CordeValle and 17-Mile Drive.

Chapter 44

Breaking the Bank

Another inaccessible golf course on the list is located in Stillwater, Oklahoma. It is very difficult to combine a trip to this location with another venue. If doing it again, I might add Barton Creek in Texas. By itself, the golf required round-trip airfare to Tulsa (not cheap), a car rental and hotel (not too expensive) and a comparatively high greens fee ($300). As long as I was there, a second round seemed necessary. The cost for this long weekend was $1,166, and I had used a free airline ticket. As a result, this proved to be one of the more expensive rounds on the list.

Karsten Creek is a fascinating, somewhat exclusive facility underwritten by alumni of Oklahoma State University. As a result of the first-class facilities, this institution has been able to attract many top collegiate golfers, the most recent of which was Rickie Fowler. The OSU Golf Hall of Fame is located in the facility. With the exception of Pete Dye's French Lick Resort course, venues in the middle of the country are typically very affordable. French Lick, being tied to a casino, is subsidized by that operation. Karsten Creek, on the other hand, has no such benefit. The members apparently do not want their course overrun with riffraff, so the greens fees are kept at a level that few in the region can afford. Given local income levels, this course is comparatively more expensive than Pebble Beach to northern California residents.

Round 96 Karsten Creek Golf Course

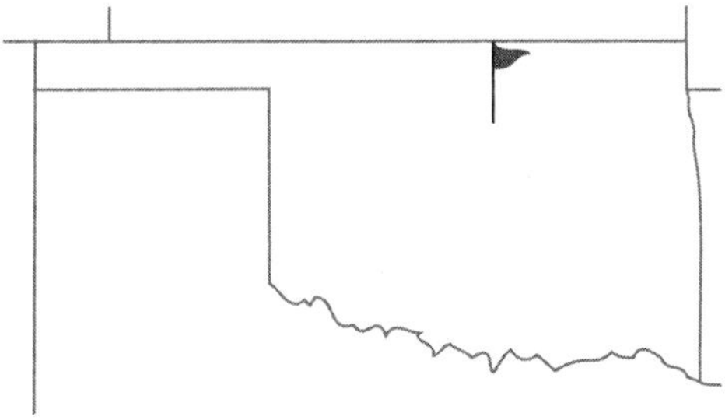

Course Rank: 69

Date Played: September 29, 2013

Starting Time: 8:20 a.m.

Weather: 48 degrees to start, rising to 70 degrees. Clear skies and minimal wind made scoring easier on the back nine.

My Score: 79

Number of Lost Balls: 3

Highlights: 1 birdie and 11 pars

Lowlights: 1 triple bogey

Excuse for Not Breaking 80: A triple bogey on No. 16 almost cost me. Fortunately, I played well enough on the rest of the course that I could afford to put one in the water on 18. Karsten Creek is much easier from the whites. The next day, playing from the blacks (141 slope), I shot 85.

Greens Fee: $300, a bit steep overall, and really high for the middle of Oklahoma.

Playing Partners: None. I nearly had the course to myself. On Monday, they only had one other tee time booked.

Practice Facilities: Way above average. The driving range was O.K., with older balls, but the putting green and practice areas were exceptional. There is also a huge practice facility for the OSU golf team.

My Rating: 8+, as the course was in terrific condition, the greens were fast but true and the staff very responsive…of course, they did not have much to do with their time. The setting is secluded, with no parallel fairways.

Absolutely Must Play: This one is a tough call. The golf course is very nice and in great condition. The high greens fees keep play to a minimum; however, a trip to Stillwater is challenging, with little else to offer in this community unless you are an OSU alumnus. Unlike Fallen Oak, there is no redeeming side trip, like New Orleans. On the other hand, this is definitely a top 50 course. It is unlikely I will return to Karsten Creek, but if I lived in the area, I would want to be a member.

Favorite Hole: All of the holes are good, but few really stood out. The Reynolds Plantation courses did a better job of incorporating the lake. The most challenging hole, and my favorite, was the par 4, No. 17, which requires a long drive over a lake. The second shot is daunting, as a miss left is likely to bounce into the water. The long approach makes this an exciting shot. Bailing out to the right leaves a very challenging downhill chip that is likely to roll off the green, and possibly into the water.

Location Characteristics: The Stillwater area is not particularly exciting; however, they found a great setting for Karsten Creek. Thick forests offering little chance to find a stray ball guard either side of the fairways. Several creeks and Lake Louise provide character, although some of the water looks to be fertile ground for mosquitoes. The course offers rolling topography, with a number of elevated tees and greens. Searching for stray balls can be challenging, and is likely to leave a number of burrs and stickers attached to your clothing. It is so thick in most spots that you might have to write off your Pro VI. Once you start you will likely never see another golfer, unless they are in front or behind. Karsten Creek occupies a serene, bucolic setting that makes for a great golf experience. Although the weather was good during my visit, they had experienced significant recent rainfall, and the course was quite wet.

Overall: I liked Karsten Creek, and, although a bit expensive—especially for the location—I am glad I was exposed to the course. The condition was virtually perfect. The large greens are difficult to putt, especially if you are on the wrong tier. All of the putts seemed to break more than expected and the balls would run out, making for challenging two-putts on many holes. The white tees seemed a bit short, but the course is really tough from the black tees. (Note: they do not put out tee markers and there are a plethora of tee boxes. As such, you could probably move up or back from either of the options.) Accuracy off the tee is imperative, as the thick forests will swallow up the errant shot. I had plenty of good holes and hit a lot of greens in regulation, but when I missed, saving bogey was difficult. I recommend playing the course a couple of times to figure out the nuances. This is especially important in reading the greens, and missing in the right locations.

Trip Summary:

Karsten Creek proved to be a very expensive proposition, as it does not match up well with any other trips. The condition and design are excellent, and Karsten Creek is definitely a top 100 venue, but a return visit is unlikely because of the logistics. If you really want to play, send your child to Oklahoma State University and make a few visits.

Chapter 45

The Good Old U.S.A.

The heartland of America is typically characterized by friendly, responsible and self-reliant folks. Previous trips to the Midwest have underscored that civility still exists in this country, despite the political bickering and ill will that often dominate the two coasts. There is no place that seems to relish traditional American values more than the town of Branson, Missouri. These God-loving people exude a stalwart faith in the American Dream that is reinforced in the many shows that comprise the entertainment in this isolated, "throwback" community. Indicative of the attitude are "Drive Friendly" signs that appear on many streets. Like it or not, a visit to this area is a breath of fresh air and an affirmation that we can achieve great things through a positive attitude, except maybe a sub-par round of golf at one of their local venues.

Likewise, Texas demonstrates a "can do" attitude, even if the larger cities are slowly being inundated with less positive outside influences. Despite the trend, Austin still allows guns in the State House. The city has grown rapidly, which may or may not be a good thing.

This is not an easy trip, but at least it starts with a flight into the world's most unique airport.

Round 97 — Branson Creek Golf Club

Course Rank: 82

Date Played: October 19, 2013

Starting Time: 8:03 a.m.

Weather: 38 degrees to start, rising to 55 degrees with 5-10 mph winds, creating a very chilly environment.

My Score: 79

Number of Lost Balls: None; I was lucky to find my second shot on 18.

Highlights: 1 birdie and 8 pars

Lowlights: None

Excuse for Not Breaking 80: None.

Greens Fee: $98

Playing Partners: Dave and Lynn from Houston, and Jeff from Tulsa. The day before I played with mini-tour player, Chase, and his father, Kenny, the golf coach at Oklahoma Baptist University. All were terrific partners, exhibiting the well-mannered Southern disposition.

Practice Facilities: Very good. There is a large range, good short game area, and two putting greens. The clubhouse, on the other hand, looks temporary. This small trailer sits adjacent to the parking lot. There is no dining facility.

My Rating: 8, for the unique setting, great views, and terrific topography. The course is very fair, with ample fairways; however, dense forests and several water features can eat up the errant shot. I found the greens very tough due to large undulations that created havoc with speed and line.

Absolutely Must Play: Yes. Although the course does not have the "wow" factor of a top 20 layout, and there is no 19th hole, the locale is unique enough to warrant a trip.

Favorite Hole: There are some terrific golf holes; however, the most dramatic is the par 5, No. 14. This 576-yard hole requires a drive placed down the left side of the fairway, to avoid a kick right into the adjoining creek. If the drive is too far left, you will have to fade the second shot around several trees. Two good shots leaves a pitching wedge to an elevated green over a creek, which crosses the fairway in front of the hole. This hole ranked as one of my all-time favorites.

Location Characteristics: Branson Creek is situated in the Ozark Mountains. This facility, along with Murder Rock Golf Course, was constructed to support the city of Branson, as well as provide golf-oriented residential housing. There are large elevation changes as you meander through the dense forests lining the fairways. The leaves were just starting to change, and I imagine the setting would be phenomenal by late October. There is one small lake and several creeks that come into play. Even more dramatic are the rock formations that may be found along some of the fairways and backing several of the greens.

Overall: I would have preferred more temperate conditions during my round at Branson Creek, but having played the day earlier, I was able to enjoy the experience fully. The city of Branson is unique and should be mandatory for those who appreciate traditional family values. Although the city can be a bit touristy, one cannot help but celebrate their love of our country. The golf itself is great. I understand Murder Rock Golf Course next door is also a fun venue. Accessing Branson takes some work, but tied into a family vacation is well worth the effort.

Round 98 — Barton Creek (Fazio Foothills)

Course Rank: *77*

Date Played: October 20, 2013

Starting Time: 9:00 a.m.

Weather: 50 degrees to start, rising to 72 degrees with clear skies and mild breezes.

My Score: 87

Number of Lost Balls: 2

Highlights: 9 pars

Lowlights: 3 double bogeys and 1 triple bogey

Excuse for Not Breaking 80: I could not play the par 5s; all three double bogeys came on these holes. The triple bogey on the difficult No. 16 did not help.

Greens Fee: Included as part of the stay-and-play package. The quoted rate is $225 on weekends and $180 during the week.

Playing Partners: Charlie, an employee of the Omni hotel chain out to inspect the operation after the recent acquisition. We were joined by Forest and Scott, two very nice gentlemen from the Dallas area.

Practice Facilities: Good, although not in great condition. Much of the course was suffering from a heavy rainstorm the previous weekend.

My Rating: 8, for a unique layout, with plenty of good golf holes. This Fazio design was much more interesting than most I have played.

Absolutely Must Play: I was going to say yes, as I thought the Fazio Canyons course would be as good, or better (not so; see next section), and the combo would definitely be worth a weekend. So now, my recommendation is somewhat qualified. I liked this course, but would probably go elsewhere first.

Favorite Hole: Three holes stood out: No. 8, No. 16 and No. 18. I think 16 was slightly more exciting. This long par 4 requires a precise tee shot, followed by a long approach over a creek, which abuts the green. No doubt, many balls have found a watery grave in this hazard.

Location Characteristics: The Fazio Foothills course is situated in the foothills above the city of Austin. This course is characterized by oak-lined fairways, which play havoc with shots drifting off line. There is enough topography to make for some elevated greens and tees, with plenty of exciting shots. This is a warm weather area that is best played in the fall and spring.

Overall: The fairways and greens were in very good condition, but the bunkers had been washed out by rains one week earlier. They should have been marked as ground under repair, but were not. Fortunately, I did not find myself in these traps, which were also pockmarked with deer prints. There was a slew of interesting golf holes, which made for a great round, as well as terrific weather. We had issues with the hotel room (the one assigned to us had been given away, so our upgraded suite was not available). The promised discount did not show up on the final hotel bill, and we had to ask. In addition, the package, which promised unlimited play on the Fazio course, was not exactly correct. One of the courses was "members only," while the promised afternoon time mysteriously disappeared, and I had to play the Crenshaw course. The good news is that Omni recently took over the operation, and if La Costa is any indication, they are committed to improving the golf experience.

Round 99 Barton Creek (Fazio Canyons)

Course Rank: 71

Date Played: October 21, 2013

Starting Time: 9:00 a.m.

Weather: 60 degrees, rising to 75 degrees, partly cloudy with mild winds

My Score: 83

Number of Lost Balls: 4

Highlights: 1 birdie and 9 pars

Lowlights: 4 double bogeys

Excuse for Not Breaking 80: The four balls I hit into the lateral hazards cost me eight strokes.

Greens Fee: Included in the package. The quoted rate is $225 on weekends and $180 during the week.

Playing Partners: Billy, Pat and Jim, three terrific retired doctors from the Fort Worth area. Pat had recently opened a winery, which appears to doing well. I will have to try something from the Brennan Vineyards in Texas.

Practice Facilities: Very good; especially the short game area.

My Rating: 7. I had expected something similar to Foothills, and was a bit disappointed. There were still some nice holes, but too many offered less of a challenge. The front nine seemed less inspired.

Absolutely Must Play: No, but I would definitely give it a shot if you visit the area, and the sister course has plenty to offer. The golf package is affordable and the resort, although I think it could stand some improvement, has a lot of amenities.

Favorite Hole: Most were good, not great. I preferred No. 15, a long par 4 with an elevated tee box, and water lurking along the right side. I boomed a drive 300 yards, and popped a nine iron 125 yards next to the pin for an easy birdie.

Location Characteristics: The location is similar to the Foothills course, except that the trees lining these fairways are more forested, with fewer oaks.

Overall: The Canyons course did not build upon my enjoyment of Foothills. Perhaps my expectations were too high. Maybe I hit so many good shots the course felt too easy. Regardless, while I can see why this is a top 100 course, it felt overrated. It will be interesting to go back some day when the bunkers have been repaired and the planned new greens are as nice as those on Foothills.

Trip Summary:

The trip to Branson and Austin proved to be an enjoyable experience. The people were terrific at both locations. Branson is accessed by my all-time favorite airport. The facilities consist of an old airline hangar that has been redesigned to look like Country Bear Jamboree at Disneyland meets Bass Pro Shop. The city of Branson is also unique in its all-American wholesomeness. You should not overlook the great golf available. This is a hidden gem that warrants a return trip.

Texas is a bit like Branson on a larger scale, although the influence of outsiders can clearly be seen. Barton Creek is a nice resort that could stand some added touches that I am sure will come now that Omni has taken over. The golf was good, if not great, and I am sure would have been more enjoyable had torrential rains not played havoc with the grounds the previous week. Austin is easily accessible, and a weekend at this resort should be somewhere on your list.

Ultimately, I believe everyone would benefit from a trip that includes a stop in Branson, with a dose of Texas hospitality thrown in.

Chapter 46

The Finish Line

Despite my nifty planning three years ago, I was thwarted in my effort to play all four Hawaiian venues when Princeville elected to replace their greens. This cost me the non-refundable airfare and necessitated a costly return trip. On the other hand, it is Hawaii, and our friends, the Strongs, were looking to celebrate Greta's 50th birthday, so we "acquiesced" to an island vacation. Our nine-day trip would afford an opportunity to revisit the top 100 courses on Maui and Lanai. Unfortunately, The Experience at Koele was being renovated, so we played The Challenge at Manele twice. There are worse things than Hawaii in February, and there is some sense of closure related to returning. Further, Joe will be joining me on this final round, just as he was there at the beginning.

This time, we booked directly with Hawaiian Airlines so as to avoid the Delta/Alaska seat fiasco of the last trip. We landed in Kauai on a Friday, with Princeville tee times scheduled for both Saturday and Monday...just to be sure. It was with great anticipation and a certain wistfulness that I headed to the Prince Course on Saturday morning to complete the final leg of the journey.

Round 100 — Princeville (Prince)

Course Rank: 22

Date Played: February 8, 2014

Starting Time: 8:40 a.m.

Weather: Overcast, light breeze, 76 degrees

My Score: 84

Number of Lost Balls: 2

Highlights: 2 birdies and 8 pars

Lowlights: 4 double bogeys and 1 triple bogey

Excuse for Not Breaking 80: Double bogeys on four of five holes, starting at No. 12. It may also have been that my socks were on the wrong feet. FootJoy recently began labeling some of their hosiery left and right, and somehow I got it backwards.

Greens Fee: $180

Playing Partners: Joe Strong.

Practice Facilities: Very nice. The driving range slopes downhill toward the ocean, which adds distance and improves the psyche. Short game area and putting green are adequate, although the putting green did not prepare us for the slow, heavily undulated greens on the course.

My Rating: 8+, for a couple of great holes, great views and plenty of topography. This is a very tough course that requires target golf. The slow greens when we played hurt the rating, even though they were in very good condition. (These are the new greens that necessitated the return trip.)

Absolutely Must Play: Yes. This may have been my favorite Hawaiian course on the list (although I really liked the unrated Experience at Koele). Kauai is a less-developed island, with some terrific scenery. There are other well-regarded courses on the island, so a week on the links is possible. (Note: there are discounted replay rates at Princeville on the day of play, as well as within seven days of your first round.)

Favorite Hole: Holes 12 and 13 are terrific challenges that kicked my butt during both rounds. However, first impressions being important, I think No. 1 was my favorite. This is a brutally tough, albeit short, par 4 that requires absolute accuracy off the tee (leave your driver in the bag) and a precise second shot.

Location Characteristics: Princeville is situated on the island of Kauai; also known as the Garden Island due to the thick vegetation. This vegetation comes without the benefit of irrigation. Kauai is subject to heavy and frequent rains, which keep everything damp. Our day, probably not unlike many others, was cart path only. This was because they had been deluged the previous week. As a result, the greens had not been recently cut, and might have been a seven on the stimpmeter. Joe, who is a great putter, left at least five efforts ten feet short. That aside, the course was lush and in great shape. Princeville covers an expansive area, with no parallel fairways. There is plenty of topography and panoramic ocean views. Many of the tees are elevated as are many of the greens. The bordering jungle will swallow the errant golf shot. If you are brave enough to venture into the underbrush, you can replenish your supply. (Unfortunately, I recovered a disproportionate number of Pinnacles and Top Flites.) You can expect trade winds, which sound relaxing but dramatically influence ball flight. The backdrop, away from the ocean, features dramatic mountains from the volcanoes that created the islands.

Overall: Princeville is a course that requires a lot of grinding. There are some open holes, but there are numerous others that require precision golf. The jungle on the back nine is a magnet for balls failing to land on the fairways and greens, and will require you to carry a few extra in your bag. Accuracy off the tee is vital, with plenty of bunkers that attract the slightly errant shot. Approaches are to large greens, which offer huge undulations. Putting is challenging, as most holes offer an excellent chance at three putts. Be prepared, as showers are likely during the round. If you are willing to brave the elements and focus your attention, however, low scores are possible. The setting is great, the facility first rate and off-course environment more than acceptable.

Trip Summary:

Not much had changed about Hawaii. My impression is that Kauai is even more laid-back than the other islands. Transplanted mainlanders dominate staffing at the hotels and restaurants. Most of these individuals are escaping the pressures of everyday life in the real world.

Hawaiian golf remains pleasurable if lacking in the dramatic. Trade winds, regular rain showers, lava and ocean views make golf in the islands different than anywhere else on the top 100 list. It is still a difficult place for the Type "A" personality who demands constant stimulation.

Departing Hawaii always seems to be a painful experience. Not because I regret leaving the islands, but there seems to be a distinct lack of service as you leave. During my last trip it was the extraordinarily unhelpful Alaska Airlines/Delta employee. This time we were regaled with a cranky counter person at Budget Car Rental. I usually avoid Budget, but it had been part of the affordable Costco package. These packages can be good; however, I often feel like a second-class citizen. Anyway, we arrived at Budget 90 minutes before the flight out of Maui, which is not a very busy airport. Due to problems with their first car, the Strongs had been given a substitute vehicle. Unfortunately, the paperwork was not transferred, so when Joe came to return the car he needed to go into the office. He waited five minutes for a customer service person, despite no one else in line. Eventually an ornery representative came over to help. After messing around on her computer for several minutes (just to get a receipt), Joe mentioned he had a flight to catch. She jumped all over him because he had not left himself two hours of lead time. Meanwhile, my wife and I had just been told for the second time that the courtesy van was full and we had to wait for the next one. My wife made the mistake of walking into the office and asking the representative, who was still working on Joe's receipt, how often the vans came, and if we might have a chance to catch one. This caused her to go ballistic again about arriving two hours before the flight. She was still yelling at Pat and Joe as they left the counter. Once again, a week's worth of vacation, spoiled by poor customer service.

Chapter 47

Getting Your Money's Worth

Having now completed *Golf Magazine*'s Top 100 Public Golf Courses, I can categorically recommend against similar insanity on your part. The good news is that by properly planning your future vacations, you can play 9 of the top 10 (all but Bethpage Black), 21 of the top 25, and more than 50 overall by structuring 10 "dream" trips. In a perfect world you would schedule two trips per year, but I recognize the veto power of a non-golfing spouse, so some of you may take 10 years. The following, in order, are the "can't miss" vacations for any golf addict:

1. MONTEREY PENINSULA

Hands down, my favorite golf trip includes Pebble Beach and Spyglass Hill, two top-ten venues. This vacation also includes Spanish Bay, another top 100 course. Within 17-Mile Drive you can also play Poppy Hills, a terrific unranked facility. This trip is great for the non-golfing spouse and can be completed in three to four days. Even better, add a couple of days to play a round at Pasatiempo and spend a night at CordeValle, which is a terrific resort.

Tips: Start at CordeValle (close to San Jose). Spend the night and visit the winery on-site. Play Pasatiempo on your way to 17-Mile Drive, and stay that evening at the Inn at Spanish Bay. This hotel is less expensive than The Lodge at Pebble Beach, but provides access to the same amenities. Book a golf package that will get you access to the big three. In a perfect world, start with Spanish Bay, as it will be a disappointment after the other two, but is a good facility on its own. Book early, as much as a year in advance, in order to ensure the best tee times. Make sure to get a walking caddie at

Pebble Beach. September and October are the prime months. Try out the restaurants in Carmel, just outside the main gate to 17-Mile Drive. Lastly, pay for everything in advance so you are not obsessing while you are there.

2. WISCONSIN/MICHIGAN

This trip may be separated into two excursions. For a lot less money than going to Scotland, you can play some of the best golf courses in the world. This trip includes two of my top 10 and two more in my top 20. Whistling Straits and Erin Hills are both major championship venues. There are eight top 100 courses on this excursion. The trip requires some travel, including a ferry across Lake Michigan, but is very doable. You can expand the trip to include the two courses located near Chicago (The Glen Club and Cog Hill) if you are adventuresome. This is a trip for your golfing buddies that will include 36 holes on most days.

Tips: Unless you are going to add the Chicago courses, fly into Milwaukee and find a hotel near Erin Hills (try Germantown). Play Erin Hills in the morning (you will have a caddie and may be worn out), and head to Whistling Straits when the round is over. Book a package at the Inn on Woodlake (it is cheaper than the American Club). After checking in, race over to to play the Blackwolf Run Meadows Valley course. Eat dinner at Blackwolf Run, and try the corn and sausage chowder. Make your reservation to play the Irish Course at Whistling Straits the next morning, with an afternoon round at the Blackwolf Run River course. Play Whistling Straits (Straits) the following morning in time to catch the SS Badger from Manitowoc to Ludington, Michigan. Check into Arcadia Bluffs. They have a limited number of rooms, and it is bit pricey, but they also have the No. 1 nineteenth hole in the country. Also, it is convenient from the ferry and the restaurant is pretty good. Book the next night at Boyne Mountain (check out their condo deals) and make a reservation to play Bay Harbor (Links and Quarry). Follow up with an afternoon round at Forest Dunes. Proceed from there to Big Rapids. Spend the night at the Country Inn and Suites. In the morning, play Tullymore before heading to Grand Rapids for your return flight. I would probably book this trip in July, since the days are longer, but humidity, bugs and lightning storms can be problematic. (Lastly, make sure you play the correct course at Tullymore.)

3. LAS VEGAS

There are no *Golf Magazine* top ten courses on this trek, nor do any host PGA events; however, it is impossible to discount the allure of Las Vegas. There are so many dining and entertainment options, and the golf is memorable. In my opinion, two of the "coolest" courses are part of this trip (Wolf Creek and Shadow Creek). The other two courses, Cascata and Wynn, are no slouches either. Also, there are plenty of non-top 100 options to entice the avid golfer.

Tips: You need to book into an MGM resort in order to play Shadow Creek. There are plenty of options you can find online. I like the MGM Signature. Allocate one day for the drive to Mesquite to play Wolf Creek. If possible play 36, although that will force an early wake-up. The next day they will chauffeur you to Shadow Creek. Wynn is on the strip. Cascata is about 30 minutes out of town. I would probably try to book during May, before the weather gets too hot, but while the days are long. Book theater tickets on the day of the show, and buy from one of the discount houses. Never pay retail. Do not try to drive down the Strip at night…way too much traffic. There are plenty of great restaurants, but check out the reviews, as some are well-located but not worth the money.

4. BANDON DUNES

Many will disagree with my selection of Bandon as No. 4. I know individuals who do not believe you can do better than the four courses that make up this facility. No doubt, it is a great golf vacation, but several of the courses have the same feel, and a visit to Bandon has little to offer besides golf. In addition, the facility is difficult to access, subject to temperamental weather and has no tournament history. Having said all this, Bandon Dunes is still a one-of-a-kind experience, with professional caddies assisting you through 36 holes a day. The setting is terrific and golf rules the day.

Tips: Make sure to go "in season" to improve the odds of acceptable weather. Fly into Southwest Oregon Regional Airport and take the shuttle to the resort. You do not need to rent a car. Book an afternoon round the day of arrival, 36 each for the next two days, and one on the day of departure. Personally, I would skip Old Macdonald, as I was underwhelmed by this layout. Bandon Trails provides the most character, but Pacific Dunes and

Bandon Dunes best emulate the Scottish golf experience. Of course, you could also book a Scotland vacation as an alternative.

5. CHARLESTON/SAVANNAH

Golf aside, the opportunity to visit Charleston, South Carolina, and Savannah, Georgia, is a treat in and of itself. Savannah is the "coolest" city in the United States. The historic squares that comprise the town make this city unique relative to any other locale. It certainly helps that this trip includes a major championship venue (Ocean Course at Kiawah) and two regular PGA sites (Harbour Town and Sea Island). The icing on the cake is a visit to the May River Plantation at Palmetto Bluffs, home of one of the most unique resorts. You are likely to fly out of Jacksonville, Florida, which means a round at TPC Sawgrass can also be included. Kiawah Island, May River and Sea Island are three exceptional resorts that enhance a great golf experience.

Tips: If you have an American Express Platinum Card, you can book Kiawah, Palmetto Bluffs and Sea Island through the Fine Hotels program. This will allow for upgrades and discounts that will make the total cost more acceptable. Plan to spend an afternoon/evening in Charleston, and take a day tour of Savannah. I strongly recommend reading *Midnight in the Garden of Good and Evil* before touring Savannah. If you can add a round at TPC Sawgrass to the agenda, it will be even more memorable.

6. THE GREAT RESORTS OF THE BLUE RIDGE/ALLEGHENY MOUNTAINS

Three of the great resorts in America are located in the mountains of Virginia and West Virginia. Primland, The Greenbrier and The Homestead are all phenomenal facilities. The Greenbrier is my personal favorite, with a top 100 golf course, in addition to a PGA venue (Old White). The Homestead has tremendous history and one of my favorite courses (Cascades). Primland is a very cool experience, and includes its own observatory. The food on this trip is great and the locations exceptional. If you are willing to travel, you can add Linville, North Carolina, and/or Williamsburg, Virginia. Both of these are must-see venues.

Tips: Add a visit to Williamsburg to the agenda. No place embodies early American history as well as historic Williamsburg. If you have the time, stay at the Eseeola Lodge in Linville and play their course. At The Homestead, eat at the 1812 Grill and visit Sam Snead's Tavern. Leave plenty of time for The Greenbrier. If you like fishing or falconry there is plenty of additional activity offered on this vacation. This is a great trip, but golf may take a back seat.

7. FLORIDA

Even without the great weather, Florida has plenty of terrific golf. You can play three of the most popular PGA venues, including TPC Sawgrass, Bay Hill and Copperhead at Innisbrook, in addition to top 100 courses at Hammock Beach and World Woods. There are other, highly regarded venues in Jacksonville and Orlando. These are comparatively flat courses and can easily be walked in most instances. If you can arrange the trip before the PGA events begin, the course conditions are likely to be fantastic.

Tips: Book the trip through one of the local golf travel agencies. Play the Conservancy Course at Hammock Beach, which is every bit as good as the Ocean Course. Consider spending the evening with some of the local sports teams. We saw the Orlando Magic and Tampa Bay Lightning, with super discounted tickets from StubHub.

8. PINEHURST

Situated in the sand hills of central North Carolina, Pinehurst has long been a favorite destination of addicted golfers. Highlighted by Pinehurst No. 2, a major championship venue, it is one of eight courses at the Pinehurst resort. No. 8 is also a top 100 venue, and No. 4 appears on *Golf Digest*'s list. The region is well known for its Donald Ross designs, with No. 2 being the most often cited example, despite a major renovation that has turned this forest course into a links design. The region benefits from other top 100 courses, Pine Needles and Tobacco Road. The local courses offer classic designs with great appeal to the golf addict. The possible exception to this is Tobacco Road, which may be the most unusual course you will ever play. Personally, I loved the "tricked up" Mike Strantz design that provides numerous blind shots, crazy greens and some of the most interesting shots you can imagine. This venue is approximately 30 minutes outside of Pinehurst, but may as well be a million miles away.

Tips: Fly into Raleigh-Durham, and plan to stay a couple of nights at the Pinehurst Resort so you can play the Pinehurst courses. Spend the remainder of the vacation at a more affordable hotel. Make sure to take the side trip to Tobacco Road. Like it or not, you will never forget this venue. Take a caddy at No. 2; you cannot drive to your ball anyway. Swing season usually works this far south, so consider saving a few bucks. Avoid the area during the hot, humid summer months. Consider a side trip to Myrtle Beach for a couple of days. It is a three-hour drive, but affords numerous additional golf options.

9. HAWAII

Logistically, golfing Hawaii can be difficult, especially considering the laid-back attitude you will adapt in the warm tropical climate. Each of the four top 100 courses are situated on different islands. Kapalua Plantation is a PGA venue with absolutely fabulous views and some of the strongest, consistent winds you will ever encounter. The Challenge at Manele also offers great views, and, in combination with The Experience at Koele, and after a ferry ride from Maui, provides a great 36-hole adventure. Mauna Kea is a classic Hawaiian layout, with a slew of nice golf holes and Princeville Prince, brings into play the rain forests of Kauai. These latter two courses will require island hopping by air if staying on Maui. The golf is fun, but the attraction remains the warm, sunny beaches of the islands.

Tips: Think about booking a package through Costco Travel. They offer great deals, which include many of the necessary extras, such as a car. If you want to play the top courses, consider a trip with several days in Kauai and the remainder in Maui. Plan a full day on Lanai, and play both The Experience and Challenge courses. These can be booked as a package. The Kapalua Bay course is also highly enjoyable if you have the time. Be prepared for a variety of weather conditions, including very warm temperatures. Practice your wind game before making the trip.

10. PHOENIX

In season, Phoenix is a terrific spot to vacation. There are more top 100 courses in this metropolitan area than any other in the country. Because this region is desert, many of the courses start to look the same, although there are many interesting golf holes, and the front nine of Boulders South is dramatic. The trip can also include a visit to TPC Scottsdale, home to the Waste Management Phoenix Open, and the rowdiest venue on the pro tour. Surprisingly, this is not a top 100 course, but is a must-play. Do not, I repeat, *do not* book this trip during the summer, and be very careful with the swing season. This is a trip that can be done with golfing buddies, or with the family. If you plan it well, it is possible to play 36 holes a day. Reminder: Arizona is on Daylight Savings Time year-round.

Tips: Book through one of the many golf tour companies. This will save a great deal of time, and allow you to avoid rebooking when some outside tournament throws off your entire schedule. Reserve a room at one of the condominiums (not hotels) in Scottsdale. These are affordable, and provide full kitchens so you can avoid some of the exorbitant meal costs. Be careful when walking in the desert areas. Some of the cacti can be especially nefarious. Plan on five-hour rounds.

HONORABLE MENTION

Reynolds Plantation/Cuscowilla offers three terrific golf courses and easy access from Atlanta. I had a hard time leaving this venue off the top 10 list, since the golf was superb. In addition, the cost is more reasonable than most. There is not much else to do in the area other than golf, so this makes sense for your golfing buddies. An added bonus is that you can access the Bobby Jones Trail, about three hours to the west. I am definitely headed back to this locale—hopefully during better weather.

Chapter 48

The Lists

Top 10 Golf Courses You Can Play (in order)

Pebble Beach

Spyglass Hill

Whistling Straits (Straits)

TPC Sawgrass

Bethpage Black

Blackwolf Run (River)

Harbour Town

Bandon Dunes/Pacific Dunes

Shadow Creek

Kiawah Island (Ocean)

Coolest Other Venues (not in order)

Wolf Creek

Caledonia Golf and Fish Club

The Homestead (Cascades)

Linville

Tobacco Road

Paa-Ko Ridge

Arcadia Bluffs

The Boulders Club (South)

Fallen Oak at Beau Rivage

Erin Hills/Chambers Bay (Links style, U.S. Open venues)

Honorable Mention

Cascata

Bandon Trails

Princeville (Prince)

Bay Harbor (Links/Quarry)

Forest Dunes

Reynolds Plantation (Oconee and Great Waters)

Atunyote at Turning Stone

Innisbrook (Copperhead)

Golf Club at Redlands Mesa

Lake of Isles (North)

There are many other great courses and terrific holes, but these were the ones that stood out. Notable absentees from the list include Pinehurst No. 2, Old Macdonald and Pasatiempo. It is not that I did not like these courses; however, each proved to be a disappointment relative to the rankings.

Best Family Vacations (with a little golf thrown in)

Bend, Oregon (Crosswater, Tetherow, Pronghorn and more)

Brainerd, Minnesota (Deacon's Run, Madden's, Cragun's)

Myrtle Beach, South Carolina (Caledonia, plus many others)

Maui/Lanai, Hawaii (Kapalua Plantation and Bay, Challenge at Manele, Experience at Koele, and more)

Orlando, Florida (Bay Hill, Disney courses)

Most Romantic (even if you ditch the significant other for golf)

Monterey Peninsula (Pebble Beach, Spyglass, Spanish Bay)

Blue Ridge/Allegheny Mountains (Greenbrier, Homestead, Primland and Linville)

Maui/Lanai (see above)

Charleston/Savannah (Kiawah, May River, Harbour Town)

Las Vegas (Shadow Creek, Cascata, Wynn and Wolf Creek)

Best Resorts/Lodging

The Greenbrier

The Inn at Palmetto Bluffs

The Homestead

Pebble Beach Lodge/Inn at Spanish Bay

CordeValle

The Sanctuary Hotel at Kiawah Island

Eseeola Lodge at Linville

The Lodge and Suites at Primland

The Broadmoor

Coeur d'Alene Resort

Best Meals*

Zino Ristorante (Edwards, CO)

Eseeola Lodge (Linville, NC)

Commander's Palace (New Orleans, LA)

1766 Grille (Hot Springs, VA)

Chinook Steak, Pasta & Spirits (Worley, ID)

Pour Richard's (Bluffton, SC)

Pine Crest Inn (Pinehurst, NC)

Tomasso (Kiawah, SC)

Shields Tavern (Williamsburg, VA)

Michael Anthony's (Jersey City, NJ)

**Perhaps should be restated as "Most Interesting."*

Best Food Specialties

Villa Ristorante Italiano (bread spread) (Petoskey, MI)

Blackwolf Run (corn and sausage chowder) (Kohler, WI)

The Silver Moon (chocolate croissant bread pudding) (Eatonton, GA)

Mrs. Mac's Kitchen (Key lime pie) (Key Largo, FL)

Birdies

Southwest Airlines' "Bags Fly Free" policy

Hampton Inn (except Terre Haute)

Country Inn & Suites

Enterprise Rent-A-Car

Cascata Golf Course operation

Fallen Oak Golf Club operation

Arcadia Bluffs lodging and 19th hole

French Lick Resort customer service

Coeur d'Alene, Pebble Beach, Princeville, French Lick complimentary bag tags

Branson, Missouri airport

Donny, the waiter at McCormick & Schmick's, Atlantic City, NJ

The caddie line-up at Whistling Straits

Bogeys

Terre Haute Hampton Inn/Expedia mess

Delta/Alaska Airlines Seat fiasco

Nasty United Airlines lady at San Diego Airport

Budget Car Rental, Kahului (Maui) Airport

Miami, Florida drivers

Tee time reservation policies that do not allow out-of-area residents to book 30 days in advance.

Inability to follow my own schedule at Tullymore

Hat selection at Sunday River (red only)

Chapter 49

Parting Words

The journey to play America's top 100 courses available to the public began in the heat of La Quinta with a par on No. 1 at the Mountain Course, and ended with a sand save par on the number one handicap (18th hole) at Princeville. I was fortunate to have Joe Strong along on both of these occasions. In between, there were plenty of pars and a few birdies, but too many double bogeys and worse.

People ask me, "In addition to being crazy, what does it take to play the top 100 courses?" Perhaps the most important requirement is time. Over the nearly four years to complete the journey, I was on the road for more than 150 days, not including side trips to Alaska, Scotland and the First Tee Open. Due to weather considerations, most of the traveling will occur between May and October, unless you are really cheap like me and challenge the less expensive "swing" seasons. Fortunately, I have a quality staff holding down the fort back home. The adventure would have been easier to accomplish over 5 to 10 years; however, my compulsive nature would not allow for such lollygagging.

You must be able to handle the travel. During the course of the four years, I visited 44 states, including all but South Dakota, Utah, Kansas, Wyoming, Montana and Arkansas. Granted, in several instances I merely passed through the state on my way to another course. I landed at 46 different airports, many of them on multiple occasions, and went through the TSA line 64 times. I rented 28 automobiles. Based upon my calculations, I flew 87,814 miles and drove another 17,051 miles in completing the journey.

You must be patient. This is not something at which I excel. The assorted logistical nightmares that accompany any vacation are magnified when you are on a tight schedule. Further, you need to build in flexibility to handle weather issues, institutional incompetence and flight delays, just to mention a few. I cannot imagine a situation in which you could play all 100 courses without at least a few missteps. Ultimately, I had to return to five locales because of weather, course closures or my own incompetence (see Tullymore).

You need to have a few extra bucks lying around. Many of my trips were made during the swing season, resulting in reduced greens fees. In addition, my huge expenses garnered me mileage credits that resulted in a number of free flights. I looked for discount package deals and generally tried to save where I could. I had originally budgeted $150,000, but my final tally for travel, greens fees and accommodations was only $69,691. (Just over one year of private college education for my daughter.) Of course, meals, travel companion tickets, wife's shopping and spa days, other tourism excursions and bonus days probably increased this figure to closer to $100,000.

Ultimately, you must have an addiction to the game of golf. I put up with two bad elbows, a bad back, frozen shoulder, iffy wrist and other assorted ailments to complete the project. This does not include the numerous bug bites, sunburns, cuts and bruises and head colds. I took 8,333 strokes, including 3,180 putts, and lost 117 Pro VIs. Despite the derisive comments behind my back, despite the travel hassles, the senior moments, the food poisoning and the course closures, I would not have changed a thing. I had the opportunity to play with some great people, both old friends and new acquaintances, and I got a first-hand look at much of this great country of ours. Hey, I am ready to do it again.

ACKNOWLEDGMENTS

For my wife, Patricia, who "suffered" through many of the journeys while I completed my trek. Her ability to survive stays at Pebble Beach, The Greenbrier, The Homestead, The Broadmoor, Inn at Palmetto Bluffs, and the Coeur d'Alene Resort (to name a few) is testimony to her unending patience and good humor with her golf addict husband.

Special kudos to my son Charlie, who really did "suffer" by being dragged along to many of the locales where my wife took a pass. I am sure he will never forget Gothenburg, Nebraska, or the sub-arctic temperatures in Opelika, Alabama.

To my daughter, Christy, and Mint Marketing, for the wonderfully creative website (tophundredgolf.com), but more for her patience explaining the idiosyncrasies of social media. What is Facebook again?

Thanks to Mark Russell and the great team at Elevate Publishing for having the vision to take a chance on an author who was clearly more obsessed with something other than this book. A special thanks to my editor, Anna McHargue, who ultimately made sense out my crazy and verbose ramblings. Also, thanks to Bobby Kuber for masterminding the marketing process. I also want to acknowledge James Cahill, golf addict in training, for his insights into the publishing business.

I especially wish to thank my "enablers," without whom I would probably be playing tennis. My brother Andy captured the award for most rounds suffering my company (24). To my other brothers, John and Chris, who joined me on several major excursions. I appreciate that you did not make me reciprocate by going on your fishing expeditions.

Enormous thanks to Joe Strong (co-founder of the Greater Turkey Open), who was there at the very beginning, as well as on my final round, joining me for 23 adventures, including the North Carolina/South Carolina craziness. His wife, Greta, also deserves recognition for her sacrifices on the project, and for keeping my wife company during those times Joe and I were navigating the links.

Thanks to Dr. Scott Rand and his wife, Leasa, for making the Midwest tolerable and for arranging the Rand Chauffeuring Service. Similarly, a shout out to brother-in-law, Tom Longar, who provided guide services through northern Minnesota. Special thanks are also in order for Dale Dreps and Jim Markowski, who worked the phones in New York to secure a starting time at Bethpage Black.

To Charlie Wilde and Greg Strong, who nearly cured me of the golf addiction in Pinehurst with their relentless pursuit of more golf holes, which resulted in a scary overdose, and to Ray Adams for generously treating me to a round at Torrey Pines.

I would be remiss not thank the 7:00 a.m. Dew Sweepers at La Costa, a large group of similarly inclined golf addicts who continue to take my money every week, and for that reason, do nothing to try and dissuade me from continuing to flail away on the links.

Lastly, special recognition to the great staff at Omni's La Costa Resort and Spa, who pretend to find me amusing. (Think laugh *at*, not with.)

SUMMIT FREE PUBLIC LIBRARY
3 9547 00405 7183